Taking Education Really Seriously

Michael Fielding has edited a timely and much needed review of four years of Labour government education policy, with contributions from authoritative friends and critics of the administration. This will provide analytic and critical purchase on the surprisingly conservative continuities and modern paradoxes of New Labour's educational policies, as well as some indications of alternatives to which it might wisely give the careful attention which is provided here.

Professor David Bridges, University of East Anglia

The now familiar 'education, education, education' as a statement of the New Labour government's priorities for national renewal has a substantial international significance. Many countries across the world see education as a key resource in the development of a vibrant knowledge economy on which they depend for their well-being and their success. The opportunity to reflect on the effectiveness or otherwise of a government that came to power with such singleness of purpose, such widespread support, and so many high hopes, particularly in the field of education, thus has a resonance that goes well beyond the shores of the UK.

In a book of considerable power, substantial insight and occasional beauty, leading writers from a range of educational fields examine New Labour's policy intentions against the varied realities of their fulfilment. A decidedly mixed picture emerges from the book's six sections

- The modernising agenda
- Alternative perspectives, particular values
- Feeling policy realities on the pulses
- Levers of change
- Rethinking the roles and realities of educational research
- International perspectives

Within the overwhelming majority of the contributions there is genuinely felt goodwill and substantial admiration for the degree of commitment and tenacity shown by the Labour administration: this is a government that clearly cares about a positive, challenging, educational experience for *all* students.

However, there are serious puzzles and challenges here too. Is there, as one leading commentator puts it, a 'crisis of identity' in the Labour government's approach to education? Or is this perception the inevitable fallout of a government brave enough and determined enough to intervene judiciously and tenaciously to ensure 'High Expectations and Standards for All, No Matter What' in pursuit of a world class education system?

Michael Fielding is Reader in Education at the University of Sussex, where he is in the process of setting up a Centre for Educational Innovation.

Taking Education Really Seriously

Four Years' Hard Labour

**Edited by
Michael Fielding**

London and New York

First published 2001
by RoutledgeFalmer
11 New Fetter Lane, London EC4P 4EE

Simultaneously published in the USA and Canada
by RoutledgeFalmer
29 West 35th Street, New York, NY 10001

RoutledgeFalmer is an imprint of the Taylor & Francis Group

© 2001 Edited by Michael Fielding

Typeset in Sabon by
Keystroke, Jacaranda Lodge, Wolverhampton
Printed and bound in Great Britain by
TJ International Ltd, Padstow, Cornwall

British Library Cataloguing in Publication Data
A catalogue record for this book is available from the British Library

Library of Congress Cataloging in Publication Data
Taking education really seriously : four years' hard labour/edited by Michael
Fielding.
    p. cm.
Includes bibliographical references and index.
1. Education and state–Great Britain–History–20th century. 2. Politics and
education–Great Britain–History–20th century. 3. Labour Party (Great
Britain)–History. I. Fielding, Michael, 1945–
LC93.G7 T35 2001
379.41—dc21   2001019110

ISBN 0–415–25210–5

Contents

Figures and tables

Figures

Tables

Contributors

Michael Barber is Director of the Standards and Effectiveness Unit and Chief Adviser on School Standards to the Secretary of State for Education and Employment, David Blunkett, at the Department for Education and Employment. Among his responsibilities are the National Literacy and Numeracy Strategies, tackling school failure, modernising secondary education in the large cities and the contracting out of failing local education authorities. Major publications include *The Learning Game* (1997), *How to do the Impossible* (1997) and *A World Class Education Service for the Twenty-first Century* (1999).

Stephen J. Ball is Karl Mannheim Professor of the Sociology of Education at the Institute of Education, University of London. He is author of several books on education policy and edits the *Journal of Education Policy*.

Tom Bentley is Director of Demos, the independent UK-based think tank. He has worked as an adviser to the British on education and youth policy, and is active in education debates around the world. His publications include *Learning beyond the Classroom* (1998), *Destination Unknown* (1999) and *The Creative Age* (with Kim Seltzer, 1999).

Mike Davies's headships in rural Scotland, inner London and Milton Keynes gave rise to two parallel passions: school-based curriculum development and pedagogy, and the reculturing of large secondary schools on a human scale. Board membership of the British Curriculum Foundation and Human Scale Education Movement reflects these long-term quests.

Paul Doherty is a senior research officer with the National Foundation for Educational Research. He left school with few formal educational qualifications and returned to study as an adult, eventually being awarded a Ph.D. studentship at the Centre for Applied Research in Education (CARE) at the University of East Anglia. Here he has worked alongside John Elliott, developing interests in student disaffection, in case study and collaborative research methodology and in the ways in which educational research informs (or fails to inform) practice.

Gwyn Edwards is Associate Professor in the Department of Curriculum Studies, University of Hong Kong. His teaching and research interests include geographical education, the humanities curriculum, curriculum change and action research. He is co-author of *Change and the Curriculum* (with Geva M. Blenkin and A. V. Kelly, 1992) and co-editor of *Education and Experience* (with A. V. Kelly, 1998).

John Elliott is Professor of Education within the Centre for Applied Research in Education at the University of East Anglia. He is the author and editor of a number of publications in the fields of curriculum and teacher professional development. He is currently an Advisory Professor to the Hong Kong Institute of Education and a consultant to the Hong Kong government.

Michael Fielding is Reader in Education at the University of Sussex where he is currently setting up a Centre for Educational Innovation. His two main research interests are the development of the 'Person Centred School' and the radical potential of student voice in educational transformation.

Dean Fink is a former secondary Head and senior educational official in Ontario. He is an associate of the International Centre for Educational Change at the University of Toronto and a visiting fellow of the International Centre for Leadership at the University of Hull. His chief areas of interest are educational change and school leadership. He has consulted in twenty-seven countries in the past few years and is the author or co-author of *Changing our Schools* (with Louise Stoll, 1996); *Good Schools/Real Schools* (2000) and *It's about Learning* (with Louise Stoll and Lorna Earl, 2001).

Helen M. Gunter is Senior Lecturer in the School of Education at the University of Birmingham. Her research interests include the history of leadership and management studies. Helen is the author of *Rethinking Education* (1997) and *Leaders and Leadership in Education* (2001).

Valerie Hannon is an Honorary Professor in Education at the University of Sheffield, and an independent consultant and researcher in education policy and management. She was formerly Director of Education for Derbyshire County Council and adviser to the Local Government Association. Her related publications include 'Local government and schools' in *Modern Educational Myths*, ed. B. O'Hagan (1999). She is working on a series of projects to develop and support creativity in education.

David H. Hargreaves is Chief Executive of the Qualifications and Curriculum Authority and a member of the National Educational Research Forum.

Bob Jeffrey is a Research Fellow at the Open University focusing on primary schools and using qualitative methodology to investigate the creative practices of teachers and children and teachers' experiences of work. He is the author, with Peter Woods, of *Teachable Moments* (1996), *Testing Teachers* (1998) and *Restructuring Schools, Reconstructing Teachers* (with Geoff Troman and Mari Boyle, 1997). He has recently co-edited *Creativity in Education* (2001).

Ann Limb, formerly Principal of Cambridge Regional College, has recently been appointed as Chief Executive of the University for industry. Her interests focus on learning and leadership. She has published two textbooks (1980, 1982) on language learning and numerous articles on strategic and change management, leadership and post-16 education and training.

Peter Moss is Professor of Early Childhood Provision at the Institute of Education, University of London. His main interests are children's services and the relation between care and employment. Recent books include *Beyond Quality in Early Childhood Education and Care* (with Gunilla Dahlberg and Alan Pence, 1999) and *Parental Leave* (co-edited with Fred Deven, 2000).

Richard Smith is Director of Combined Social Sciences, University of Durham. His main interest is the philosophy of education, particularly how education counters the prevailing culture of performativity and rediscovers a sense of value. His most recent book is *Education in an Age of Nihilism* (with Nigel Blake, Paul Smeyers and Paul Standish, 2000).

John Smyth is Professor of Teacher Education at Flinders University of South Australia and Director of the Flinders Institute for the Study of Teaching. His research interests are in socio-critical policy analyses of education, and the sociology and politics of teachers' work. His recent works have appeared in the *British Educational Research Journal*, the *Journal of Education and Work*, the *Journal of Education Policy* and the *British Journal of Sociology of Education*. He is author or editor of fourteen books, the most recent of which is *A Critical Politics of Teachers' Work* (2001).

Paul Standish is Senior Lecturer in Education at the University of Dundee and editor of the *Journal of Philosophy of Education*. His main research interest is the relationship between analytical and Continental philosophy and its significance for education. His recent books include *Education in an Age of Nihilism* (with Nigel Blake, Paul Smeyers and Richard Smith, 2000), *Education at the Interface* (ed., with Nigel Blake, 2000), *Lyotard: Just Education* (ed., with Pradeep Dhillon, 2000) and *Universities Remembering Europe* (ed., with Francis Crawley and Paul Smeyers, 2000).

James Tooley is Professor of Education Policy at the University of Newcastle upon Tyne, where he directs the Centre for Market Solutions in Education. His publications include *The Global Education Industry* (1999) and *Reclaiming Education* (2000). He is researching the nature and developmental impact of private schools for the poor in India and Africa.

Geoff Troman is a Research Fellow and Associate Lecturer in the Faculty of Education and Language Studies at the Open University. His Ph.D. research was an ethnography of primary school restructuring. He is conducting research into the social construction of teacher stress. Among his publications is *Primary Teachers' Stress* (with Peter Woods, 2001).

Mel West is Professor of Educational Leadership at the Manchester Business School and also at the Faculty of Education, University of Manchester. He has written a number of books and articles on educational management topics and has a particular interest in strategies for school improvement both in the UK and abroad.

Peter Woods is a Research Professor in Education at the University of Plymouth, and also at the Open University, where he was formerly Director of the Centre for Sociology and Social Research. He has been researching 'creative teaching in primary schools' since the 1980s. His latest books, *Critical Events in Teaching and Learning* (1993), *Creative Teachers in Primary Schools* (1995), *Teachable Moments* (with Bob Jeffrey, 1996) and *Multicultural Children in the Early Years* (with Mari Boyle and Nick Hubbard, 1999) are products of this research. He has also published work on qualitative methodology, the most recent being *Researching the Art of Teaching* (1996) and *Successful Writing for Qualitative Researchers* (1999).

1 Taking education really seriously

Four years' hard labour

Michael Fielding

Origins and architecture

The now familiar 'Education, education, education' as a statement of the incoming Labour government's priorities for national renewal has a substantial international significance. Many countries across the world see education as a key resource in the development of a vibrant knowledge economy on which they depend for their well-being and success. The opportunity to reflect on the effectiveness or otherwise of a government that came to power with such singleness of purpose, such widespread support and so many high hopes, particularly within the field of education, thus has a resonance that goes well beyond the shores of the United Kingdom. That resonance is amplified still further by the sheer energy of its initial engagement – '50 or so policies' articulated 'Within 67 days of the government being elected' (Barber and Sebba 1999) – and the resoluteness and tenacity of its commitment.

The chapters of this book spring initially from a preliminary taking stock after two years of the Labour government's term of office. The special issue of the *Cambridge Journal of Education* in which they were published quickly sold out and many of the papers that appeared in it were widely referenced in the ongoing debate. Most of the original papers[1] have been slightly revised to take account of subsequent developments, but, with one exception,[2] none substantially. This is an indicator of the enduring nature of their particular contributions, not just because the government has remained steadfast in its intent, but also because the issues they touch on are rooted in debates about education and the good life that have deep historical roots and continuing significance. The additional invited contributions[3] serve to widen the range of the debate and extend its international engagement.

The book is organised into six parts. The first, 'The modernising agenda', consists solely of the contribution from Michael Barber, head of the UK government's Standards and Effectiveness Unit at the Department for Education and Employment (DfEE). In a chapter of wide international reference and relevance he sets out the Labour government's aspirations, reflects on their progress to date and ends by suggesting a number of future prospects which transcend the boundaries of a single nation state.

The second, 'Alternative perspectives, particular values', contains two chapters. Coming at their task from quite different theoretical frameworks and quite different value standpoints, Stephen Ball and James Tooley engage with the intellectual grounding and practical realities of Labour's education policy. As with Michael Barber's contribution, the multiple threads of international economic development weave their way through the fabric of their texts.

Part III, 'Feeling policy realities on the pulses', addresses different aspects of policy realisation through a consideration of how different sectors of provision have been affected in the four years of Labour government. Peter Moss looks at early years education and Peter Woods, Bob Jeffrey and Geoff Troman examine the experience of those in the primary (elementary) sector. Mike Davies and Gwyn Edwards focus on curriculum thinking and practice, largely, though by no means exclusively, from a secondary (high school) perspective and Ann Limb reflects on changes in further education. Richard Smith and Paul Standish consider developments and aspirations in higher education and Tom Bentley extends horizons to lifelong learning and the adequacy or otherwise of contemporary schools as institutions of learning in the twenty-first century.

The issue of transformation is taken up by the subsequent four chapters focusing on some of the Labour government's key 'Levers of change'. In this fourth part Michael Fielding looks in something akin to disbelief at the virtually unchallenged reputation of target setting as panacea for multiple educational and other human dilemmas. Helen Gunter examines the Labour government's modernising agenda for the preparation and training of headteachers (principals), Mel West considers the North American and other evidence for performance management and Valerie Hannon asks some searching questions of the values and perspectives that have led to the transformation and near extinction of Local Education Authorities (Districts).

The two chapters that comprise Part V, 'Rethinking the role and realities of educational research', take forward a debate that has been running for some time on both sides of the Atlantic, in Australia, in New Zealand and in many other countries throughout the world. David Hargreaves on the one hand and John Elliott and Paul Doherty on the other take very different views of the move towards evidence-informed practice and its helpfulness or otherwise in realising the synergy between research and daily practice in education and other fields of social scientific enquiry.

The 'International perspectives' that conclude the book bring us full circle to the worldwide aspirations with which Michael Barber began. The two contributors who have strong international reputations as well as a good knowledge of the English education system are Dean Fink from Canada and John Smyth from Australia. Both examine the international evidence for much of that to which English and many other educational systems aspire. In focusing particularly on the potential gap between policy makers and policy implementers and on the questionable evidence base for the self-managing school the volume ends as it began, with strong feeling, firmly held values and, above all else, a commitment to education as the most compelling agent of human transformation and well-being currently at our disposal.

Part I The modernising agenda

Michael Barber's chapter, based on a presentation in Washington DC, in May 2000, opens by locating the challenges facing many governments across the world today. Whilst the title, 'High expectations and standards for all, no matter what', articulates both standards-based continuities with New Labour's Conservative predecessors and an equity-informed insistence on new departures, his subtitle, 'Creating a world class education service in England', echoes aspirations that transcend national boundaries. The impetus and energy of his international orientations drive insistently through his advocacy and commitment. The high challenge, high support motif of New Labour policy orientation applies in equal measure to his manner of writing: the tone is upbeat; the aspirations both wide-ranging and focused; the data compelling in detail and presentation; and the pace and substance of argument urgent in its moral and economic resonance. The message is clear: a modernised education system is the key to economic vitality and international competitiveness, and if this is to be achieved then governments need to intervene judiciously and bravely to liberate energies and capacities in new ways through new combinations and partnerships. The only acceptable arbiter is a rigorous and undeviating insistence on what works.

Part II Alternative perspectives, particular values

The necessity of a transnational dimension in any contemporary debate about education policy is picked up both by Stephen Ball and James Tooley, though their frames of reference and values orientation are markedly different. Whilst both acknowledge positive dimensions of New Labour's approach, both are searchingly critical of the degree to which, on the one hand, the UK government has been captured or, on the other hand, insufficiently influenced by the development of an inevitably international and, in the words of Richard Sennett (1998) increasingly 'energetic' twenty-first-century capitalism.

For Stephen Ball the labour government's education policy is intelligible only within the wider international context, currently dominated by neo-liberal economics. In 'Labour, learning and the economy: a "policy sociology" perspective' he argues, not only that Labour's chosen approach to education policy is more than compatible with that of the previous administration and the requirements of international agencies such as the World Bank and OECD, but also that their narrow approach to learning and the increasing influence of the ideology and practice of performativity on the daily realities and discursive arenas of schooling are actually antithetical to the high skills knowledge economy to which they are so fervently committed.

For James Tooley, too, Labour's errors reside, at least in part, in a mistakenly narrow conception and practice of learning, though for him the mistake lies not in an unimaginative or narrow pedagogy but in the monopoly of state-run formal schooling in defining the only legitimate site and framework within which learning can take place. Whilst applauding aspects of Labour policy the overall verdict of his 'The good, the bad and the ugly: on three years' Labour education policy' is ambivalent. At best, Labour's approach is seen as schizophrenic, standing as much chance of making things worse as of making them better. At worst, its full blooded dirigism is seen to be indefensibly presumptuous, intellectually untenable and practically unrealisable.

Part III Feeling policy reality on the pulses

Peter Moss's 'Renewed hopes and lost opportunities: early childhood in the early years of the Labour government' is both generous in its praise and incisive in its philosophical and practical insights. Whilst acknowledging the 'unparalleled and invigorating change of climate' together with a welcome preparedness to spend significant amounts of money, there is also a sense of regret, of an opportunity missed as well as positive steps taken. What is missing is a philosophically coherent vision of childhood education. In its stead there seems to be an enlarged employment-led child care system where educational purposes are tagged on at the end, rather than integral to the process itself.

Peter Woods, Bob Jeffrey and Geoff Troman also identify a significant set of dilemmas and tensions that await a fuller resolution over time. 'The impact of New Labour's educational policy on primary schools' includes reference to some signs of a broadening of perspective and a more differentiated approach to the challenge of school improvement through inspection. These are, not however, the dominant motifs of their research. Well intentioned reforms are seen as likely to produce divisiveness and a further erosion of trust, and the strong tradition of child-centred education remains as embattled as it ever was under the previous Conservative administration: the reductionist backdrop of performativity seems an improbable agent of a more creative or fulfilling practice.

These continuities are picked up by Mike Davies and Gwyn Edwards in 'Will the curriculum caterpillar ever learn to fly?' If there is development it is seen as largely regressive: curriculum is seen to be replaced by 'standards' and pedagogy has become a legitimate site of explicit government intervention and requirement. None of this is seen as adequate for the inevitable flux and creative possibilities offered by a twenty-first-century context, and the chapter ends with a quite different set of questions and responses from those currently sanctioned by the Labour government.

In contrast, Ann Limb's 'Further education under New Labour: translating the language of aspiration into a springboard for achievement' sees more positive progress made against a widespread backdrop of indifference or ignorance in many sectors of society. Her subtitle, 'Translating the language of aspiration into a springboard for achievement', is indicative of her upbeat assessment of current changes and future possibilities. Here we have a government unequivocally committed to 'implementing radical reform which delivers results and brings about lasting change', its continued progress predicated on its capacity to listen and learn from those working in the field.

'It lifted my sights: revaluing higher education in an age of new technology' is also cautiously optimistic about and appreciative of more recent developments. Richard Smith and Paul Standish remark on significant changes that connect very strongly with a quite different, positive set of values and aspirations from those often articulated as appropriate to other sectors of the education service. Whilst they see a degree of ambivalence and contradiction in government policy, they are nonetheless heartened by the vibrant sense of possibility, particularly with regard to the use of ICT.

In 'The creative society: reuniting schools and lifelong learning' Tom Bentley argues strongly that schools as currently conceived and experienced are incapable of doing what is required of them in terms of meeting the likely needs of twenty-first century learners. In an advocacy that resonates strongly with the curriculum thinking articulated earlier in this volume by Mike Davies and Gwyn Edwards he suggests that governments need to work on a long-term vision that involves schools turning themselves inside out, reconnecting strongly with the communities they serve.

Part IV Levers of change

The issue of transformation is taken up by the subsequent four chapters focusing on some of the Labour government's key levers of change. Michael Fielding's 'Target setting, policy pathology and student perspectives: learning to labour in new times', whilst not anti-target setting, nonetheless argues that if it is to achieve its educative potential then target setting should be less arrogant in its ambitions, less strident in its approach and more explicitly reciprocal in its understanding of the learning process. Students should be the agents of their own learning, not the objects of their teachers' ambitions or anxieties.

Agency, values and the struggle to develop and sustain a voice are also central to Helen Gunter's 'Modernising headteachers as leaders: an analysis of the NPQH'. In examining the Labour government's modernising agenda for the preparation and training of headteachers (principals) she looks with care at the kind of tensions and dilemmas facing candidates who wish to retain a commitment to democratic and humane traditions of public service. If we are to attract creative people the NPQH needs to rest explicitly on a view of headship that transcends the current technicist trend and in its stead re-establishes a stronger connection with the social and moral dimensions of both management and leadership

Mel West focuses on another part of the government's strategy for developing a more rigorous accountability and a more differentiated motivation within the profession. 'Reforming teachers' pay: crossing the threshold' considers arguments for the reform of existing arrangements before drawing on and critiquing international evidence from the United States on the wisdom or otherwise of performance-related pay. Both critical and supportive, like other contributors to this volume he underscores the necessity of closer dialogue with those who are most affected by its day-to-day operation.

The central importance of values is key to much of the chapter ' "Modernising" LEAs: a changing framework of values' by Valerie Hannon. Her three foci concern pluralism, achievement and equality of opportunity. Of these, pluralism is seen as particularly important, since within its ambit rests the legitimacy and future health of local democracy at regional and district level, and yet, unsurprisingly for a government that saw itself as leading a 'crusade', the status and strength of pluralism as a key orientation seem increasingly weak.

Part V Rethinking the role and realities of educational research

David Hargreaves's 'Revitalising educational research: past lessons and future prospects' opens with a series of quotations each of which underscores the debilitating gap between the expectations of social science researchers on the one hand and policy makers and practitioners on the other. Through an imaginative historical analysis of the debate over the past sixty years his chapter leads to a vigorous advocacy of the Labour government's pragmatic approach to 'what works', the rapid dissemination of good practice throughout the education service and the advent of evidence-informed practice.

The adequacy or otherwise of evidence-informed practice as a hegemonic motif for the immediate future of educational research is explored energetically in John Elliott and Paul Doherty's 'Restructuring educational research for the "Third Way"?' They argue not only that there are serious question marks over the political innocence of a 'what works' ideology, but also that the government has yet to find a genuinely Third Way in education that breaks the mould of a narrow neo-liberal agenda.

Part VI International perspectives

Dean Fink's 'The two solitudes: policy makers and policy implementers' identifies the gap between policy makers and policy implementers, tellingly described as 'a dialogue of the deaf', as a matter of serious concern, not just because it endangers the longevity of important changes but, more seriously, because it threatens to undermine the credibility of state-supported education itself. Central to his intention to restore our several capacities to hear, to listen and to learn from each other is the necessity of a shift from control to capacity building and a willingness to attend with as much imagination and commitment to the process as to the content of change.

Some of the most interesting aspects of John Smyth's 'Managing the myth of the self-managing school as an international education reform' are that his challenge to current government thinking on the legitimacy or viability of the self-managing school rests partly on his exposure of the staggering paucity of evidence to substantiate the considerable claims of the self-managing school approach (see Sennett 1998: 50 for a similar exposé of current macroeconomic equivalents) and partly on his unearthing of its heavily ideological base. For governments to extend and develop the self-managing school as a key strand of educational renewal is seen as a serious mistake with far-reaching adverse consequences for the future viability of publicly funded education provision.

Critique

Within the overwhelming majority of the contributions to this volume there is genuinely felt goodwill and substantial admiration for the degree of commitment and tenacity shown by the Labour administration: this is a government that clearly cares about a positive, challenging educational experience for all students. Where critique is offered it is done with a view to furthering real, responsive and responsible education policy and practice that has an emancipatory, not an inquisitorial, intent. It is offered in the spirit of genuine dialogue which is the *sine qua non* of real, responsive and responsible democracy.

However, there are a number of puzzles here that are exacerbated by reference to a wider set of reference points. Standing back and reflecting on the wave of informed support that the Labour government received when it first came into power one cannot now fail to be struck, not only by the substantial achievements to which it can legitimately lay claim, but also by the equally strong set of concerns that have grown over time, even from its supporters. Why has the government ended up in a situation where close allies have talked of 'a feeling of deep disgust' (Simon 2000: 91) and 'a feeling close to contempt' (Davies 2000: vi)? Why have we ended up in a situation where, in the words of one commentator, 'We have . . . six year olds being coached for SATs in the name of improvement . . . parents haranguing teachers for not giving their children enough homework . . . and teenagers who just stop going to school' (Moore 2000: 17). Why, in the still compelling words of another writing some sixty-five years ago, is it still the case that 'We have immense power, and immense resources; we worship efficiency and success: and *we do not know how to live finely*' (Macmurray 1935: 76, my italics)?

My own view is that there are six main reasons, not only for the puzzles and disappointments expressed above, but also, and more particularly, for the reservations that emerge from many of the contributors to this volume. These six sources of concern amount to what Clyde Chitty has called a 'crisis of identity' (2000: 89) in the Labour government's approach to education.

Six concerns

The first source of concern is *ontological*. By this I mean that within government policy there is no adequately articulated understanding of human being, of what it is to be and become a person. This has at least two seriously damaging consequences. First, without a coherent ontology it has and can have no adequately articulated understanding of what education is ultimately and immediately about beyond the insistent imperatives of economic production. Second, the processes through which the government seeks to achieve its modernising transformation are too often likely to go awry because it has not adequately addressed the specifically human dimension of change processes. Michael Barber's 'high challenge, high support' model does not provide the kind of contemporary anthropology on which its intended success depends. In Richard Sennett's words, 'Operationally, everything is so clear; emotionally so illegible' (1998: 68).

The second concern is that Labour's approach to education struggles *morally*, not because it is morally indifferent, but rather because it is morally indiscriminate. It is deeply compromised by the strength of its links with a newly energetic international capitalism which is at best morally disengaged and at worst morally corrosive not only of character (Sennett 1998), but of the very service (i.e. education) in which the development of character has its most appropriate and compelling place. Despite its laudable and authentic commitment to social justice, the unremitting emphasis on performance, 'no matter what', marginalises the subtlety and complexity of the means of our engagement. The moral ambivalence of ambition and 'the chameleon values of the new economy' (Sennett 1998: 26) replace the ethical transparency of service and the enduring values of commitment.

It is also *aesthetically* weak in both a substantive and a discursive way. Not only is its record on the arts woefully hesitant and uncertain, its discourse, its way of expressing its aspirations and articulating its requirements, is deeply and damagingly dull. Too much is metallic and managerialist, too often enunciated in ways which are overbearing and overconfident in their insistence. Why is it that we have such little confidence in the capacity of the much more subtle, ethically nuanced language of education to express what is important to us as teachers and learners? Why do we feel impelled to borrow the disfiguring language of performativity, which has neither the capacity nor the inclination to articulate what matters most to us in our daily work and our enduring intentions? The discourse of performance and the now regrettably familiar 'delivery' is not only offensive, it is dishonest:

offensive because it violates both our interpersonal realities and our intellectual self-respect; dishonest because one can no more deliver learning than one can, with integrity, reduce the richness and complexity of vibrant professional practice to 'the effective management of performance'.

Unsurprisingly, it also fails *existentially*; there seems no place for either the language or the experience of joy, of spontaneity, of life lived in ways that are vibrant and fulfilling rather than watchfully earnest, focused and productive of economic activity. Nor does there seem to be a place for an aspiring narrative of human experience, for 'a sustainable sense of self' (Sennett 1998: 27). It is understandable that the robust realities of policy realisation exemplified in the abrasive abruptness and unsurprising dislocation of bullet point thinking leave little room for nuance, or for the openness and attentive reciprocity of dialogue that we need to make sense of our lives together. However, it is regrettable that there is so little that reminds us of the legitimacy, let alone the necessity, of such exploratory undertakings. Whilst I recognise that the suggestion that 'Changing the metaphor changes the theory' (Sergiovanni, 1994) is to overstate the case, it is not to overstate it by very much. If we began to talk to each other in a language that is more attuned to the intellectual and emotional realities which we all now face, we would begin to think and feel differently about what we do and why we do it. We would be able more often and more insistently to open up intellectual and practical spaces that challenge the conspicuous common sense of world class targets. It is not that, of themselves, aspirations to be world leaders in education are necessarily inappropriate (though some would argue they are that too). Rather it is that they are inadequate, humanly inadequate.

It is deeply ironic that a fifth source of concern is and will continue to be its failure on its own terms of educational *productivity*. The Labour government will not and cannot deliver genuinely educational goods unless it does so by accident or default or for reasons its own presumptions do not properly understand or value. Productivity in terms of certain kinds of measurable results is quite obviously and absurdly incomplete, both because it takes little account of wider aspirations and because it necessarily relies upon them (Fielding 2000a). Inevitably and dishonestly parasitic upon the richness of human encounter, such productivity is as likely to be destructive as constructive of educational progress, producing situations 'where unjustifiable educational practices are not only possible, but encouraged' (Reay and Wiliam 1999: 353) Indeed, '[t]he more specific the Government is about what it is that schools are to achieve, the more likely it is to get it, but the less likely it is to mean anything' (ibid.).

What these five sources of concern point to is an overarching *intellectual* inadequacy that adversely affects the quality and realisation of Labour's educational project. It is here, at its intellectual heart, that Labour's approach to education is most comprehensively and damagingly mistaken. At the most basic and fundamental level it seems to me that there are two key questions that, more than any others, expose the profundity of the challenge that needs to be faced and the distance that still needs to be travelled before it can be properly grasped or practically addressed. These are 'What is education for?' and 'How might we best achieve our educational purposes?' In other words, they concern the nature of educational ends and the proper relationship between those ends and the means we use to achieve them.

On the practical necessity of philosophy

What is education for?

With regard to ends, to the vision to which considerable government effort and commitment are directed, the most puzzling concern continues to be whether the vision is primarily an economic one with the occasional bit of social adhesive stuck on to ensure the enterprise remains viable, or whether the vision is one in which economics is the servant of a wider and deeper human flourishing. The differences between the two are profound, but show no evidence of having been acknowledged or properly understood. Certainly, Michael Barber has suggested elsewhere (1999: 17) that a world class education system is not an end in itself, and that 'It is a key element of achieving the Government's goals of a more productive economy, a more cohesive society, a more successful democracy and more fulfilled individuals' (ibid.), but this does nothing to help us understand the relationship between these things. A list is no substitute for argument: there are tensions to be acknowledged and properly addressed here. There are, as Maxine Greene (1997: 64) points out:

> two contradictory tendencies in education today: one has to do with shaping malleable young people to serve the needs of technology in a post-industrial society; the other has to do with educating young people to grow and become different, to find their individual voices, and to participate in a community in the making.

and we are in grave danger of the 'tyranny of the technical' winning out over the more complex, more profound human developments to which she points a contrasting finger. What we do about this tension is, of course, an immensely difficult matter. But what we cannot do is pretend it does not exist, wish it away by sheer strength of will, or simply fail to see there is a fundamentally important issue to be addressed.

Relating ends and means

Because there is substantial ambivalence about the philosophical nature of the vision to which the government is committed there remains equally substantial ambivalence about the relationship between means and ends. This goes to the heart of the current malaise, exemplified by the still dominant place of the school effectiveness movement in the government's educational imagination. It is, after all, a movement which remains an intellectually timid articulation of a largely frightened society (Elliott, 1996). When those who would in all probability wish to support what is a demonstrably well-intentioned government end up saying, 'All I know is that what is being done in the name of education is not what I would call education at all. It is about fear and pettiness and deliberate social exclusion' (Moore, 1999: 17), something has gone seriously awry. Similarly, the deeply felt anger in many primary (elementary) schools about what they saw as the political manipulation of booster funding arrangements had its roots firmly in the soil of an indignation that was neither self-righteous nor self-serving and was connected with what was seen as the questionable morality of the means rather than the ends of policy.

There are ways of addressing issues concerned with the integrity of means and ends, but they lie outside the intellectual arena of performativity. However, unless they are addressed at a fundamental philosophical level no amount of commitment will make a jot of difference. Joined-up policies, much trumpeted by those in power, require joined-up thinking that transcends more superficial continuities. Unless and until this is done teachers and their students will continue to feel and respond as objects rather than as agents of policy and their value will continue to reside and, what is equally damaging, be seen to reside in school performance rather than personal or communal significance.

'The functional is for the sake of the personal; the personal is through the functional'

It is a measure of the government's seriousness of purpose that the dialogue it has prompted delves deep into purposes and values and the relationship between them as well as into matters of a more transient relevance. These kinds of questions are undoubtedly the most difficult: they are, of course, primarily philosophical matters and it is to one of the UK's most profound and most neglected philosophers, John Macmurray, that we need to turn, both for their proper articulation and for their most likely resolution.

Macmurray argued that, broadly speaking, human beings enter into two kinds of relation with each other: functional relations which are essentially instrumental in nature and personal relations which have no purpose other than to enable us to be ourselves, as, for example in friendship or family. These two very different kinds of relationship will always remain different:

> They are opposites, with a tension between them. They are inseparable and limit one another. They are essential to one another and form a unity. Any attempt to fuse them or absorb one into another will fail because they are opposites. Any attempt to separate them will fail because they limit one another. Any effort to run them parallel with one

another without relating them will break down because they form an essential unity.

(Macmurray, 1941: 5)

Both functional and personal relations are necessary. However – and here is the centrally important point – the personal is the more important of the two. In Macmurray's view, the meaning of the functional lies in the personal, and not the other way round. The functional life is for the sake of the personal life: 'an economic efficiency which is achieved at the expense of the personal life is self-condemned, and in the end self-frustrating . . . the economic is for the sake of the personal' (1961: 187). However, the personal also needs the functional to become real. Whilst it is true that the functional life is for the sake of the personal life, it is also true that the personal life is through the functional life. Unless it were so the personal life, the life of community, would be merely well intentioned rhetoric.

The consequences of these insights seem to me profound and of substantial importance in helping us to identify why some aspects of current policy are successful and why some are not working in ways which had been anticipated or hoped. They also suggest a number of ways in which things might not only be done differently, but done better. Above all they suggest why teaching within the context of education must be understood and practised as a personal and not a technical activity, why schools should aspire to be vibrant learning communities and not merely effective learning organisations, and why education policy should rest upon values and understandings which ensure that economic activity is expressive of human flourishing, not its intended or *de facto* master (Fielding 2000a).

This line of argument points to the necessity of a radical break from the still dominant but increasingly moribund paradigm of school effectiveness. Here, and elsewhere in our society, we have utterly misunderstood the proper relationship between the functional and the personal. Here, in the 'high-performance organisation' or effective school model (Fielding 2000b: 53–4) the personal is used for the sake of the functional, community is primarily a convenient tool to achieve organisational purposes. Following Macmurray, I would suggest that the relationship should be completely reversed. Instead of schools as 'high-performance organisations' we need schools as 'person-centred communities'. Here the functional is for the sake of and expressive of the personal: organisation exists for the sake of community, not the other way round. The destructive and myopic obsession with outcomes is replaced by a commitment to schools as both morally and instrumentally successful (ibid.).

Whether the radical break I suggest is necessary follows my own suggestion of the 'person-centred school' or some other model which places human flourishing at the heart of our chosen educational processes remains to be seen. What we cannot do is continue as we are but more persistently and more intensely. The example offered by Governor Paul Patton of Kentucky, who ups the stakes by repeating 'Education, education, education, and education' four times rather than the now familiar three is unlikely to provide the lead we require: repetition is seldom the harbinger of new departures, and it is genuinely new departures we now need. It is undoubtedly true that we do need to remind ourselves of the importance of attending to the demands of 'what works': the worth of the philosophy, policy and practice of any approach to education is, of course, most appropriately judged by its impact on the realities of people's experience in the world. However, such a test must be complex rather than crude, patient rather than perfunctory or populist, creative rather than controlling, and productive in a richer and more wide-ranging sense than the dominant discourse currently allows. We have to break free from current modes of thinking and exhibit what in his contribution to this volume John Smyth calls 'a preparedness to think radically outside the frame'. Unless we do so we will fail profoundly and persistently to educate ourselves, our contemporaries and our children's children. At this juncture our most important tasks are intellectual. We are operating in the wrong frame of reference and as a consequence our lives will continue to become more busy, more exhausting, less humanly productive or satisfying and increasingly devoid of meaning. Alternative frameworks exist that are likely to serve our human needs more profoundly and more engagingly: it would be foolish to ignore them.

Notes

1 The special issue of the *Cambridge Journal of Education* 29, 3 (June 1999) contained papers by Stephen Ball, Michael Barber and Judy Sebba, Mike Davies and Gwyn Edwards, Michael Fielding, Helen Gunter, Valerie Hannon, David Hargreaves, Ann Limb and Peter Moss.
2 Michael Barber and Judy Sebba's paper now appears as a singly authored chapter by Michael Barber
3 Authors contributing new chapters to this book are Tom Bentley, John Elliott and Paul Doherty, Dean Fink, John Smyth, Richard Smith and Paul Standish, James Tooley, Mel West, and Peter Woods, Bob Jeffrey and Geoff Troman.

References

Barber, M. (1999) 'Teachers' place in the big picture', *Times Educational Supplement*, 12 February, p. 17.
Barber, M. and Sebba, J. (1999) 'Reflections on progress towards a world class education system', *Cambridge Journal of Education* 29 (3), 183–93.
Chitty, C. (2000) 'Crisis of identity', *Forum* 42 (3), 89–90.
Davies, N. (2000) *The School Report: Why Britain's Schools are Failing*, London: Vintage.
Elliott, J. (1996) 'School effectiveness research and its critics: alternative visions of schooling', *Cambridge Journal of Education* 26 (2), 199–224.
Fielding, M. (2000a) 'Community, philosophy and education policy: against the immiseration of contemporary schooling', *Journal of Education Policy* 15 (4), 397–415.

Fielding, M. (2000b) 'The person centred school', *Forum* 42 (2), 51–4.

Greene, M. (1997) 'Art and imagination: reclaiming a sense of the possible', in E. Clinch (ed.) *Transforming Public Education: a new course for America's future*, New York: Teachers' College Press, pp. 145–53.

Macmurray, J. (1935) *Reason and Emotion*, London: Faber.

Macmurray, J. (1941) 'Persons and Functions'. Outline document for a series of radio talks submitted to the BBC, 19 September. Unpublished manuscript.

Macmurray, J. (1961) *Persons in Relation*, London: Faber.

Moore, S. (1999) 'I'd rather sacrifice my children to my political beliefs than for the sake of an A-level grade or two', *New Statesman*, 26 February, p. 17.

Moore, S. (2000) 'Summerhill has filled the powers that be with fear of naked, feral children who never attend lessons', *New Statesman*, 27 March, p. 17.

Reay, D. and Wiliam, D. (1999) '"I'll be a nothing": structure, agency and the construction of identity through assessment', *British Educational Research Journal* 25 (3), 343–54.

Sennett, R. (1998) *The Corrosion of Character: The Personal Consequences of Work in the New Capitalism*, London: Norton.

Sergiovanni, T. J. (1994) 'Organizations or communities? Changing the metaphor changes the theory', *Educational Administration Quarterly* 30 (2), 214–26.

Simon, B. (2000) 'Blair on education', *Forum* 42 (3), 91–2.

Part I
The modernising agenda

2   High expectations and standards for all, no matter what

Creating a world class education service in England

Michael Barber

The vision

The determination of the Blair government to pursue education reform and bring about a step change in the performance of the education service is not in doubt. Ever since it was elected in May 1997 the Labour government has sought, with passion and purpose, to turn into a reality Blair's commitment in opposition to make 'Education, education and education' his three priorities.

The vision is a world class education service: one which matches the best anywhere on the planet. It should be achieved, not at some indeterminate date in the future, but as soon as possible within the decade that has just begun. The sense of urgency comes, not just from the belief that every passing day when a child's education is less than optimal is another day lost, but also from the belief that time is running out for public education to prove its worth. The danger is that as the economies of developed countries grow, more and more people will see private education for their children as a rational lifestyle option. If this were to occur, they would become less and less willing to pay taxes to fund public education, which over time would become, in the devastating phrase of the sociologist Richard Titmuss (1968) a generation ago, a poor service for poor people. It is hard to imagine how social cohesion could be achieved and how cascading, ever-growing inequality from one generation to another could be prevented under these circumstances.

Only if public education delivers, and is seen to deliver real quality, can this unwelcome prospect be avoided. We believe that successful reform is possible, that public education can meet not just the needs but the aspirations of all students in our diverse, modern societies; and that it need not take for ever. That is the vision before us.

The opportunity

In England we have an opportunity, possibly unique, to achieve that vision across an entire system of 24,000 schools and 7 million students. In its first term of office the government had a large majority and real power. Expenditure on education is increasing in real terms year on year – over 5 per cent real growth in the year 1999–2000, over 8 per cent in the year 2000–01 and three further years of real growth already promised (HM Treasury, 2000).

Furthermore, a combination of macroeconomic policy and changes in the tax and benefit system will mean that, by the end of the fiscal year 2000–01 over 1.2 million children will have been taken out of poverty since May 1997 with obvious benefits for education itself (Brown 2000). If it is not possible to reform education successfully in these favourable circumstances it is hard to imagine when it would be.

In seeking to achieve this vision we are highly conscious of our starting point. In a 1996 study of adult literacy (Carey *et al.* 1997), the United Kingdom fell behind most European countries and Australia, performing similarly to the United States. On maths for 13 year olds England fell below the average, as Figure 2.1 illustrates.

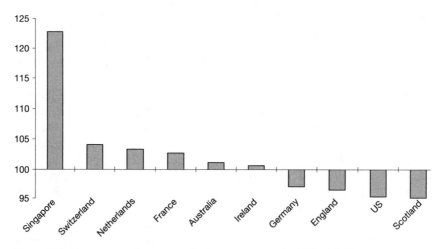

Figure 2.1 Country maths scores relative to average (= 100), 1965.
Source: derived from statistics in Keys *et al.* (1966)

Meanwhile the proportion leaving school unqualified or with low levels of qualification is unacceptably high compared with other developed countries. Clearly, this relatively poor starting point provides a greater impetus to reform. Both this starting point in terms of performance and its degree of ambition influence the extent to which any given government seeks a transformative approach to reform. After comparing our reform with eight others we arrived at the categorisation shown in Figure 2.2.

In the modern world, though, electorates are fickle and impatient. They do not take the word of politicians on trust. Why should they? They may be prepared to give a new government a little time to settle in, but only a little. Much as they may share the long-term vision of a world class education service, they will not wait patiently for five or ten years to see if it is delivered. They want immediate evidence that it is on the way. Hence the central

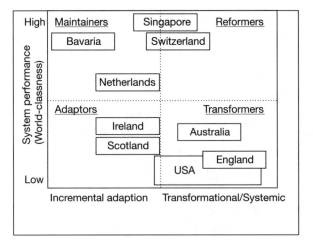

Figure 2.2 English education relative to other countries'

paradox facing education reformers in a democracy: a long-term strategy will succeed only if it delivers short-term results.

High challenge, high support

In order to move from the evidently underperforming system of the mid-1990s to the world class vision, and to do so while generating short-term results, we have developed a policy approach best described as 'high challenge, high support', which is illustrated in Figure 2.3. It is possible, by generalising ruthlessly, to see this diagram representing twenty-five years of educational history in England: ten years of low challenge and low support until, in the mid-1980s, the Thatcher government turned its formidable attention to the problems of the education service. Their answer? Increase the challenge: new standards, new tests, new school inspection and new publication of school test scores. Ten years of high challenge, low support followed. The increased challenge was not matched by investment in teachers' pay, smaller classes, improved technology, professional development or better school buildings. Nor was enough done to address the social circumstances that, particularly in declining industrial areas and large cities, made the daily job of educators more difficult. The result was some improvement but also conflict and demoralisation. During those conflicts many educators waited for the election of a Labour government that, the historical evidence suggested, would reduce the challenge and increase the support. But the Blair government did not believe the old approach would deliver either the long-term vision or the short-term results. Instead it built on the Conservative government's reforms, sharpened the challenge and, crucially, added the support. Hence high challenge, high support. The principles of this approach can be summarised briefly.

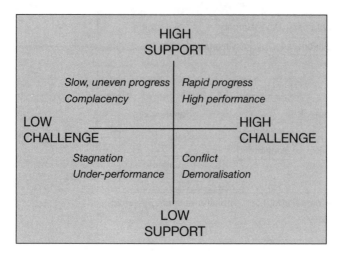

Figure 2.3 Policy approach of English education.
Source: Barber and Phillips (2000)

All students can achieve

- Set high standards and expect every student to meet them.
- Recognise that for some students, in some circumstances, reaching those high standards is more difficult: give them the extra assistance and time they need.

Easton (2000) summarises this approach excellently: if standards of achievement are the constant, then all the other factors in the equation – time, place, teaching approach and resource – must become variables.

Don't compromise on quality: invest in it

- Expect schools and teachers to do an excellent job: hold them to account for their performance.
- Reward success, challenge failure.
- Recognise that if teachers are to perform excellently they need the encouragement, the rewards, the support, the materials, the buildings and, above all, the professional development that makes sustained excellence possible.
- Recognise that, for some schools and some pupils, the challenge of meeting high standards is more demanding and provide the necessary targeted support.

A government that demands quality must provide it too

- Constantly restate the big picture and strategically manage reform so that the substantial demands of radical change are seen by headteachers and teachers as an investment in a better future rather than a series of unconnected initiatives which are here today and gone tomorrow.

- Create a culture in which everyone takes responsibility for student outcomes, including the Secretary of State for Education and in which problems, however intractable, are out in the open being tackled rather than being swept under the carpet.
- Invest steadily and ensure that, to use the Blair soundbite, all money is for modernisation.

The framework of continuous improvement

The way in which these principles of high challenge, high support are turned into practical policies which will drive school improvement is summarised in Figure 2.4. The policies for each segment (starting at twelve o'clock) are set out in Table 2.1. There are many parallels between this approach and what is known in the United States as standards-based reform. We are confident that in the medium and long term this framework for continuous improvement will work. The emerging evidence (Blunkett 2000) reinforces our confidence: the number of failing schools has fallen; the average time it takes to turn a failing school round has dropped from twenty-five months to under eighteen months; the percentage of students meeting standards at 16 and 18 has risen slowly but steadily; and the percentage of students leaving school with no qualifications has dropped significantly (from 8 per cent of the cohort to less than 6 per cent), though it is still too high.

Figure 2.4 Principles and policies (see Table 2.1)

Table 2.1 Policies for the segments of Figure 2.4

Ambitious standards
High standards set out in the National Curriculum
National Tests at age 7, 11, 14, 16
Detailed teaching programmes based on best practice
Optional World Class Tests based on the best 10 per cent in the 1995 TIMSS

Devolved responsibility
School as unit of accountability
Devolution of resources and employment powers to schools
Pupil-led formula funding
Open enrolment

Good data/clear targets
Individual pupil-level data collected nationally
Analysis of performance in national tests
Benchmark data annually for every school
Comparisons with all other schools with similar intake
Statutory target setting at district and school level

Access to best practice and quality professional development
Universal professional development in national priorities (literacy, numeracy, ICT)
Leadership development as an entitlement
Standards Site (http://www.standards.dfee.gov.uk)
Beacon Schools
LEA (district) responsibility
Devolved funding for professional development at school level
Reform of education research

Accountability
National inspection system for schools and LEAs (districts)
Every school inspected every four to six years
All inspection reports published
Publication annually of school/district-level performance data and targets

Intervention in inverse proportion to success (rewards, assistance, consequences)

For successful schools
Beacon status
Celebration events
Recognition
School Achievement Awards scheme
Greater autonomy

For all schools
Post-inspection action plan
School Improvement Grant to assist implementation of action plan
Monitoring of performance by LEA (district)

For underperforming schools
More prescriptive action plan
Possible withdrawal of devolved budget and responsibility
National and LEA monitoring of performance

Table 2.1 continued

Additional funding to assist turn-round (but only for practical improvement measures)

For failing schools
As for underperforming schools, plus:
Early consideration of closure
District plan for school, with target date for completing turn-round (maximum two years)
National monitoring three times a year
Possible Fresh Start or City Academy

For failing LEAs (districts)
Intervention by central government
Possible contracting out of functions to the private sector

Our welcome for this progress is tempered by the knowledge that it is neither rapid nor dramatic enough to convince us, or more importantly the citizens of our country, that we are on track to achieve world class standards within the next few years. In order to achieve the step change we require, in addition, three broad strategies have been developed and implemented, each one of which is aligned with and reinforces the framework for continuous improvement:

- the National Literacy and Numeracy Strategies at primary (elementary) level;
- the transformation of secondary education;
- the modernisation of the teaching profession.

The national literacy and numeracy strategies

The education system will never be world class unless virtually all children learn to read, write and calculate to high standards before they leave primary (elementary) school. At the time of the 1997 election the national data showed how far we were from achieving this goal. Only just over half of 11 year olds were meeting the standards set for their age in literacy and numeracy.

During 1996–7 Labour in opposition developed a national strategy to tackle this unacceptable state of affairs immediately after an election. Within a few days of that election therefore the new government was able to set ambitious national targets for the year 2002: that in literacy 80 per cent and in numeracy 75 per cent of 11 year olds should meet the standards set for their age. These targets are staging posts on the way to even higher levels of performance by the middle of this decade.

Our assumption, based on a review of the international research (e.g. Beard 1998; Literacy Task Force 1997) is that about 80 per cent of children will achieve those standards simply as a result of being taught well by teachers who know, understand and are able to use proven best practice. A further 15 per cent have a good chance of meeting the standards if, in addition, they receive extra small group tuition should they fall behind their peers. The remaining 5 per cent are likely from time to time to need one-to-one tuition, preferably early in their school career (i.e. before age 8). Some of these will prove able to meet the standards: for a very small percentage we do not yet have the knowledge or the capacity to enable them to meet the standards, but we will not give up trying.

To achieve these ambitious objectives we have progressively put in place what the leading Canadian educator Michael Fullan has called (Earl *et al.* 2000) the most ambitious, comprehensive and aligned national strategies anywhere in the world. The chief elements of the strategies are as follows:

- a nationally prepared project plan for both literacy and numeracy, setting out actions, responsibilities and deadlines through to 2002;
- a substantial investment sustained over at least six years and skewed towards those schools which need most help;
- a project infrastructure involving national direction from the Standards and Effectiveness Unit, fifteen regional directors and over 300 expert consultants at local level for each of the two strategies;
- an expectation that every class will have a daily maths lesson and a daily literacy hour;
- a detailed teaching programme covering every school year from age 5 to 11;
- an emphasis on early intervention and catch-up for pupils who fall behind;
- a professional development programme designed to enable every primary teacher to learn to understand and use proven best practice in both curriculum areas;
- the appointment of over 2,000 leading maths teachers and hundreds of expert literacy teachers, who have the time and skill to model best practice for their peers;
- the provision of 'intensive support' to around half of all schools where the most progress is required;
- a major investment in books for schools (over 23 million new books in the system since May 1997);
- the removal of barriers to implementation (especially a huge reduction in prescribed curriculum content outside the core subjects);
- regular monitoring and extensive evaluation by the national inspection agency, Ofsted;
- a National Curriculum for initial teacher training requiring all providers to prepare new primary teachers to teach the daily maths lesson and the literacy hour;
- a problem-solving philosophy involving early identification of difficulties as they emerge and the provision of rapid solutions or intervention where necessary;

- the provision of extra after-school, weekend and holiday booster classes for those who need extra help to reach the standard.

The impact of the strategies so far is evident in the national test results over 1997–2000. Figure 2.5 shows the progress towards the 2002 target in literacy. Figure 2.6 shows the impact of the government's numeracy strategy, with a fall in 1998 when a new mental arithmetic element was introduced to the test, followed by large rises in 1999 and 2000.

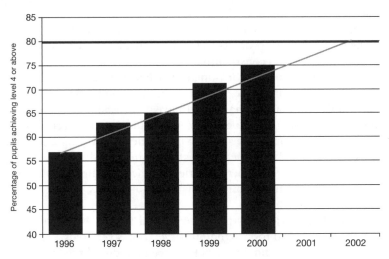

Figure 2.5 Pupils at level 4 or above in KS2 English tests.
Source: DfEE (2000)

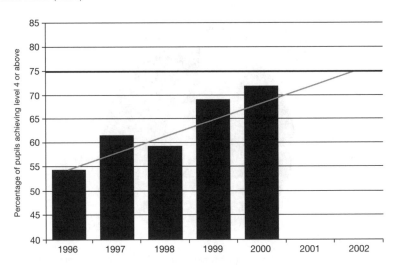

Figure 2.6 Pupils at level 4 or above in KS2 mathematics tests.
Source: DfEE (2000)

It is important to remember, though, that test results are only a representation. In the case of the tests we use they are a good representation, but what matters most is the reality of what students in schools know, understand and are able to do. The most heartening evidence so far of the impact of the strategy is not last year's test scores but the fact that teachers and Heads can see the difference day-to-day in the capacity of their students. Figures 2.7–8, taken from an independent opinion poll (BMRB 2000) shows what primary headteachers think about the impact of the strategies on standards. Sixty per cent believe the literacy programme has had 'quite a lot of impact' or more. In numeracy they are more positive still.

Secondary headteachers confirm these findings: they can see the difference in their new cohorts. The progress so far is only the beginning. Our intention is to pursue the strategies consistently, to refine them constantly and to invest in professional development for primary teachers through to 2004 at least. Each year the professional development programme will be based on analysis of what pupils and teachers have (and have not) been able to do well the previous year. Precision targeting of professional development across a system is one of our most important strategy innovations, ensuring both quality and cost effectiveness. While the overall strategy impacts directly on teaching, learning and student achievement, a series of other measures are designed to provide the necessary underpinning:

- Pre-school education has been introduced for all 4 year olds whose parents want it and for around 60 per cent of 3 year olds.
- Class sizes for 5, 6 and 7 year olds are being reduced to a maximum of thirty across the system. The latest average infant class size figure has dropped to 24.5.

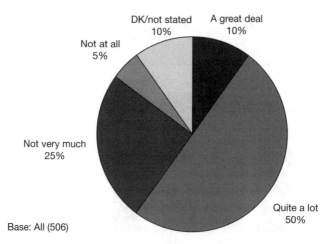

DK/not stated 10%
A great deal 10%
Not at all 5%
Not very much 25%
Quite a lot 50%
Base: All (506)

Figure 2.7 Do primary school headteachers think the National Literacy Strategy is raising standards?
Source: BMRB (2000)

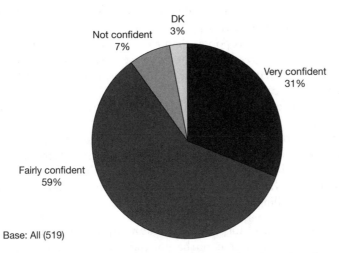

Figure 2.8 How confident are primary school headteachers that the National
        Numeracy Strategy will raise standards?
Source: BMRB (2000)

- Learning mentors (school-based counsellors) are being provided to help
  remove barriers to learning outside school from thousands of primary
  age pupils in the disadvantaged parts of large cities.
- After-school and/or summer learning opportunities are being offered in
  over 25 per cent of primary schools.
- Campaigns, including government-funded television advertisements, have
  been run to promote parental support for reading and mathematics.
- The National Year of Reading (in 1998–9) and Maths Year 2000 opened
  up opportunities for businesses, community groups, libraries, Churches
  and others to join the national crusade.
- Family literacy schemes are supporting parents whose own levels of
  literacy prevent them from assisting their children as much as they would
  like.
- Growing investment, year on year, is being made to provide extra assistance in literacy and maths for children whose first language is not English.

The result of these measures is not only to strengthen the capacity of the
system to deliver the demanding reward targets but also to take all the excuses
off the table.

The transformation of secondary education

In our drive for world class performance the next phase demands that we
modernise secondary education so that it builds on the growing success
of the primary sector rather than, as at present, dissipating it. Our data show
that currently in the middle years (age 11 to 14):

- Around 40 per cent of pupils made no progress or regressed in English and maths a year after leaving primary school.
- The quality of teaching is poorer than for any other age group.
- Pupils make less progress than in other phases, especially in science.
- The gap in performance between girls and boys, already evident at age 11, widens significantly.
- The performance of African-Caribbean pupils, especially boys, slips dramatically.
- Secondary schools with concentrations of pupils whose prior experience of learning has been uninspiring and whose present social circumstances are characterised by poverty face an enormous challenge.
- There is immense variation in performance among our secondary schools, even after controlling for intake.

In these circumstances it is not surprising that many aspirant parents of all classes, especially in the large conurbations, are sceptical about publicly provided secondary education. A key goal politically, socially and educationally is to convince this group that we can deliver a service which meets the needs and the aspirations of their children. Our strategy for doing so has two elements:

- a universal strategy to improve the quality of teaching and learning and therefore improve achievement for all pupils aged 11 to 14;
- a targeted programme called 'Excellence in Cities' designed to promote both equity and diversity in England's major conurbations.

Teaching and learning in the middle years (age 11–14)

Our intention over 2001–4 is to design and implement a strategy for the middle years which will be of comparable thoroughness and quality to the National Literacy and Numeracy Strategies at primary level but which takes account of the greater complexity of secondary schools and the secondary curriculum. Its main characteristics will be:

- new annual targets for schools and LEAs relating to the performance of 14 year olds and national targets for 2004;
- new tests for age 12 and 13 (in addition to those already in place for 11 and 14 year olds) to check that all pupils are making progress and that those who had not met national standards in literacy and numeracy by age 11 are catching up;
- extending the primary school strategies for literacy and numeracy into the middle years, including materials, a professional development programme and extra assistance for schools facing the greatest challenge;
- improving transfer arrangements from primary to secondary schools, including funding summer school provision aimed at transferring pupils in almost half of secondary schools;

- new teaching programmes for all curriculum subjects available electronically and in hard copy;
- the preparation and provision of professional development opportunities for all teachers in every subject;
- the preparation and provision of professional development opportunities in 'transforming teaching and learning' available to all secondary teachers and including the teaching of thinking skills, assessment against standards, student engagement and individual student-level target setting.

Each aspect of this comprehensive programme will be trialled over the next two years. It started in just over 200 secondary schools in September 2000. From September 2001 it will be extended and by September 2002 the full programme should be in place and making an impact on every one of our 4,000 secondary schools.

Excellence in Cities

Excellence in Cities (EiC) is a programme designed to transform both the reality and the perception of secondary education in England's largest conurbations. Its purpose is to convince both parents and students that publicly provided education can meet both their needs and their aspirations. If the programme is to succeed, it will need to guarantee high standards for all in the essential core of learning and, simultaneously, open up individual pathways and aspirations for each student. In short it will need to provide both *equity* and *diversity*. From the point of view of the individual student Figure 2.9 depicts precisely what we aim to achieve for each individual student.

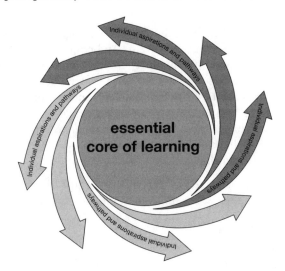

Figure 2.9 The aims of EiC for the individual student.
Source: Barber and Phillips (2000)

We have developed four core beliefs that inform every decision from national level to individual classroom. The statement sent to participating schools reads as follows:

High expectations of every individual
EiC will encourage all schools to have high expectations of every individual pupil and all young people to have high expectations of themselves. It will seek to meet the needs and aspirations of all young people, whatever their gifts and talents and to remove systematically the barriers to their learning, whether inside or outside the school. No pupil's education should be confined or restricted because of the school they happen to attend.

Diversity
EiC is designed to increase the diversity of provision in secondary education in the major conurbations. Diversity will differ dramatically from the past in two important respects. First – as with the Government's wider approach – it is not for a few at the expense of the many. Through the establishment of more specialist schools, more beacon schools, more EAZs and through City Learning Centres, many secondary schools will take on specialist functions in addition to their core function of providing a good rounded education for all their pupils.

Second, the additional resources a school receives under the programme are designed to bring higher performance, not just to that school, but to other schools in the area too.

Networks
EiC is based firmly on the belief that schools working together, collaboratively, can achieve more for pupils, parents and communities than schools working in isolation. Of course, each individual school is responsible for continuously improving its own performance. But by working with others to share best practice, tackle common problems and offer specialist opportunities to pupils from a range of schools, each school can help to enhance performance across an area. Promoting diversity, recognising excellence and disseminating good practice are essential to these networks working effectively.

Each pupil should see him or herself as a member, not just of a specific school community, but of a wider learning community committed to his or her success.

Extending opportunity
Some schools in large conurbations have always succeeded. Yet others, often close by, have suffered. The EiC programme is intended to bring success to every school rather than concentrate it in a few locations. The

investment that the EiC programme brings to an area should therefore extend opportunity. Rather than reinforcing current inequalities, it should enhance quality. Its purpose is to make Excellence for Everyone a reality rather than just a slogan.

To turn these beliefs into reality there are seven strands of the policy:

- *The gifted and talented*. Each participating school provides a teaching programme for the most gifted and talented 10 per cent of students at the school. Each school is part of a national training programme designed to enable them to do so.
- *Removing barriers to learning*. Each school provides a learning mentor – a trained, dedicated adult – whose job is to remove, for those pupils who require it, problems outside school that prevent learning in school.
- *Behaviour support*. New provision within schools of learning support units which strengthen a school's capacity to deal with disruptive students.
- *Beacon schools*. Schools of proven success, each given a funding and responsibility to provide professional development to other schools in the Excellence in Cities area; these schools are part of the IBM Wired for Learning initiative.
- *Specialist schools*. Schools that receive additional funding in order to provide a specialist focus in either technology, modern foreign languages, sports or arts and a responsibility to share that resource and expertise with others.
- *New City Learning Centres*. Centres, based at schools, designed to take advantage of the latest developments in technology and provide learning to students of all ages across a community during evenings, weekends and holidays as well as school time.
- *Education Action Zones*. Small networks of schools, in pockets of severe deprivation within large cities, focused on integrating primary and secondary education more effectively and also co-ordinating education, health and social services in those areas.

The programme started only in September 1999 but already there have been substantial reductions in truancy and exclusion and improvements in pupil attitude. It has broken down the isolation of many inner-city schools and encouraged a new sense of shared endeavour. We believe these are 'vital signs' of improvement. Ultimately the programme should result in a complete re-engineering of secondary education. Instead of fitting students into the system as we did in the twentieth century, we would build the system around the needs and aspirations of students.

The modernisation of the teaching profession

No matter how coherent our framework for school improvement is, no matter how successful our policies to strengthen primary and secondary education, world class standards will elude us unless we can recruit, retain and develop teachers and school leaders of real quality. There are major challenges in doing so:

- There are major teacher shortages in some secondary subjects including science, maths, modern foreign languages and music.
- Schools in challenging circumstances face particular recruitment and retention difficulties.
- There is a shortage of good candidates for leadership positions, especially at primary levels.
- These factors are particularly acute in London and the south-east, where the cost of living is much higher.

Beyond the challenges of recruitment and retention are other serious problems. While at the cutting edge of change there are growing numbers of teachers and school leaders who are embracing reform, the general culture in the profession is characterised by anxiety about change, sensitivity to criticism, and a sense of being overburdened. In addition, there is a pervasive belief, to some extent justified, that society does not value teachers sufficiently. The government's reform programme, with its powerful critique of the *status quo*, is simultaneously the short-term cause of some of this and the long-term solution. Either way, it is evident that as the economy continues to boom the education service will find itself competing ever more fiercely with the rapidly growing demands of the new economy for talented graduates. It is against this background that the government is implementing the most radical reform of the teaching profession since the Second World War.

In order to address these problems, some immediate, others still emerging, before they became acute the government published proposals for a comprehensive reform of the teaching profession in December 1998 (DfEE, 1998). The programme outlined at that time, modified slightly in the light of consultation, is currently being implemented. The new vision of a modernised teaching profession has five aspects.

Strengthening leadership

The framework for school improvement, with its emphasis on schools themselves taking responsibility for their own destiny, puts a high premium on leadership. It may be a simplification to say that the difference between success and failure is the quality of the headteacher, but it is not far from the truth. In the improvement of failing schools, for example, a change of headteacher has taken place in just over half of cases (Gray 2000; Stark 1998). The systemic problem is clear. The people currently in, or on the brink of, leadership positions have been promoted expecting to administer the traditional education system, only to reach the top and find it in a process of radical transformation. Their careers have prepared them to manage a system that no longer exists. Instead of managing stability they have to lead change. In place of an emphasis on smooth administration they find an unrelenting focus on pupil outcomes.

Our tasks as a government are to attract and develop a new generation of school leaders and to enable the present generation to adapt to this radically new and demanding world. To do so we have:

- created a new qualification for aspiring headteachers (the National Professional Qualification for Headship) which sets new standards and combines workplace learning with scholarship;
- provided all newly appointed headteachers with a £2000 voucher to spend on professional development, invited them every year to a major, high-profile conference in London and linked them with an online learning community in which they can debate among themselves and with internationally known education experts;
- established a new qualification for mid-career headteachers (the Leadership Programme for Serving Heads) which requires them to engage in vigorous, externally validated self-assessment;
- established a new National College for School Leadership which will have a state-of-the-art building on a university campus, develop an online as well as traditional presence, and will link our school headteachers with leaders in other sectors and their peers in other countries;
- worked with business to provide business mentors for thousands of school headteachers;
- improved headteachers' pay and capacity to earn performance bonuses;
- created a new leadership tier in each school;
- established a £50 million fund to enable the removal or retirement of headteachers who are not ready for the new challenge.

Linking pay and performance for teachers

The central challenge for us, as for many other education systems, is to recruit good people into teaching, enable those who are demonstrably successful to rise rapidly and improve the status of teachers in their own eyes and those of the public. Linking teachers' pay with their performance is the key to achieving these objectives. In addition to raising the pay of all teachers by more than inflation (a 3.5 per cent pay increase in 2001 with inflation around 2 per cent), we will introduce in the course of 2001:

- a new performance threshold for teachers seven years into their career or earlier if they are exceptional: their performance will be assessed by their headteacher and an external assessor against published standards (see below) which include the impact of their work on pupil performance; all those who meet the standard will receive a £2,000 pay rise (about 8 per cent extra for the average teacher) which will be consolidated permanently into their pay;

- a performance management system under which headteachers must assess every teacher's contribution annually in improving the performance of both the pupils and the school;
- two routes to higher pay above the threshold, one for taking on management and administration, the other for being an outstanding teacher; the historic complaint of teachers ('The only way to get promoted is to stop teaching') has thus been answered;
- a School Achievement Award scheme which will provide lump sum bonuses to be distributed among the staff of those schools which have demonstrated substantial improvement or sustained excellence; about 30 per cent of schools will benefit.

The threshold standards

Teachers should:

- have a thorough and up-to-date knowledge of the teaching of their subject(s) and take account of wider curriculum developments which are relevant to their work;
- consistently and effectively plan lessons and sequences of lessons to meet pupils' individual learning needs;
- consistently and effectively use a range of appropriate strategies for teaching and classroom management;
- consistently and effectively use information about prior attainment to set well-grounded expectations for pupils and monitor progress to give clear and constructive feedback;
- show that, as a result of their teaching, their pupils achieve well relative to the pupils' prior attainment, making progress as good as or better than similar pupils nationally;
- take responsibility for their professional development and use the outcomes to improve their teaching and pupils' learning;
- make an active contribution to the policies and aspirations of the school.

These proposals have been highly controversial within the teaching profession, but broadly supported outside it. The flashpoint has been the government's insistence that pupil outcomes must be taken into account in assessing a teacher's performance. We have done so partly because, to anyone outside the teaching profession, it is simply not credible to leave the central purpose of an activity out of the assessment of it, and partly because our wider objective is to create a culture in the education service in which everyone, whatever their role, takes responsibility for pupil performance.

Improving professional development

For most teachers professional development has traditionally been haphazard, off-site, barely relevant, poorly provided and a chore at best. I exaggerate, but not much. If we are to create an education service capable of both achieving world class standards and changing rapidly, we know we have to do much better. We are significantly increasing investment in professional development year on year, but the issue is at least as much one of the nature and quality of provision. Across the country as a whole, expenditure on professional development is likely to exceed 5 per cent of the total teachers' salary bill for the first time in 2001. To improve quality as well as quantity we have:

- developed the capacity to organise and deliver professional development of quality to all teachers on themes of high national priority, such as literacy and numeracy in primary schools;
- begun to put in place arrangements to ensure that each school, in addition to its mainstream devolved budget, has a clearly identified, separate pot of money for professional development designed to support its own improvement strategy;
- developed programmes, most currently in their pilot phase, to encourage individual teachers to see their own professional development as both a right and a responsibility. Among them are state-funded individual learning accounts for teachers in disadvantaged areas, research scholarships and international exchange opportunities;
- sought to enhance the capacity of teachers to provide professional development for their peers through the creation of beacon schools, advanced skills teacher posts and, for national priorities, the creation of networks of exemplary professionals such as our 2,000 leading maths teachers, each given several days a year to share good teaching practice with colleagues in other schools;
- established a General Teaching Council to promote higher professional standards and improve the status of the profession.

Strengthening the preparation of teachers

While our professional development reforms are improving the skills of the existing teaching force, we are also seeking to improve the training and preparation of new entrants. Our reforms to date have:

- imposed a new National Curriculum for initial teacher training setting out the standards and content of training courses which all providers must follow;
- introduced training salaries of £6,000 (£13,000 for teachers of shortage subjects) for good graduates doing postgraduate training or for mature entrants joining teaching through the employment-based routes;
- required for all newly qualified teachers an induction year with a lighter timetable and clear standards for achievement by the end of the year;
- run television and cinema advertising promoting teaching as a career;

- developed plans for a fast-track route into teaching for exceptional candidates of any age, with extra intensive training, extra pay and extra responsibility.

These measures are designed to lead into the wider reforms allowing talented teachers to progress more rapidly than ever. It is too early to say what their impact will be but applications for initial teacher training are up significantly since the new training salaries were announced.

Providing greater support

Teaching is demanding work at any time. During a period of rapid change and high public profile it is exceptionally demanding. If teachers are to be successful in the future, we will need to enable them to prioritise teaching, learning and their own professional development and simultaneously to relieve them of the other demands on their time. So far we have not achieved the balance we would want, but a number of measures are beginning to make a difference:

- a major investment in school buildings (11,000 improved since May 1997), staff facilities and information and communications technology;
- the provision of standards, teaching materials, planning guidance, data and best practice advice through the internet (the standards site had 17,000 pages searched on Christmas Day!);
- making provision for, and encouraging, the use of technical expertise to maintain ICT systems, manage school budgets, etc;
- training and developing over 20,000 additional teaching assistants, particularly to support literacy and numeracy teaching in primary schools;
- reducing bureaucratic burdens on schools and teachers by streamlining administrative systems.

The problems

I work for the government. It is my job to promote policies, show their coherence and expect them to work. By any standards the programme is an ambitious one and I believe it will work and achieve our objective of creating a world class system. No one, however, is likely to believe my account or share my optimism unless I draw attention to the problems and 'messiness' which accompany this reform, just as they accompany any major programme of change. Indeed, just over three years on, it would not be no exaggeration to say it is at a critical stage. A great many elements are currently in intensive implementation – literacy, numeracy, the pay threshold, performance management and training for ICT, for example. The capacity of the system (not to mention many individual headteachers and teachers), is stretched to the limit. Only if each element of the reform is well planned and implemented can we achieve successful and irreversible reform.

In the meantime, the challenges remain substantial:

- Too few teachers see the big picture of reform and the experience of the past decade leaves them sceptical about whether any government ever sees a reform through.
- In order to promote radical change the government has to spell out a compelling critique of the present but, in doing so, too often portrays schools and teachers negatively.
- The sustained drive from central government is perceived as an entirely top-down reform with its associated pressure to conform, whereas all evidence suggests that successful reform requires a combination of top down and bottom up change.
- The growing assertiveness of central government, on the one hand, and of headteachers of successful schools, on the other, has placed local education authorities, the middle tier, in an uncomfortable position, criticised from the school end for being interfering bureaucrats and from the centre for not being sufficiently effective in implementing reform.
- The system for funding schools has been too complex, has lacked sufficient transparency and has been a cause of tension; too often it provides an excuse for schools or LEAs not to take responsibility for reform and, from a central government point of view, does not always deliver the substantial extra resources to the front line where it makes most difference.
- And, of course, even highly competent governments make mistakes occasionally, which, even in a context of broadly successful progress, create 'noise' and frustration in the system.

Our success in bringing about irreversible reform will depend on our ability to address these problems, and minimise their negative consequences, while sustaining the implementation of the overall strategy until all students achieve high standards, no matter what.

Conclusion

The present phase of reform is all-embracing and urgent but, even as it is implemented, it is important to look ahead and to anticipate the shape of reform to come. I want to finish this chapter with some speculations about the future.

The first task is to see things through

The first task in the next three to five years is to embed the reforms currently being put in place and ensure they become irreversible. The literacy and numeracy strategies at primary level need to be constantly refined and built upon for at least another four years so that every primary teacher's skills reach high levels. The performance management system needs to ensure that every teacher is focused on the quality of their teaching so that all students achieve high standards. The system needs to develop the capacity to prevent failure as well as to tackle it after it has occurred.

All this is not about new reforms but ensuring the present ones work. The last twenty years of education reform are littered with programmes which have been inadequately implemented or abandoned by governments without the courage or strategic sense to see them through to impact on student performance. We will not make that mistake.

If it all works, the result will be schools with high autonomy and high performance

The policy principle of intervention in inverse proportion to success is being applied steadily. If our overall strategy works, as more schools succeed, so they will have greater autonomy and reward. Ultimately each school will have very substantial autonomy. Each would have responsibility for meeting standards in the core areas of learning, but also for making a distinctive contribution to the system as a whole. The autonomy would not be unconditional. It would have been earned, because performance had been demonstrated. Government's role in these circumstances would shift from driving reform to creating the conditions, and crucially the culture, for a transformation that would be led and created by the schools themselves. This is precisely the shift that has happened in successful businesses, with the centre shaping overall direction and culture while front-line units lead innovation and respond to ever higher customer demands.

School reform will globalise

Just as financial services globalised in the 1980s, and media and communications in the 1990s, so in the 2000 we will see education reform globalising. The impact of the international comparisons of the 1990s, such as TIMSS, was profound. Increasingly researchers and policy makers have extended their horizons beyond national boundaries in the search for solutions. This process will go much further as technological change and globalisation gather pace. The death of distance, best characterised by e-business, will not leave education untouched. We will see the globalisation of large elements of the curriculum. We, in England, will want to be sure that our 14 year olds are as well as educated as students in the United States, Germany or Singapore, not least because ultimately they will be competing in a global job market. In any case, physics is the same in Kentucky as in Kent. Media and communications organisations will prepare and market internationally excellent interactive materials that will influence curriculum, standards, pedagogy and assessment across international boundaries. They will also re-engineer where and how learning takes place. It is hard to predict how this will happen: successful school systems will be those open-minded and sensitive enough to spot it when it does.

The school will remain crucial, providing the foundation of learning, the induction into democratic society and the constant support that every individual student needs, but it will cease to be the provider of all learning for each student. Instead, while it will provide some, it will also seek learning opportunities in other schools, in out-of-school learning settings (such as museums), in the community, in the workplace or over the internet. It will be an advocate for the student and a guarantor of quality. Increasingly teachers and headteachers will think not just outside the boundaries of their school building, but beyond their city and their country too. To anticipate this in England we intend to provide international exchange opportunities for 5,000 teachers a year and from next year through the new Leadership College offer every headteacher the opportunity to link to their peers abroad.

The central question for public authorities will cease to be 'Who provides?' Instead they will ask, 'How is the public interest to be secured?'

We must ask ourselves from where the energy, knowledge, imagination, skill and investment will come to meet the immense challenge of education reform over the next decade.

For most of the twentieth century the drive for educational progress came from the public sector, often in combination with the religious or voluntary sectors. Towards the end of the twentieth century, as frustration with existing systems grew, this legacy was challenged by a growing vibrant private sector, especially in the United States, but also in many other parts of the world, including China, Africa and South America. The challenge for the twenty-first century is surely to seek out what works. The issue is not whether the public, private or voluntary sector alone will shape the future, but what partnerships and combinations of the three will make the most difference to student performance.

There is a rich field for research and development here and we need to know more. In England we are consciously experimenting by creating new vehicles for partnership with the private sector, for example through the Private Finance Initiative bringing private capital into school building and the seventy Education Action Zones bringing private and public sectors together to raise standards in areas of disadvantage. The 550 beacon schools, some linked with IBM's Wired for Learning and 569 specialist schools which play an important role in sharing best practice, also involve business partners.

We are also intentionally breaking the mould in our relations with the voluntary and religious sectors by, for example, providing for the first time state funding for Muslim, Sikh and Seventh Day Adventist schools as well as Catholic, Anglican and Jewish schools, which have received state funding for over a century.

The central challenge is to build social coalitions in the drive for higher standards and radical reform. It is clear in Hong Kong and elsewhere that the business and religious sectors are strong allies. This is true in the United States too, where, in cities like Philadelphia, the Churches provide real energy and drive for educational progress. It is clear in eastern Europe, where the Soros Foundation is investing heavily in early years education. Each a different combination, each fit for a purpose and each shifting the public policy question from 'Who provides education?' to 'How can the public interest in education be secured?'

Public authorities will need to invest more in education than ever before, partly because of technology and pressure to improve teachers' pay, conditions and professional development, but mainly because they will be striving to achieve much higher performance standards for *all*, not just some, students. Meanwhile, those parents able to will spend more money than ever on their children's education. Some may choose private schools, depending on the quality of public provision locally, but many will spend on resources for the home and on out-of-school learning opportunities of all kinds.

The challenge for government will therefore be, not only to provide high-quality schools, but also to provide the equivalent of the home and out-of-school learning opportunities for those students whose parents do not have the will or the means to provide them. This will be crucial from an equity as well as from a performance point of view, and opens up an entirely new area for public policy.

References

Barber, M. and Phillips, V. (2000) 'The fusion of pressure and support', *Journal of Educational Change* 1 (3), 277–81.

Beard, R. (1998) *National Literacy Strategy: Review of Research and other Related Evidence*, London: DfEE.

Blunkett, D. (2000) 'Raising Aspirations in the Twenty-first Century', speech given at the North of England Education Conference, 6 January, London: DfEE.

British Market Research Bureau (2000) *The National Literacy Strategy Survey of Head Teachers Report*, London: BMRB Social Research.

Brown, G. (2000) Chancellor of the Exchequer's Budget Statement, 21 March, Hansard, vol. 346, p. 865.

Carey, S., Low, S. and Hansbro, J. (1997) *Adult Literacy in Britain*, London: ONS.

Department for Education and Employment (1998) *Teachers: Meeting the Challenge of Change*, Green Paper Cm 4164, London: Stationery Office.

Department for Education and Employment (2000) *Statistics of Education: Statistical Bulletin*, London: Stationery Office.

Earl, L., Fullan, M., Leithwood, K., Watson, N. with Jantzi, D., Levin, B. and Torrance, N. (2000) *Watching and Learning*, first annual report of the OISE/UT evaluation of the implementation of the National Literacy and Numeracy Strategies, Nottingham: DfEE Publications.

Easton, L. (2000) 'If standards are absolute', *Education Week* 19 (31), 50–3.

Gray, J. (2000) *Schools causing Concern but Improving*, London: DfEE Publications.

Keys, W., Harris, S. and Fernandes, C. (1996) *Third International Mathematics and Science Study, First National Report*, Part 1, *Achievement in Mathematics and Science at Age 13 in England*, Slough: NFER.

Literacy Task Force (1997) *The Implementation of the National Literacy Strategy*, London: DfEE.

Stark, M. (1998) 'No slow fixes, either: how failing schools in England are being restored to health', in L. Stoll and K. Myers (eds) *No Quick Fixes: Perspectives on Schools in Difficulty*, Lewes: Falmer Press.

Titmuss, R. M. (1968) *Commitment to Welfare*, London: Allen & Unwin.

HM Treasury (2000) *Prudent for a Purpose: Working for a Stronger and Fairer Britain*, London: Stationery Office.

Acknowledgements

Shorter versions of this chapter appeared in B. Lucas and T. Greany (eds) *Schools in the Learning Age*, London: Campaign for Learning (2000), and the *Times Educational Supplement*, 7 July 2000.

Part II
Alternative perspectives, particular values

3 Labour, learning and the economy

A 'policy sociology' perspective

Stephen J. Ball

Whatever else one would want to say about Labour's education policies there is certainly no shortage of them! At the 1998 Labour Party Annual Conference a briefing paper for delegates (*Pledges into Action: Education and Employment*, Labour Party Policy Unit) listed forty-seven education-related policies, initiatives and funding decisions announced since the 1997 election victory. There have been still more moves and announcements since the conference. A great number of these policy activities are aimed at remediating the neglect and omissions of the previous Conservative administrations: protecting school playing fields, cutting class sizes, additional funding for Local Education Authorities (LEAs), £2 billion for school repairs, etc. Another group cluster round the issues of school improvement and the raising of educational 'achievement' – I shall return to the use of the quotation marks later – including 'a new national literacy framework', 'improved teacher training', a 'fresh start' for 'failing schools', 'an expanded specialist school programme' (the Secretary of State hopes to see the number of such schools rise to 450), 'Education Action Zones', 'national numeracy targets' and 'support projects to improve school attendance', etc. All of this amounts to a cash injection over three years of £19 billion, according to government figures. Interestingly, however, relatively little of previous Conservative policy, of which there was also a great deal, has been dispensed with. The phasing out of the assisted places scheme, the compromise over grant maintained school status, the closing of the Funding Agency for Schools and the abandoning of the nursery voucher scheme are the notable exceptions. Furthermore, the three key non-governmental agency figures from the previous Conservative administration have been retained, Woodhead at the Office for Standards in Education (OfStEd), Tate at the Qualifications and Curriculum Authority (QCA) and Millett at the Teacher Training Agency (TTA). It is hardly a startling conclusion, then, to suggest that despite the flurry of policy activity in and around education under Labour we need to attend as much to the continuities as to the differences between Labour and the Conservatives.[1] Crump (1998), David (1998) and Whitty (1998) make much the same point. The significance of continuity was evident in Labour's stance in opposition and explicit in the election manifesto: 'Some things the

Conservatives got right. We will not change them' (Tony Blair, Manifesto, p. 3).

In this chapter I want to consider Labour's education policy portfolio in two loosely related ways. First, I argue for the need to see the policy continuities noted above in an international context and to suggest that in a sense Labour's policies are not specific to Labour at all; they are local manifestations of global policy paradigms – policyscapes. Second, I begin to sketch out an argument which suggests that in one key respect Labour's policy thrust is contradictory in its own terms, i.e. the overriding emphasis on education's role in contributing to economic competitiveness rests on a set of pedagogical strategies the effects of which are actually antithetical to the needs of a 'high skills' economy. As an aside here I will also suggest that this contradiction arises in part from an inherited, and ultimately self-defeating, impoverished view of 'learning'. I shall also point to some of the effects of *performativity* (Ball 1998c) in relation to teaching and learning.

I am not attempting to arrive at a finished or definitive position in the chapter. Rather, I offer some ways of thinking about Labour education policy, some initial moves which may open up useful avenues of analysis or which may turn out to be dead ends!

Global local policies

To a great extent, despite issues of levels of funding and the specificity of some individual schemes and initiatives – I shall return to the question of specificity later – the basic organising principles of educational provision have been taken over from the Conservatives untouched and unquestioned. There are three primary interrelating principles:

- *Choice and competition.* The commodification and consumerisation of education.
- *Autonomy and performativity.* The managerialisation and commercialisation of education.
- *Centralisation and prescription.* The imposition of centrally determined assessments, schemes of work and classroom methods.

An examination of Labour's policy rhetoric might suggest the development of a fourth organising principle, around 'equality of opportunity' (or 'fairness' or 'tackling the spiral of disadvantage' – the lexicon varies between documents and between speeches). However, it is difficult to see this as a principle convincingly embedded in the practices and structures of provision. Indeed, policies like specialisation and selection and the support of 'setting' in schools and the unquestioning acceptance of 'choice' suggest a confused or at best weak commitment to social justice (see Edwards 1998). The explicit commitment to tackling exclusion does not seem to be matched by efforts to maximise inclusion. What I mean by that is that the excluding effects of educational processes themselves remain unaddressed. As Whitty (1998: 2) puts it: 'The government has adopted a fairly conventional view of educational knowledge and avoided awkward sociological questions about its selective nature and social functions'. O'Brien (1998: 3) points out that Labour's education policies can be understood and analysed as 'a synthesis between market and social democratic values' or rather a dichotomy 'informed by two separated strands of philosophical thought', although Jones (1996) prefers the term 'bricolage'. Indeed, in some ways parallel to Thatcherism, Blairism or New Labour rests upon a set of tensions between traditional Labour values and 'think-tank radicalism'. Of course, the 'Third Way' is intended to provide the post-socialist resolution of this dialectic. Within all this, equity issues do not so much disappear entirely as become 'framed and reframed'; 'competing discourses are "stitched together" in the new policies' (Taylor and Risvi, 1997: 9). The meanings of equity are refracted, reworked and realised in new ways, 'glossing over the different perspectives of key players' (p. 10).

Clearly, the emphasis between the three organising principles differs between Labour and Conservative, as it does in other national political contexts, but all three currently remain as unassailable bases of the organisation and delivery of education and all are clearly represented in Labour's current policies. (I shall have to leave the reader to match up specific policies to principles.) However, I am not suggesting that these continuities are simply an example of a Labour government having succumbed to the political and ideological project of the 'New Right'. Rather, New Labour and the political and ideological project of the New Right are, in many respects – again, not all – different manifestations of the globalisation of 'ideological discourses which frame education policies at the national level' (Taylor and Risvi, 1997: 61). The differences are matters of emphasis rather than distinctiveness.

What is happening within this ensemble of policies is the modelling of the internal and external relations of schooling and public service provision more generally upon those of commercial, market institutions. In the process 'the structure and culture of public services are recast . . .'. These policies introduce 'new orientations, remodel existing relations of power and affect how and where social policy choices are made' (Clarke *et al.*, 1994: 4). They play a key role in the wearing away of professional/ethical regimes that were dominant in schools and bringing about their replacement by entrepreneurial/ competitive regimes. They are also involved in the increasing subordination of education to 'the economic' and the rendering of education itself into the commodity form, i.e. 'education systems have been made objects of micro-economic reform with educational activities being turned into saleable or corporatised market products as part of a national efficiency drive' (Taylor and Risvi, 1997: 77). Educational provision is itself increasingly made susceptible to profit, and educational processes play their part in the creation of the enterprise culture and the cultivation of enterprising subjects (see Kenway *et al.* 1993). In both relational senses the classification and framing of educational organisation and culture are weakened. Schools become more like businesses and more business-like. Educational knowledge is reworked in terms of the skills, competences and dispositions required by the economy (although see the discussion of this in the next section). Parents and students are positioned as consumers (see Ball 1998a for an extended discussion) and entreated to compare schools in terms of published performance indicators. Competition between schools for market share is encouraged. As Bernstein (1996: 75) puts it: 'the steps taken to measure and maintain performance, for the survival of the institution, is likely to facilitate a state-promoted instrumentality'. In each respect education is increasingly subject to 'the normative assumptions and prescriptions' (Linguard *et al.* 1998: 84) of 'economism' and 'the kind of "culture" the school is and can be' is articulated in its terms.

Now, whatever else I say here, I am not suggesting that Labour's education policies can be read off in their entirety from a global educational agenda or that Labour has no real control over its policy decisions, set as they are within the logic of the global market. Education has a complex set of relationships with and within the processes of globalisation. However, I do want to suggest that there is a process of convergence of education and social welfare policies between countries which have very different political and social welfare histories. I do not mean by this what might be called 'simple convergence', i.e. exactly the same policies being invoked in very different national settings, but rather a 'paradigm convergence', the invocation of policies with common underlying principles, similar operational mechanisms and similar first and second-order effects: first-order effects in terms of their impact on prac- titioners, practice and institutional procedures and second-order effects in terms of social justice – patterns of access, opportunity and outcome. (See also Whitty *et al.* 1998: 39–42, for a discussion of convergence.)

> In terms of the interplay between the national and the global in education policy what I am suggesting is a 'relational' analysis; 'globalisation invades local context but does not destroy them'.
>
> (Giddens, 1996)

> Policies need to be understood as the product of a nexus of influences and interdependencies, resulting in 'interconnectedness, multiplexity and hybridisation'.
>
> (Amin 1997: 129)

> . . . the intermingling of global, distant and local logics.
>
> (Ball 1998c: 133)

It is possible to analyse and discuss the education 'policy epidemic' with an emphasis either on the global similarities or on the local differences. Levin (1998) and Whitty and Edwards (1998) among others emphasise the latter. I intend to focus on the former and attend to what one of my students calls 'commonality within difference' (Marques Cardoso 1998) or what Sweeting and Morris (1993) call 'exogenous trends'.

Carter and O'Neil (1995) summarise evidence on the state of education policy making in their two-volume collection on international perspectives on educational reform by identifying what they call 'the new orthodoxy' – 'a shift is taking place', they say, 'in the relationship between politics, government and education in complex Westernised post-industrialised countries at least' (p. 9). They cite five main elements to this new orthodoxy:

- improving national economics by tightening a connection between schooling, employment, productivity and trade;
- enhancing student outcomes in employment-related skills and competences;
- attaining more direct control over curriculum content and assessment;
- reducing the costs to government of education;
- increasing community input to education by more direct involvement in school decision making and pressure of market choice.

Levin (1998: 131) identifies what he calls 'an epidemic of education policy' and six themes 'which seem common across many jurisdictions'. These map almost perfectly on Carter's list with the addition of the point that:

> Educational change is occurring in the context of large-scale criticism of schools. Government policy documents typically take the view that schools systems have failed to deliver what is required and that the failure is lamentable in view of the high level of spending on education. The general tone underlying much reform is negative. . . .

This comment would certainly be appropriate to the United Kingdom. The one point of divergence in Labour policy from these lists is the increase in education funding noted above.

In part at least the establishment of a global policy paradigm in education and social welfare could be identified with the activities of certain key supranational agencies (World Bank, IMF, OECD).[2] For example, Philip Jones (1998) argues that the World Bank's 'preconditions for education can only be understood as an ideological stance, in promoting an integrated world system along market lines'. The role of such agencies can be seen as partly that of enforcement, but also partly the legitimation of market policies as economic common sense and as the only logical format for public service provision (Vanegas 1998). However, the most immediate impact of World Bank policies is on debtor and developing nations rather than the Western and Asian developed economies. Perhaps what is more significant for our concerns is the way in which the World Bank, the OECD, etc., represent the accepted, collective wisdom of 'the West'. As Cerny (1990: 205) puts it, the stance and policies of these agencies define 'the very nature of economics and therefore the potential range and scope of policies themselves'.

These agencies are strongly committed to the market form, as noted by Jones (see also Unterhalter 1996). The World Bank and OECD have also been powerful advocates of the use of performance indicators in education. And the 1988 OECD conference 'Education and the Economy in a Changing Society':

> took as its theme the convergence of education and economic functions in the new global context, arguing the centrality of the 'human factor' as an element in production: 'the skills and qualifications of workers are coming to be viewed as critical determinants of effective performance of enterprises and economies'.
>
> (Taylor and Risvi, 1997: 69)

However, these agencies are not the only vehicles disseminating the 'new orthodoxy'. Academic networks and academic entrepreneurs also play a key role in the international flow of policy solutions (Ball 1998a). There also arises a complex but always selective inter-borrowing of mutually reinforcing ideas about and models for education (e.g. 'Blunkett takes a lesson from Swiss on teaching 3 Rs', *Times*, 14 May 1997; see Brown *et al.* 1998). The general fearfulness about and the political usefulness of 'crises' in international competitiveness encourage this inter-borrowing and contribute to convergence (see also below on 'New Growth Theory').

Politicians, policy makers and planners learn to think policy within the discourse of 'economism' which 'recognises no other form of interest' (Bourdieu 1990: 112). The discourse of economism constructs the topic – the 'problem' of education – and, as with any discourse, it appears across a range of texts, forms of conduct and at a number of different sites at any one time. Discursive events 'refer to the one and the same object . . . there is a regular style and . . . constancy of concepts . . . and "strategy" and a common institutional, administrative or political drift and pattern' (Cousins and Hussain 1984: 84–5).

Learned incompetence

The general orientation of Labour education policy to the global competitiveness of the economy is very clear and recurs constantly in policy texts of various kinds. Clearly, again, this orientation can be seen in itself as part of a global flow of policy concepts related to fairly abstract conceptions about the shift towards 'knowledge-based', 'high-skills' economies and a consequential realignment of education policies, i.e. the substitution of 'labour-focused' policies for 'capital-focused' ones. More specifically in the case of New Labour, this policy realignment may also be understood as resulting from the impact of 'New Growth Theory' thinking, 'borrowed' in turn from US Democratic Party interest in and use of the work of economists like Robert Reich. New Growth Theory puts an end to 'the cleavage between economic and social policies' (Reich 1983: xx) – the triumph of economism!

White's (1998) discussion of the Third Way represents this as 'empl[...] centred social policy' – 'a prime example of the dual commitment to the [...] of opportunity and personal responsibility' (p. 6). In effect, social [...] educational policies are collapsed into economic and industrial policy. Su[...] collapses are often indicated in policy condensates like 'The Learning Society' (in the United Kingdom) or 'The Clever Country' (Australia). Or as David Blunkett explained in his 1998 Labour Party Conference speech:

> We recognise the very real challenge facing manufacturing industry in this country and the way in which we need to support and work with them for skilling and re-skilling for what Tony Blair has described as the best economic policy we have – 'education'.

The issue I want to raise in relation to this is a substantive one. If we accept the argument of a 'synthesis' or 'collapse' of policies, how should we evaluate the effectiveness of current school-related policies in terms of meeting the needs of the economy and international competitiveness? Labour's approach to this question is a highly technocratic one based on a black-box, input/output approach to educational planning.[3] The inputs take various forms, most obviously and pertinently such things as 'a greater focus on mental arithmetic', 'the new Literacy Hour' and a 'dedicated Numeracy Hour'. There is also the 'strong focus on effective teaching in literacy and numeracy' in 'improved teacher training'. Schemes of work are being written for National Curriculum subjects. The Numeracy and Literacy Hours are 'supported' by step-by-step manuals and how-to-do-it videos. The outputs are also various. They range from setting 'national numeracy targets' – '75 per cent of all 11 year olds to reach Level 4 for 2002' – to the publication of school National Test results and the continuing use of raw GCSE performance scores as the basis of local league tables of secondary schools. Locked inside the black box, an absent presence, out of sight in this policy panopticon, is LEARNING!

Now Labour's stance towards learning can be viewed in two ways. Either as based upon the antiquated, pre-theoretical, transmission mode conception of the learning process (which has been reinforced by various international borrowings) – the banking concept of learning, as Friere once called it. Indeed, there is a certain degree of support for this, as we shall see. Or as representing an aversion to learning – having no conception at all of the processes and meaning of learning. A quick perusal of the Green Paper *The Learning Age* would tend to support this latter position. There is no explicit discussion of learning as such at all. The acquisition of skills and dispositions is effectively stripped of social and psychological meaning. This might also be seen as a point of continuity with the Conservatives[4] and ties in with the TTA's attempts to proscribe work on learning theories in initial teacher training.

Also inside the black box teachers are caught between the imperatives of prescription and the disciplines of performance. Their practice 'steered' *and* 'rowed' – overdetermined! Paradoxically, the managerial models and techniques which are being used to redesign teaching practices draw upon

mode of regulation and control (Fox 1974). As Hanlon
issue of trust, who is trusted, and why they are trusted
ill the case that teachers are not trusted.

e is that rather than 'raising standards' in any real
1 producing skills and attributes relevant to a
ny, the overdetermined New Labour classroom may
1 of young people marred by what Hugh Lauder

...ucal issue must surely be in part a question not only of test results but how they are arrived at. . . . In England the problem of how to raise basic educational standards while preserving or developing creativity is not even part of the public debate . . . if we are not careful policy settings which emphasise results at the expense of methods will lead to a trained incapacity to think openly and critically about problems that will confront us in ten or twenty years time throughout the system.

(Lauder *et al.*, 1998: 15)

How does this happen? In the simplest sense it is a problem of 'teaching to the test'. Drilling students, individually and competitively, in and for specific, context-bound, abstract tasks. An emphasis that is on repetitive, short-term memory tactics and narrowly focused, classroom-based knowledge and skills aimed at maximising test or examination performance. (See Askew *et al.* 1997 for a research-based critique of transmission methods and Brown *et al.* 1998 on the lack of a research base for the National Numeracy Strategy.) The pressures of performance act back upon pedagogy and the curriculum, both narrowing the classroom experience of all students and encouraging teachers to attend specifically to those students likely to 'make a difference' to the aggregate performance figures of the class and the school. Hence, for example, in secondary schools, the focus of attention on students on the C/D boundary of GCSE performance.[5] In primary schools, the QCA is concerned that those schools which have demonstrated most improvement in National Test results are those which have 'narrowed' their curriculum most markedly, and early evidence suggests that the Numeracy and Literacy Hours relegate other activities and areas of the curriculum to the fringes of the school day. Our recent research, admittedly done in secondary schools during the last Conservative administration, began to identify a number of ways in which teachers, against their better judgement, were shaping their pedagogy and curricula specifically to maximise test scores. Included in this, the teachers reported 'less emphasis on responding to the interests of children, the cultivation of relationships and the *process* of learning . . .' (Gewirtz and Ball 1999: 20). There are many reasons to believe that these trends have continued and may be developed further under Labour.

All this sits in stark contrast with recent work in learning theory and indeed with developments in mathematics and science pedagogies in the 1980s, which were developed with a clear orientation to the needs of the 'new economy'.

In the case of the former I am thinking of the work of Jean Lave (1988) and Rogoff (1990) and also what Heath and McLaughlin (1994) call 'curricular authenticity' (p. 487) which rests on the 'ever regenerative present of an up-close and tangible possible world' (p. 476). In the case of the latter I am referring to what I have called elsewhere 'vocational progressivism' (Ball 1990: 101–13) – for example, the development and use of 'investigations' in mathematics and science, the use of cross-curricular, open-ended, real-world, problem-solving tasks to encourage group work, creativity, initiative and the application and transfer of learning. As Bentley (1998: 81) puts it, 'the true test of understanding becomes what you are able to do with the knowledge you possess'.[6]

Street (1998) airs a very similar set of concerns in relation to the National Literacy Strategy and argues that 'Employers' concerns, then, are with communicative skills of a broader kind and with "counterbalancing" social strengths to those indicated by tests of traditional literacy' (p. 5). The National Literacy Strategy looks unlikely to be able to deliver what Street calls 'the mix of decoding skills' which 'people are going to have to learn in order to be "literate" in the future' (p. 8).

Conclusion

There are a set of paradoxes here, then. Labour are attempting to realise economic policy in education by creating a model of schooling which is essentially Fordist and micro-managed. This is based on a decontextualised, 'basic skills' approach which stands in stark contrast to the 'high-skills', knowledge-based, post-Fordist economy portrayed in Labour's own policy texts and policy rhetorics. In effect, using Jamieson's (1986) terms, Labour appear to have rebuilt 'the edifice of didacticism' (p. 37) in schools: a strengthening of the classification and framing of educational knowledge, set over and against the weakening of cultural boundaries noted earlier. While Labour may see themselves responding to employers' concerns about students' basic skill deficiencies and the needs of international competition they may well be paying attention to the wrong messages.

One of the key elements in the new policy panopticon is the use of highly prescriptive systems of accountability – performance indicators, inspections, league tables, achievement targets. Schools are rated and compared in terms of student 'achievement' measured by tests and examinations, for which students are carefully prepared. Institutional and national increases in test scores are then taken to be indicators of rising standards and improvements in schooling. However, the question that is avoided here is whether these indicators actually 'stand for' and thus 'represent' valid, worthwhile or meaningful outputs. Does the increased emphasis on preparation for the tests and the adaptation of pedagogies and curricula to the requirements of test performance constitute worthwhile effects of 'improvement'? In terms of economic competitiveness is what is measured here what is needed?

In all of this social justice issues seem peripheral. As previously, concerns about equity are tagged on to the list of Labour's priorities and are not central to their content or planning decisions about education. Further, the 'what works' ideology of the Third Way, which is presented as 'beyond' politics, obscures the class politics of current education policies.

I have also suggested that Labour's policy stance in education has a paradigmatic similarity to education policies in many other developed nations, that New Labour is part of the 'new orthodoxy'. To reiterate, I am not intending to suggest that we need not attend to the specificities of Labour's local educational concerns and projects, quite the opposite (the Third Way in particular needs careful examination), but I do want to 'place' Labour's policies in a global context. To underline the need to see these policies, in part at least, as embedded in powerful, coherent global *policyscapes*.

Notes

1 The same point could have been made about the Conservatives in the period 1979–1981 but there was relatively little policy activity around education under the previous Labour government. There was very little to put a stop to.
2 Although altogether there are 'a very large number of agencies using a variety of instruments to push and pull country policy and practice in often very different directions' (Deacon *et al.* 1997: 22).
3 At its most mechanistic this approach uses international comparisons of performance as the basis for selecting 'successful' pedagogies or curricula (see, for example, Reynolds and Farrell 1996). See also Brown (1998) on Sig Prais's arguments and influence.
4 Kenneth Clarke's 1991 Westminster lecture to the Tory Reform Group, 'Education in a Classless Society' is an interesting document in this respect.
5 The new league table indicators will have different effects.
6 Bentley (1998) sees 'deschooling' or what he calls 'complex systems of learning' as the key to achieving the 'learning society'.

References

Amin, A. (1997) 'Placing globalisation', *Theory, Culture and Society* 14 (2), 123–37.
Askew, M., Brown, M., Rhodes, V., Johnson, D., and Wiliam, D. (1997) *Effective Teachers of Numeracy*, London: King's College, University of London.
Ball, S. J. (1990) *Politics and Policymaking in Education*, London: Routledge.
Ball, S.J. (1998a) 'Big policies/small world: an introduction to international perspectives in education policy', *Comparative Education* 34 (2), 119–29.
Ball, S. J. (1998b) 'Educational studies, policy entrepreneurship and social theory', in R. Slee, G. Weiner and S. Tomlinson (eds) *School Effectiveness for Whom? Challenges to the School Effectiveness and School Improvement Movements*, London: Falmer Press.
Ball, S. J. (1998c) 'Performativity and fragmentation in "postmodern schooling", in J. Carter (ed.) *Postmodernity and the Fragmentation of Welfare*, London: Routledge.
Bentley, T. (1998) 'Learning beyond the classroom', in I. Christie and I. Hargreaves (eds) *Tomorrow's Politics: the Third Way and Beyond*, London: Demos.
Bernstein, B. (1996) *Pedagogy, Symbolic Control and Identity*, London: Taylor & Francis.

Blunkett, D. (1998) Speech to the Labour Party Conference.

Bourdieu, P. (1990) *The Logic of Practice*, Cambridge: Polity Press.

Brown, M. (1998) 'The tyranny of the international horse race', in R. Slee, G. Weiner and S. Tomlinson (eds) *School Effectiveness for Whom? Challenges to the School Effectiveness and School Improvement Movements*, London: Falmer Press.

Brown, M., Askew, M., Baker, D., Denvir, H. and Millett, A. (1998) 'Is the National Numeracy Strategy research-based?' *British Journal of Educational Studies* 46, 362–85.

Carter, D. S. G., and O'Niel, M. H. (1995) *International Perspectives on Educational Reform and Policy Implementation*, London: Falmer Press.

Cerny, P. (1990) *The Changing Architecture of Politics: Structure, Agency and the Future of the State*, London: Sage.

Clarke, J., Cochrane, A., and McLaughlin, E. (1994) *Managing Social Policy*, London: Sage.

Cousins, M., and Hussain, A. (1984) *Michel Foucault*, London: Macmillan.

Crump, S. (1998) 'New Labour, old Conservatism', in *Education in the Continuous Present*, Sydney: Faculty of Education, University of Sydney.

David, M. E. (1998) 'Education, education, education', in H. Jones and S. MacGregor (eds) *Social Issues and Party Policy*, London: Routledge.

Deacon, B., Hulse, M., and Stubbs, P. (1997) *Global Social Policy: International Organizations and the Future of Welfare*, London: Sage.

Edwards, T. (1998) *Specialisation without Selection*, Briefing No. 1, London: RISE.

Fox, A. (1974) *Beyond Contract: Work, Power and Trust Relations*, London: Faber.

Gewirtz, S., and Ball, S. J. (1999) 'Schools, Cultures and Values: the Impact of the Conservative Education Reforms in the 1980s and 1990s in England', ESRC Values and Cultures project paper, London: King's College, University of London.

Hanlon, G. (1998) 'Professionalism as enterprise', *Sociology* 32 (1), 43–63.

Heath, S. B., and McLaughlin, M. (1994) 'Learning for anything every day', *Journal of Curriculum Studies* 26, 471–89.

Jamieson, I. (1986) 'Corporate hegemony or pedagogic liberation? The schools/industry movement in England and Wales', in R. Dale (ed.) *Education, Training and Employment*, Oxford: Pergamon.

Jones, K. (1996) 'Cultural politics and education in the 1990s', in R. Hatcher and K. Jones (eds) *Education after the Conservatives*, Stoke on Trent: Trentham Books.

Jones, P. W. (1998) 'Globalisation and internationalism: democratic prospects for world education', *Comparative Education* 34 (2), 143–55.

Kenway, J., Bigum, C., and Fitzclarence, L. (1993) 'Marketing education in the postmodern age', *Journal of Education Policy* 8 (2), 105–22.

Lauder, H., Jamieson, I., and Wikeley, F. (1998) 'Models of effective schools: limits and capabilities', in R. Slee, G. Weiner and S. Tomlinson (eds) *School Effectiveness for Whom? Challenges to the School Effectiveness and School Improvement Movements*, London: Falmer Press.

Lave, J. (1988) *Cognition in Practice*, New York: Cambridge University Press.

Levin, B. (1998) 'An epidemic of education policy: what can we learn from each other?' *Comparative Education*, 34 (2), 131–42.

Linguard, B., Ladwig, J., and Luke, A. (1998) 'School effects in postmodern conditions', in R. Slee., G. Weiner and S. Tomlinson (eds) *School Effectiveness for Whom? Challenges to the School Effectiveness and School Improvement Movements*, London: Falmer Press.

Marques Cardoso, C. (1998) *Reforms of School Management and Governance: Portugal and England, 1986–96*, London: King's College, University of London.

O'Brien, S. (1998) 'New Labour, New Approach? A Critical View of Educational Theory', paper presented at the BERA Annual Meeting, Belfast: Queen's University.

Reich, R. (1983) *The Next American Frontier*, Harmondsworth: Penguin.

Reynolds, D., and Farrell, S. (1996) *Worlds Apart? A Review of International Surveys of Educational Achievement involving England*, London: HMSO.

Rogoff, B. (1990) *Apprenticeship in Thinking*, New York: Oxford University Press.

Street, B. (1998) 'New Literacies in Theory and Practice: What are the Implications for Language in Education?' Inaugural professorial lecture, School of Education, King's College, University of London.

Sweeting, A. E., and Morris, P. (1993) 'Educational reform in post-war Hong Kong: planning and crisis intervention', *International Journal of Educational Development* 13 (3), 210–16.

Taylor, S. and Rizvi, F. (1997) *Educational Policy and the Politics of Change*, London: Routledge.

Unterhalter, E. (1996) 'States, households and the market in World Bank discourses, 1985–95: a feminist critique', *Discourse* 17, 389–401.

Vanegas, P. (1998) *Education Reform in Colombia*, London: School of Education, King's College, University of London.

White, S. (1998) *Interpreting the 'Third Way': a Tentative Overview*, Cambridge MA: Department of Political Science, MIT.

Whitty, G. (1998) *New Labour, Education and Disadvantage*, London: Policy Studies Unit, Institute of Education, University of London.

Whitty, G., and Edwards, T. (1998) 'School choices policies in England and the United States: an exploration of their origins and significance', *Comparative Education* 34 (2), 211–27.

Witty, G., Power, S., and Halpin, D. (1998) *Devolution and Choice in Education*, Buckingham: Open University Press.

Addendum

Since this chapter was completed the Labour government has announced a number of schemes, programmes and initiatives which certainly indicate a commitment to social justice. In some cases considerable sums of money are involved, for example £500 million to tackle truancy and exclusions, £540 million for the Sure Start scheme, £41.5 million for nursery places for 3 year olds. Key 'problem' areas are being addressed like truancy, child care for further education students, changes in the relationship between the Careers Service and further education, etc. The sheer volume of money and effort has to be acknowledged. Generally, though, such developments still appear to be addressing the symptoms rather than the causes of inequality. Further initiatives are in the pipeline; the analysis may have to change.

Acknowledgements

The writer is grateful to Margaret Brown, Miriam David, Brian Street and Carol Vincent for making this a better chapter.

4 The good, the bad and the ugly

On four years' Labour education policy

James Tooley

From my 'classical liberal' perspective[1] there is much one can admire in New Labour's education policy, including the potentially liberalising measures contained within Education Action Zones and the first steps towards the privatisation of failing local education authorities and, through 'City Academies', failing schools. But New Labour is schizophrenic in its education policy. Along with these liberalising measures, the government's dirigism is writ large in the greater control it seeks over the curriculum. In this way, however, it is only continuing the traditions inherited from the previous Conservative government. In this, I suspect, one can detect the biases and predilections of the more permanent civil servants in the DfEE, rather than the underlying philosophy of either party.[2]

This chapter briefly comments on the 'good', the potentially liberalising measures such as the first steps towards privatisation of LEAs and schools more generally, before moving to a more in-depth critique of the 'bad and the ugly', the government's centralising curriculum measures. It focuses on citizenship education as a prime example of this dirigism, but suggests that the criticisms can be more widely applied. Finally, it briefly points to ways in which education policy could move forward, whether under Labour or any other government, in ways which could satisfy this classical liberal perspective.

The 'good': Labour's privatisation policies

Since Labour has come to power there have been a whole raft of proposals which have led, or will lead, to the undermining of the power of Local Education Authorities (LEAs), and the concomitant privatisation of educational management and curriculum delivery. The first part clearly follows on from Conservative government reforms, building on the 1988 Education Reform Act, which introduced 'local management of schools' (LMS), giving schools control of their budgets. The second part has been an interesting development which not many of us could have predicted and which, although one suspected it was in keeping with Conservative government philosophy, was not something which the Conservatives seemed to dare to introduce. In this way, again, Labour education policy provides an interesting extension of what has gone before.

Three relevant proposals were set out in the Schools Standards and Framework Act 1998. The first is the Education Action Zone model. The intention was to create a zone around two secondary schools and their feeder primary schools where almost 'anything goes', including opting out of the National Curriculum, teachers' pay and conditions, to allow maximum flexibility and innovation.

Initially the action zone proposal was almost a classic case of the way in which vested producer interests can 'capture' a reform and transform it for their own ends – and if nothing else had changed would make me rather pessimistic about their potential. It was made clear by the influential Michael Barber, head of the Standards and Effectiveness Unit at the Department for Education and Employment (DfEE), on announcing the zones policy, that zones were there in part to give schools freedom from LEA control. However, *all but one* of the initial zone proposals submitted were from LEAs. Why? The way the application form was drawn up, under advice from key educational providers, made it rather difficult for any body other than an LEA to get the required information in time for the deadline. And if any school showed an inclination to 'go it alone' without the LEA, there were reports of strong-arm tactics to make sure the headteacher and governors realised it was not in their interests to go that way after all. However, it is fair to say that after some disappointment about the first twenty-five zones created – that they were just LEA governance under a new (and expensive) guise – the government has moved to make it easier for schools to bid, and the next round has featured more innovative ways forward.

The second aspect of the 1998 legislation concerns individual schools which have been 'failing' (in the government's definition, involving continual low standards) for more than two years. The conditions of the 1998 Act have been translated into the policy of 'City Academies' by the Secretary of State, who has issued an invitation for any voluntary or commercial organisation to express interest in managing such schools. Recent press reports suggest that the DfEE is actively courting the US education company Edison Schools to be one such commercial organisation (*Observer*, 2 April 2000). Indeed, before the 1998 Act it was already possible for LEAs to contract failing schools out to the private sector, and before the Act became law Conservative-controlled Surrey County Council put the management of one of its failing schools, King's Manor School, out to tender. The contract was awarded to the education company 3Es. This move has been endorsed by the Labour government, although it must be noted that it had nothing to do with Labour's education legislation, although clearly it had much to do with its agenda.

Finally, there are the procedures in the 1998 Act which allow the Secretary of State to bring private education companies into the management of failing LEAs. The first such contract was awarded on 1 July 1999 to the listed Cheshire-based education company Nord Anglia to run the School Improvement Service in Hackney, while the Ethnic Minorities Achievement Service will be got into shape and similarly 'privatised' later in 2000. Close behind, the London Borough of Islington has been contracted out more or less *in toto* – not an insignificant proposal, given its £16 million turnover – to the education company Cambridge Education Associates, and it has been estimated by the DfEE that 10 per cent of all LEAs, to a lesser or greater degree, will face some privatisation over the next five years.

From this 'classical liberal' perspective, as outlined in more detail elsewhere (Tooley 1999, 2000), reforms which lead to the emergence of a strong, innovative private education sector, and which have the potential to allow the private education alternative to flourish and compete more satisfactorily with state provision, are to be applauded. For the classical liberal tradition would balk at seeing education so firmly in government control, and would seek a variety of educational suppliers, to ensure that the state's monopoly did not lead to inefficiency, the undermining of educational values and the erosion of liberty (see for example, John Stuart Mill's famous tirade against monopolistic state education, 1859). However, a classical liberal may also see some disadvantages in these moves, which are worth outlining, as they point to some of the dangers when the instruments of government are used to 'roll back' state intervention.

First, whilst bringing the private sector into the delivery of LEA services and into running failing state schools can bring a range of new incentives, investment and innovation into the state sector, and improved management and customer concern, which could lead to dramatic improvements in quality and conditions, these virtues will depend on there being *competing* companies running geographically contiguous schools, enabling genuine choice of several educational brand names. So it would be less advantageous if a UK version of Edison Schools, say, had all its schools in the south-east and Nord Anglia all its in the north-west.

There is also less potential advantage if a single education company gets to run, say, Liverpool or Islington LEA, the model the government seems to be moving towards, for a private monopoly can be almost as bad as a public one. Again, however, provided that there are competing education companies in the country as a whole, there will be some competitive influences brought to bear. For the company awarded one of these LEAs is also likely to be seeking further education ventures, and its performance in that LEA will be compared with the performance of other contractors, so this will influence whether it can expand further into other spheres.

The second danger is that this kind of contracting out could create rather cosy relations between the state (local or national) and the education companies, which then might begin to undermine innovation and excellence. This would be rather in the way that the close symbiotic relationship between the Ministry of Defence and key defence industries in many countries is blamed for high prices and lengthy delays in arms products. In terms of education, would it be in any company's interest, for example, to help point out that there is a considerable amount of fat within government spending on education, to schools and LEAs? Or would it rather be in their interest to keep quiet about it or, indeed, to say that *more* state funds needed to be devoted to education, in order to help inflate profits? There is also the potential for corruption too, with deals being done between central or local government and education companies which might not bear scrutiny.

Whether companies could get away with this would depend upon how open the supply side was – for if a couple of companies pretended that more funds were needed, there is an obvious market niche for a company to show how it could create high quality at less cost to the government. In the United Kingdom the DfEE has created a group of ten companies on its Approved List. Perhaps ten is large enough to stop companies colluding to keep costs high. But it is a real danger, and a definite down side to these types of moves. There are positive precedents to suggest that privatisation of state-subsidised services in the United Kingdom will not necessarily lead to this happening. When the railways were privatised, companies were given subsidies for many routes, but on a diminishing basis, to be eliminated completely in a few years' time. And when the private company Stagecoach Holdings took over the ailing Sheffield Super-tram it cut operating losses from £3 million to £1.4 million in its first year of operation. Experts suggest that it will eliminate operating losses altogether in the next two years – all without being forced to do so by the local authority, which would have been prepared to continue the massive subsidy.[3]

Third, there is the danger of setting the current system in stone, and now with new vested interests to help preserve the *status quo*. It is my impression, for example, that the consultants drawing up the procedures for the privatisation of the LEAs in the United Kingdom seem to have proceeded in a distinctly unimaginative fashion, seeking simply to contract out everything as it currently is. But it may well be that things as they are now are actually undermining educational aspirations and standards, and contracting them out could simply reinforce that process.

Fourth, there is also the danger of the types of performance contract that will be brought to bear for the education companies taking over schools and LEA services. All companies will be in favour of performance-related rewards, of course. But performance could be very narrowly drawn up in terms of what is easily measured, and may not be what is necessarily desirable in terms of educational outcomes. This could be in terms of getting teachers simply to teach to the test, in order to ensure the terms of the contract are met. Or it could be in terms of more arcane terms within the contract. For example, when one London borough was conducting market research to see whether it was worth contracting out its Education Welfare Service (EWS – the service which is there to combat truancy) it was adamant that its performance indicator for the service must be the number of parents taken quickly to court for not having their children in school. A few discrete indicators like that might completely undermine a holistic view of an LEA's greater role in improving educational opportunities for all.

These difficulties point to a typical 'classical liberal' dilemma: that in order to diminish the role of the state in education – for the sake of improving efficiency, educational efficacy and innovation, and bringing liberty – if one is using the state to do so it can lead to other problems, some of which could be as bad as those the reforms are seeking to address. One way around this dilemma is touched on in the final section of this chapter, pointing to pressures within the education system, many of which are recognised by the Labour government, which can help bring the desired change without distorting the policies.

However, such qualms about these liberalising measures may seem rather querulous, given the nature of the reforms which are taking place elsewhere under Labour government policy, which would be decidedly less appealing to a classical liberal. To explore these, we turn to the government's proposals for compulsory citizenship education.

The 'bad' – curriculum dirgism – and its 'ugly' implications

The Conservatives introduced the National Curriculum in 1988 and, despite its difficulties, it is clear that Labour policy makers are in favour of the concept. Michael Barber, for example, argues that the only alternative to a national curriculum is the 'blind alley' of 'professional autonomy and control over what is taught in schools' (1996: 164). But this alternative is unsatisfactory because of *democratic* needs:

> What is taught in schools not only helps to define the country's culture and democracy: it is also a critical element in building its future. Why should teachers alone decide matters which are clearly relevant to every citizen?
>
> (p. 165)

It was no surprise, then, that very soon after the Labour government was elected, it proposed extending the National Curriculum, in particular 'to strengthen education for citizenship and the teaching of democracy in schools' (DfEE, London, 19 November 1997). To this end, Secretary of State David Blunkett set up an 'Advisory Group on Citizenship' and appointed Professor Bernard Crick to chair this committee, which reported in 1998. Its proposals were accepted more or less in full and will be introduced into schools from September 2000, becoming compulsory by 2002.

From the perspective of this chapter, the proposals on citizenship are exceedingly helpful in showing what is wrong with this 'dirigist' strand of Labour thinking on education policy. They provide a useful case study of the thinking which has clearly influenced the Conservatives as much as Labour, but which, I argue, is profoundly mistaken. Moreover, although the argument here can be read simply as a particular criticism of Labour's citizenship education policy, I believe that it can be adapted, *mutatis mutandis*, to apply to any government intervention in the curriculum, as I have argued elsewhere (Tooley 1996).

What are the particular difficulties, then, with Labour's citizenship education policy? When it reported, the Advisory Group's concerns could not have been more forthright. The very first paragraph of its report reads:

> We unanimously advise the Secretary of State that citizenship and the teaching of democracy . . . is so important both for schools and the life of the nation that there must be *a statutory requirement on schools* to ensure that it is part of the entitlement of all pupils. It can no longer sensibly be left as *uncoordinated local initiatives* which vary greatly in number, content and method. This is an inadequate basis for animating the idea of a common citizenship with democratic values.
>
> (QCA 1998: 7, my emphasis)

This paragraph clearly reveals all the elements of what I have called elsewhere the fear of the *ad hoc* nature of life without state intervention, and the putting forward of a 'neat and tidy' proposal to combat that (Tooley 2000). The suggestion is that there is some genuine problem in society, and that this problem provides a justification for seeking to bring in government intervention in the curriculum.

The paragraph contains a five-point argument:

- Education for citizenship is highly important.
- 'Uncoordinated local initiatives' are not enough to provide it.
- Therefore, government must impose a national curriculum for citizenship on all students.
- Such a curriculum is best learnt in schools.
- Such government intervention will be more effective at creating effective citizens than without it.

Now, let us assume the first proposition is true, that education for citizenship is important. The second proposition is then in part an explicit statement of the objection to the *ad hoc*. I say 'in part' because by using the terminology of 'initiatives' it is clear that Labour have simply missed out a whole gamut of local, national and international activities through which education for democracy might also be conveyed, namely the newspapers, magazines, television and radio and internet input into political commentary. So what do they actually mean by the point that these 'initiatives' provide an 'inadequate basis' of education for democracy? Presumably they mean that the various 'uncoordinated' attempts are not working at preparing all young people for democracy?

I say 'presumably' – and this is absolutely crucial – because it is not explicitly spelled out. But it would seem essential for us to know *whether or not* these uncoordinated attempts are working before we turn to the state to impose an additional curriculum burden on young people and their teachers. To be fair, they do consider some evidence to this effect. But it is hardly conclusive, indeed it is contradictory, and moreover they have no counterfactual evidence to show whether or not having compulsory education for democracy would make it any better. Indeed, there are some indications that it might not, even within the evidence they present.

For example, on one hand they try to paint a picture of a serious problem regarding citizenship. We are told that young adults in the 18–24 age group are politically 'apathetic', showing 'the highest abstention rate among all age groups': 25 per cent said they would not vote in the 1992 general election, while 32 per cent abstained in the 1997 election (p. 15). Similarly, they point to the work of Demos think-tank authors Helen Wilkinson and Geoff Mulgan – now a key policy adviser to the Prime Minister – who, noting a large degree of youth alienation, present 'a powerful case that there should be a legal obligation to teach civic education alongside personal and social education' (QCA 1998: 16). Interestingly, two of the statistics given are that only minorities of young people have 'trust in society's core institutions' such as *national and local government,* and that this therefore shows the need for their political education. I think that I would also be included in the number (not of young people, of course) who don't necessarily trust these institutions of government. However, I'd like to think that this doesn't show that I particularly need any 'political education', unless it is of the Pol Pot variety, I suppose.

But, such considerations aside, how one can possibly make the assumption that this lack of desire to vote, encapsulated as it is in general youth 'alienation and cynicism', has anything to do with a lack of *compulsory education for democracy?* The Advisory Group notes that this youth alienation is also embodied in such things as 'Truancy, vandalism, random violence, pre-meditated crime and habitual drug-taking' (p. 15). But others have also noted that youth alienation has been linked with the rise of youth culture, which in itself has been blamed on the form which compulsory schooling takes (see Rutter and Smith 1995; Hargreaves 1994). So adding to the burden within compulsory schooling, as the Advisory Group proposes to do, could simply make matters worse, not better – undermining the fifth proposition above, that government intervention will make things better, not worse.

In any case, even on this point their evidence is muddled. For they note that research conducted by the Trust for the Study of Adolescence in 1997 found that 'a majority of its sample had been involved in some form of political or community action the previous year' (p. 15) – suggesting that perhaps the picture was not as bleak as their initial suggestions, and that, in fact, the 'uncoordinated local initiatives' may well have been having at least some impact. Similarly they note that a 1996 Social and Community Planning Research (SCPR) survey commissioned by Barnardo's also warned caution about some of the doom-and-gloom headline figures: 'The survey data are ambiguous. . . . young people . . . do seem one way or another to have secured some basic but important political facts' (quoted p. 15). Basic facts about the constitution and political parties were indeed known by the majority of young people in the survey. They conclude, 'These may be simple propositions, but the accuracy of the response suggests basic information does get ingested, *whatever the source*' (quoted p. 15, emphasis added). (We'll return to the italicised comments shortly.)

Again, the report notes that there is some more cautionary advice proffered in another social report, this time by Roger Jowell and Alison Park. These authors questioned whether 'teenage and younger generation alienation', in terms of political participation at least, had got any worse. It was this aspect of the lecture which Crick's report focused on. But there was also the eminently sensible question: why is it surprising that younger people are less interested in politics than older people? For the researchers found the less than baffling fact that 'as people got older, concerned with taxes, mortgages and family, they began *to inform themselves* better and show more concern for public policy' (p. 16, my emphasis) (Again, we'll return to this italicised comment shortly.)

However, this wisdom cuts no ice with the committee. They agree it is not clear whether things are getting worse or not, but they do say (on the basis only of this very scant evidence) that things are 'inexcusably and damagingly bad, and could and should be remedied' (p. 16). And the remedy is that 'Schools should have a coherent and sequential programme of citizenship education' (p. 16).

These difficulties with justifying citizenship education are not simply ones which this particular advisory group has come up against, but show the difficulty with the whole approach: I suggest that it would be difficult for *any* such advisory group to actually do better. How could anyone adequately find evidence of whether or not the 'uncoordinated', '*ad hoc*' solutions are enough to provide education for citizenship? There would seem to be so many possible sources for this education (local initiatives, national and local press, radio, television, the internet, political meetings and debates, conversation in the pub, etc.), and so many confounding variables (such as youth alienation, and its possible relationship with compulsory schooling) that it would seem impossible to devise a model which could adequately demonstrate that the *ad hoc* was not good enough. It would seem that any such advisory group would have to move to the third proposition, that 'government must impose a national curriculum for citizenship on all students' on the basis of prejudice and faith, rather than adequate evidence.

From here, the Advisory Group does not even attempt to provide evidence or argument for the fourth and fifth propositions. Having got thus far with some argument, the *status quo* commonsense assumptions allow them to take for granted that 'Such a curriculum is best learnt in schools' and that 'Such government intervention will be more effective at creating effective citizens than without it.' But could these assumptions be justified – in general, by this or any other advisory group?

We italicised two comments in the evidence above which are relevant here. Young people, it was noted, clearly had learnt aspects of politics '*whatever the source'*. Moreover, when they acquired the accoutrements of adult life young people would be likely *'to inform themselves'* of the necessary details of the political process. The Crick committee clearly assumes that the only way that young people can acquire the conditions required for citizenship is through schooling, and it all has to be accomplished by the time they reach age 16. But *why* does it make these assumptions?

At one point it does mention that 'many of the key concepts, values and dispositions, and, to a much lesser extent, skills, aptitudes, knowledge and understanding already are or can be developed and applied within other parts of the curriculum' (p. 43), in other words, in other parts of the *school* curriculum. But it does not occur to the committee, apparently wedded to a conflation of schooling and education, that they might also better be acquired *outside* the context of schooling, and not necessarily by the age when compulsory schooling expires.

However, there does seem to be one suggestion pointing to this conclusion in the report, in an appendix, which indicates how 'New information and communications technologies' can impact on Education for Citizenship. The appendix, written by Dr Stephen Coleman,[4] Director of Studies at the Hansard Society for Parliamentary Government, seeks to demonstrate that:

- New information and communication technologies (ICTs), specifically the Internet, are growing fast as an educational tool, particularly amongst young people.
- Many opportunities to become better informed about citizenship and to participate in democratic discussion exist on the Internet.
- The interactive character of the Internet provides opportunities for invigorating citizenship education, although some notes of caution need to be considered.

(p. 67)

Some of the key features of interest for educationalists include that 'the technologies are interactive: users are not expected to simply imbibe information, but are usually able to add to it or contest it', that 'on-line discussions offer people a sense of not simply hearing about or being spectators of civic affairs, but becoming involved as deliberating participants', that this can lead to global awareness, and that 'on-line discussion allows citizens to become familiar with the rules . . . of democratic debate' (p. 69). All very positive aspects of the new technology, one would agree, for education for democracy.

Now one interpretation of these observations would be to note that these opportunities are available in the world *outside* schooling, and that if there is a problem with universal access (which is one of the report's key 'notes of caution') then ways to overcome this should be sought, perhaps by the provision of state and/or philanthropic subsidised networked computers in community centres or student cafes. But the key point would be that all these new technological opportunities can go a long way to overcoming the problem (if such exists) of political apathy among young people. And, very positively, we would note that young people have much greater facility with these kinds of technology, and so young people will probably have a much greater edge when it comes to the new form of education for democracy.[5]

But the report does not draw these obvious conclusions. It notes, 'Overall a strong case can be made for the use of ICTs as an integral part of education for citizenship. *However, at present, there are few signs that schools and colleges are realising or have the resources to realise the full potential of this important link with the curriculum*' (p. 71, emphasis added). And it continues: 'Much of the potential is dependent on the competence and confidence of *teachers* using ICTs as a teaching and learning tool and a resource.' (p. 71, emphasis added).

A more dramatic example of the conflation of schooling and education, and the assumption that young people learn only when there are teachers around, would be harder to find – and in a context which simply cries out for an alternative explanation.

I suppose Professor Crick and his Advisory Group would not have much sympathy with these kinds of objections for one major reason. It is to do with the untidiness of the alternative. I suggested above that 'there is absolutely no reason to believe that *all* the aspects of citizenship education enumerated in this report could not be better learnt under some other environment than the school'. Except then, the Advisory Group could point out, outside the school, government would not be able to control it. And it is government control that is the key here. For if it is not compulsory, then what guarantees have we that all would receive their entitlement?

This argument has a rather obvious rebuttal, to question why it is assumed that with government compulsion the neat-and-tidy outcome will arise in practice, rather than in theory. Take the case of compulsory education itself. The glib assumption is that because there is universal schooling in law then there must be universal education in practice. But even in terms of schooling this is clearly not the case. Tom Bentley, using figures estimated by Tim Brighouse, Chief Education Officer of Birmingham, suggests that currently one in ten of all young people – 10 per cent – are not in school (Bentley 1999: 75). The Department for Education and Employment's own figures (1999: 47) are that there were 12,700 pupils permanently excluded during 1996/97. Dr Dennis O'Keefe of the University of North London reports that over 30 per cent of students regularly or sometimes play truant from school (O'Keefe 1994). But then when we come to ask about universal *education*, even these figures overstate the case. For in Britain 40 per cent of 21 year olds *admit* to difficulties with writing and spelling, nearly 30 per cent difficulties with numeracy, and 20 per cent difficulties with reading and writing (Central Statistical Office 1995: 58). Similarly in a survey conducted in Canada, Germany, the Netherlands, Poland, Switzerland (French and German) and the United States – all countries with (legal) universal schooling – 'roughly a fifth of the populations' of all of these countries 'were found to be barely literate – unable, for instance, to read and grasp a bus schedule' (Coulson 1999: 9). So legal universal state schooling does *not* imply that all are in school, nor, most significantly, does it imply that all receive the benefits of education.

Exactly the same argument can be given against the notion that compulsory citizenship schooling will lead to all young people becoming educated in citizenship. Just because there is a 'neat and tidy' solution does not mean that all will receive their entitlement curriculum.

There is one final implication with the Labour government's approach to citizenship education which is worth mentioning in passing – and here I believe it does get rather 'ugly'. For there is something rather worrying about the language in which the 'entitlement' to the education for citizenship is conveyed in the government's documents. It is argued that only with that entitlement will young people have the 'values and dispositions', 'skills and aptitudes' and 'knowledge and understanding' which are 'appropriate' for citizenship (p. 41). The curriculum provides *'essential elements'* (p. 44) of citizenship. In other words, the neat and tidy solution is required because, unless all young people are brought up to be good citizens in this way, democracy will suffer. But if it is so essential to democracy to have all young people educated for citizenship, so much so that government can intervene to make it compulsory, then what should happen to those who do not master this education? I have argued elsewhere that the answer may be profoundly disturbing and illiberal (Tooley 2000: section 5). For if education for citizenship is so important for democracy that we need the state to make it compulsory, then I argue that the logical implication has to be that those who *do not* get their education for democracy should *not be allowed to vote* in the democracy. It is precisely the same argument as when we say that certain skills and knowledge are necessary for driving on public roads, so we need a compulsory driving licence. In this case, certain skills and knowledge (and values and dispositions) are necessary for participation in a democracy – that is the Advisory Group's argument – so we need a compulsory democracy licence. And if one does not accept this, that there are greater values such as political liberty which lead to the cancelling out of this desire, then this leads to a *reductio ad absurdum* of the idea of requiring a compulsory citizenship curriculum in the first place. Such is the argument I have put forward elsewhere, in any case.

Moving on from New Labour

New Labour certainly has not been the calamity that many feared in libertarian and classical liberal circles. It has been simply a case of a 'more of the same' combination of some important and welcome liberalisation (although replete with dangers) with further centralisation and central control with which we became familiar under the Conservatives. Indeed, there would seem to be powerful theoretical reasons from public choice theory why such democratic reforms are likely to be of this form, rather than more truly liberating (see Tooley 1996).

Does this then mean there is no hope of moving towards a more radical educational programme, one which could satisfy the libertarian and classical liberal desire to see an undermining of state monopoly provision? Actually, I don't think we need be so pessimistic. For there is an alternative route towards educational liberation, which does not require governments to initiative policy reforms, but only requires them to be sensitive to political pressure from below. I like to believe this route is there in embryo in the work of influential Labour thinkers too, although how much it can influence policy remains to be seen. For example, although the final chapter of Michael Barber's important and influential *Learning Game* (1996) is all about what the *state* should do to bring about the learning society, he ends on a note which is out of character with this conclusion. For he concludes with some-thing which he clearly thinks is very important (he has saved it till last) and has *no potential for government intervention at all* (at least, I'm assuming that is his intention!). It is all about individuals taking their own proud first steps towards the 'learning revolution': 'through changing . . . language people can change society' (p. 304). So he says we should use language to begin to create the learning society. Instead of asking acquaintances, 'What do you do?' as we generally do at dinner parties and the like, we might instead try asking, 'What did you *learn today?*' Barber tried it, he tells us, and the 'effect was electrifying. I had more fun and learnt more than at any other event I can remember' (p. 305). The point of what he is saying is that, while he thinks government has a very important role, 'ultimately' it is all down to us, it 'depends on everyone playing their part. Most of all, the learning society . . . is the speech of the people' (p. 305).

Again, the same germ of the idea is to be found in the work of another of the influential Labour policy analysts, Tom Bentley, the Director of Demos. All the examples he gives to illustrate his desirable types of learning are of individuals and organisations providing opportunities outside the state, not prompted by the state, but because they have seen a need to move in this way. And I also note something else of interest for my purposes in Bentley's writings. Each of his examples shares the striking characteristic that the valued type of learning takes place in what may be called the *interstices* of compulsory schooling – before school, after school, at weekends and in the vacation away from school and for groups who are excluded from mainstream schooling.

These considerations provide the basis of my solution to the problem of undermining state education without using the state to do it. Those interested in further details can see the last chapter of my *Reclaiming Education*, where I dub the solution, with apologies to Nike, the 'Just do it' route (Tooley 2000). It is to chisel away into the interstices of state schooling, from all angles and directions, until one day there are no more bricks left in that particular wall. Some of these fissures, in no particular order, include: the rise of alternative educational routes for the education of long-term sick[6] and excluded children, showing what is possible outside of schooling, using advanced technology; the marketing of attractive but affordable alternatives for after-school and weekend clubs, extended when the desirability of their methods become apparent to full-time 'schooling' alternatives; private education companies contracting out parts of the curriculum within schools so that, as time passes, more and more of the curriculum is offered by specialist companies, until the time comes when some *state* schools become empty shells in which private companies deliver the goods; the rise of the teacher-entrepreneur, who sees numerous opportunities outside state schooling, in the new private chains, in distance teaching, in the virtual global education market; the rise of home schooling, growing at an extraordinary rate in the United States and United Kingdom as a response to dissatisfaction with the quality of state schooling; a new awareness of the opportunity costs of schooling, with children who currently have to tread water for several of the years of secondary schooling wondering why they cannot move more quickly and get out of school, particularly as they have access to more and more flexible curriculum offerings, and as education companies and teacher entrepreneurs market courses to them.

Each of these and other fissures will, I suggest, lead to the demand for a solution to the 'paying twice' dilemma: if so many parents and children are gaining the most desirable educational opportunities outside the state, why should they still be paying for state schooling through taxation? With this demand will come the obvious notion of an educational tax credit and, with that, the unleashing of educational demand.

Through each of these ways the activities of politicians, whether Labour or Conservative, will become less significant. Is four more years' Hard Labour unattractive to libertarians and classical liberals? About as attractive as four more years' Hard Conservatism. Indeed, it is hard to spot the difference, and harder still to believe that politicians of any colour can resist the changes in education which are about to confront them now.

Notes

1 The foundations of my, possibly idiosyncratic, classical liberal perspective are outlined in Tooley (2000), from which this chapter draws heavily. Others may be happier calling it a libertarian perspective, and in this chapter I use both terms freely.

2 See Ball (1990) for a provocative discussion of the ways in which the interests of the DfEE became dominant over those of the party in power in terms of education policy during the Thatcher years.

3 'Stagecoach to propose new Sheffield line', *Tramways and Urban Transit*, 739, (July 1999), p. 247.

4 Appendix B of the Crick report.

5 I have visited a particularly interesting project along these lines in New Delhi, India, where the computer education company NIIT has created a 'hole in the wall' internet computer, and has witnessed illiterate slum children teaching themselves and their peers how to get connected.

6 This is the somewhat awkward official terminology.

References

Ball, S. J. (1990) *Politics and Policymaking in Education*, London: Routledge.

Barber, Michael (1996) *The Learning Game: Arguments for an Education Revolution*, London: Gollancz.

Bentley, Tom (1999) *Learning beyond the Classroom*, London: Routledge.

Central Statistical Office (1995) *Social Trends, 1995*, London: HMSO.

Coulson, Andrew (1999) *Market Education: The Unknown History*, New Brunswick NJ and London: Transaction.

Department for Education and Employment and Office for Standards in Education (1999) *Departmental Report: The Government's Expenditure Plans, 1999–00 to 2001–02*, London: HMSO.

Hargreaves, David (1994) *The Mosaic of Learning*, London: Demos.

Mill, John Stuart ([1859], 1972), *On Liberty*, London: Dent.

O'Keefe, D. J. (1994) *Truancy in English Secondary Schools*, London: HMSO.

Qualifications and Curriculum Authority (1998) *Education for Citizenship and the Teaching of Democracy in Schools*, Final Report of the Advisory Group on Citizenship, 22 September, London: QCA.

Rutter, Michael, and Smith, David J. (1995) *Psychosocial Disorders in Young People: Time Trends and their Causes*, Chichester: Wiley.

Tooley, James (1996) *Education without the State*, London: Institute of Economic Affairs.

Tooley, James (1999) *The Global Education Industry*, London: IEA in association with the IFC.

Tooley, James (2000) *Reclaiming Education*, London and New York: Continuum.

Part III

Feeling policy realities on the pulses

5 Renewed hopes and lost opportunities

Early childhood in the early years of the Labour government

Peter Moss

Transformation or reformation?

The first thirty-six months of the Labour government have seen unparalleled attention and resources devoted to early childhood services.[1] Educational provision has been made for all 4 year olds and is to be extended to at least two-thirds of 3 year olds by 2002; a National Childcare Strategy has been proposed, and is being implemented by early years development and child care partnerships, informed and guided by child care audits and local early years development and child care plans; the *Sure Start* initiative targets children under 3 and their families in disadvantaged areas, with 250 local programmes envisaged by the end of 2002; a programme of Centres of Early Excellence, intended to highlight 'best practice', has been launched; new sources of funding have been provided, including a child care tax credit introduced in October 1999; two of the existing systems for regulating early years education and child care in the voluntary and private sectors (inspections by OfStEd under section 122 of the Nursery Education and Grant Maintained Schools Act 1996 and by social services under the Children Act 1989) are being brought together within OfStEd, and a new set of national standards is being drafted; desirable learning outcomes have been replaced by early learning goals 'which set out what most children are expected to achieve by the end of the reception year' (QCA 1999a: 3), backed up with guidance on delivering this foundation stage (QCA 2000); and the QCA together with the National Training Organisation (NTO) has produced a national Qualifications and Training Framework for the early years (QCA 1999b).

Faced by such evidence, no one can doubt that early childhood services are a priority of government, or the determination of government to increase access to and standards in these services. However, the theme of this chapter is that behind the current flurry of activity a larger opportunity has been slipping away: the opportunity to *trans*form a neglected and incoherent confusion of services into an 'integrated and coherent early years service' (the words used in a pre-election Labour Party policy document (Labour Party 1997: 9)). Instead we have settled for a process of *re*formation, driven not so much by concern for early childhood as an important stage of life in its own right for young children as a social group as by the imperatives of two major projects of the new administration. Rather than thinking the unthinkable, government has opted for more and better of the same.

A troubled legacy

The early childhood services that the Labour government inherited were in urgent need of change. A mountain of publications testified to past neglect and current inadequacies. Much quoted comparisons with other European countries showed the low level of publicly funded provision in Britain (e.g. EC Childcare Network 1996a). But they also showed another difference, less often noticed but just as significant. In Britain the compulsory school age is 5, with many children actually starting primary school reception class earlier – before which, if lucky, some may have had three terms of part-time nursery education. By contrast, the European norm has been settling at three years or more of publicly funded nursery schooling or kindergarten prior to compulsory school at age 6.

Early childhood 'school-based' provision – in nursery or reception classes – is only one part of Britain's split system of early childhood services, which has produced inequalities and inconsistencies in almost every way imaginable – regulation, opening hours, staffing, funding, access and so on (for a full inventory see Moss and Penn 1996). The other part consists of a range of 'day care' or 'child care' services (e.g. nurseries, playgroups, family centres, childminders). Providing for more young children than the education system, and with access overwhelmingly dependent on parents' ability to pay fees, these services have been the responsibility of social welfare. Underpinning this part of the early childhood system has been a poorly trained and poorly paid work force, which enabled the development of a large American-style private market, ranging from 'for profit' nurseries to 'voluntary' playgroups.

Issues unaddressed

What would have constituted a transformation to a genuinely integrated and coherent early childhood service? Certainly, great attention paid to a mass of detail. But at least six major issues involving concepts, principles and basic structures also needed to be fully addressed. So far, however, they have not been.

First and foremost, what constitutes 'early childhood'? The present British situation – compulsory school age of 5, but most 4 year olds admitted on a voluntary basis to primary school – is not the result of a recent and principled decision. Its origins lie in long-forgotten nineteenth century political considerations, compounded by a subsequent desire to use surplus primary school places and most recently the need of schools to recruit young entrants. The consequences have proved problematic: the possibility of some 4 and 5 year olds being in inappropriate settings; discontinuity in the lives of many 3–5 year olds, who within twenty-four months may move from playgroup to nursery class to reception class; and, perhaps most significant yet least appreciated, a truncated and weakened early childhood system, increasingly subservient to the needs and concerns of compulsory schooling. Such considerations, with no obvious offsetting benefits such as enhanced educational attainment at older ages, have led some commentators to propose raising compulsory school age to 6 (Ball 1994; Moss and Penn 1997).

Shifts in the basic structure of schooling are major undertakings, but possible. In 1997, for example, as part of a major reform of the whole education system, the Norwegian government lowered compulsory school age from 7 years to 6. This required major changes – in buildings, staffing, curriculum and, perhaps most significant in the long run, in the ethos of schools, which have had to open themselves to the pedagogical methods of the kindergarten sector from which 6 year olds have been transferred. Consequently, rather than a 'take-over' by schools, the reform has led to new thinking about the education of children from 6 to 10, bringing together perspectives and methods from both kindergarten and school.

In its newly produced early learning goals the QCA (1999a) has treated nursery education and the reception year (approximately from 3 to 6 years) as a distinct stage. While welcome recognition of the need to rethink, this is modest stuff. Government has neither envisaged a change in compulsory school age nor the possibility of 3–6 constituting an early childhood stage of the education system, separate from primary schooling. The opportunity has been missed to consider the transformatory possibility of establishing early childhood, *from birth (not 3) to 6 years of age, as the first stage of the education system*, with children having the opportunity to attend early childhood services for at least three years – and on a full-time basis rather than the part-time shift system that has long predominated. (The government's extension of early years education not only envisages a relatively short period of such education, two years, but does not question a long-standing tenet of education policy, the superiority of *part-time* attendance; for an alternative view that proposes the pedagogical benefits of less time-governed attendance see Dahlberg *et al.* 1999; Gandini 1993; Moss and Penn 1996.)

The principle of early childhood – defined as the first six years of life – constituting the first stage of the education system was adopted in Spain in 1990 as part of a general educational reform. Early childhood is now an equal but autonomous and distinct stage in the Spanish education system, viewed not just as a preparation for the next primary stage, but considered 'to be a separate and self-contained stage in education, with its own characteristics and intrinsic value' (Moss and Penn 1996: 128). This is not to argue that the early childhood stage should not be in relationship with primary schooling, but to question the nature of that relationship and to assert the need for it to be based on equality and mutuality.

Second, an integrated and coherent early childhood service based on recognising birth to 6 years as the first stage of the education system requires administrative expression, through the integration of responsibility within the education structure, both nationally and locally. At local level, an increasing number of local authorities have integrated responsibility for early childhood services, often within education departments. At a national level, the Labour government early on took the important step of transferring responsibility for 'day care' services from the Department of Health to the Department for Education and Employment. But instead of bringing 'day care' and 'school-based' services for young children into one strong and integrated 'early childhood' division, responsibility has remained divided between two parts of DfEE – the 'early years division' and the 'child care unit'. (In addition, there is now also a Sure Start Unit, located within DfEE.)

Certainly government policy emphasises the close relationship between care and education. But underlying thinking often appears to be still compartmentalised. This is reflected not only in the continuing split of responsibility at national level, but in the continuing use of the language of 'child care' and the emphasis attached to a 'National Childcare Strategy', as well as the exception of early years education and teachers in the maintained school sector from the reforms of early years regulation (see above) and training (see below). These and other signs appear to add up to a decision not to take the transformatory step of committing to an integrated and coherent early childhood service, covering *all* services up to compulsory schooling, education-based but with a remit well beyond education, including care and family support.

(To those who say that 'child care' and the 'child care strategy' are about more than early childhood, covering the period up to age 14, I would answer that an alternative approach would have been an 'early childhood strategy', incorporating early childhood from 0 to 6 as the first stage of the education system, while recognising its responsibility for a wide range of other functions, including care; and a 'work/family strategy', covering the full gamut of support needed for working parents *and* other employed carers. The 'child care' needs of children over 6 might have been considered either in the 'work/family strategy' or, more radically, as part of a 'school-age' or 'older childhood strategy', covering educational, recreational, care and other needs of school-age children. My argument is that 'child care', in the sense of ensuring the safe care of children while their parents are at work, could form part of these other strategies, and does not merit its own strategy. A 'national child care strategy' therefore was not inevitable, but an option: its significance lies in what the choice of that option means for the future of early childhood services.)

Third, the continuing split in the administration and conceptualisation of early childhood services has led to a failure to transform the staffing of early childhood services. The work being undertaken by the QCA and NTO (QCA 1999b) to develop a framework for early years qualifications and training is again essentially reformatory: it is about improving what exists, rather than rethinking. So it rationalises the existing jumble of qualifications (with the important exception of teachers), grouping qualifications together according to their level and category and relating them to existing occupational groups and job roles. What is missing is any prior analysis and discussion of the nature of the work in an integrated and coherent early childhood service concerned with education, care and a wide range of other functions – and what type or types of worker might be best suited to undertake this work.

The present system of staffing, unquestioningly replicated in government documents, involves a disparate mix: an elite corps of teachers in nursery and reception classes, who have undertaken four years of post-18 training to work with children from 3 through to primary school age; and a much larger army of various types of 'child care workers' (again the explicit language of government documents), some with no basic early childhood training, others with varying types including a two-year post-16 training covering the full early childhood age range. But there are other basic options for early childhood work, for example the *pedagogue* trained to work with children from 0 to 6 (and sometimes also with older children in non-school settings), envisaged as equal to but different from the schoolteacher; or the *early childhood teacher*, trained to work specifically with children from 0 to 6 within the education system. One or other of these two options has been adopted by all other countries which have opted for a coherent and integrated early childhood service (Moss 2000). In terms of basic training, both options assume at least three years at a post-18 level, with a focus on the whole early childhood age range.

Why has there been no serious enquiry into *who* the early childhood worker should be, as a necessary precursor of further discussions about training and qualifications? Perhaps, deep down, Ministers realise they are holding a can of worms best left unopened. As already noted, current early childhood services depend mostly on a large group of poorly trained and poorly paid women workers (analysis at the Thomas Coram Research Unit of the Labour Force Survey shows that the average gross weekly wage of nursery nurses over the period 1996–8 was £147 for an average working week of thirty-one hours (Cameron *et al.* forthcoming)). The whole economy of the 'child care' part of the system, in particular the ability to provide services at a price that enough parents can afford to make a private market in services viable, depends on the continuance of this situation. Staffing is easily the main cost in early childhood services, so any fundamental disturbance of the current staffing situation, such as a transformation of training and status and hence of earnings, spells chaos – that is, unless accompanied by a rethinking of funding.

Which brings me to the fourth issue. The Labour government has directed resources to the early childhood field in a number of ways, but in particular through the new child care tax credit. Again, what is missing is any evidence of fundamental and comprehensive rethinking, closely linked with other changes (such as staffing) and concerned to promote and support an integrated, coherent and education-based early childhood service. It could be that a child care tax credit would have had a part to play in such a rethink of the funding of early childhood services, since in theory it gets help quickly to lower income parents. But then again, it could be that it did not have, since the tax credit adds yet another type of funding to an already complex area involving various disparate sources of public and private funding. Furthermore, the tax credit system offers no guarantee that the extra funding it provides will find its way to improving services through, for example, enhancing staff pay and training. (If tax credit money is to serve this purpose, services must increase their fees, as well as ensure that the resulting increased income is used for service improvement.)

But the actual pros and cons of this funding mechanism are hard to judge. There was no fundamental and comprehensive rethink of funding across the whole system of early childhood services. Consequently the child care tax credit was never offered for public scrutiny as part of a wide-ranging review of funding options for achieving an integrated and coherent early childhood service. Indeed, the term 'child care' tax relief once again is suggestive of continuing compartmentalised thinking.

Not only have various funding options, with assessments of their implications, not been set forth; there has been no discussion of the principles which might guide the choice between these options and, more broadly, the distribution of costs between government, parents and employers. One consequence is that the government uncritically espouses employer funding of 'child care' ('we want to encourage and enable more employers to support childcare' (DfEE 1998: 37)), rather than considering it as one possible funding option which some view as problematic. (For discussion of why it may be considered problematic see Moss (1992a, b); it is also worth noting that Denmark and Sweden, in building up their early childhood services, have rejected employer participation in provision or funding.) Once again, an attachment to 'employer child care' is evidence of the continuance of compartmentalised thinking about young children and their services.

The fifth issue concerns the type of early childhood services that Britain needs, both now and in the future. What currently exists, like everything else in this field, does not represent a carefully considered view of what would be best for young children and their families, their communities and society as whole. It is an accumulation of responses to past social, economic and political circumstances. The question that needs to be asked is whether a mix of part-time nursery classes and full-time reception classes, private nurseries and childminders, family centres and playgroups is really best suited to current and future circumstances and needs.

Of course, life is not that simple, and it is necessary to work in part with what already exists. However, an early childhood policy should, I would argue, take a view about the direction to be followed in the long run, including what types of service might be better suited to current and future circumstances and needs. Do we have too many of some types, and too few of others? (And within all the rhetoric of choice and diversity, it is easy to lose sight of the fact that Britain has some notable gaps, for example few nursery schools, and few public or otherwise non-profit nurseries.) And, if so, over time how can disparities be rectified? As it is, a strategy emphasising partnership and early excellence centres seems to risk avoiding making difficult decisions at a critical moment of rapid growth. The setting up of a review panel to consider just one type of provision, playgroups (DfEE 1999), adds to an impression of wanting to keep all the established players happy rather than risk some unpopularity by asking whether over the long term, to be rebuilt.

The sixth issue is perhaps the least obvious, but perhaps the most important. The government's approach to early childhood services illustrates the contention of the Italian historian Carlo Ginsburg (1989) that the Minority World lives in a culture where we are constantly being offered solutions, *before we have asked the critical questions*. Government documents are full of questions, but mostly of a technical or managerial nature – how can we best do this or that? More fundamental and critical questions about issues of value receive little attention. Who do we understand the young child to be? What sort of early childhood worker do we want? What are the purposes of early childhood services and pedagogical work? What do we want for our children, here and now and in the future? What kind of world are we living in and how should early childhood relate to that world?

By posing such questions I am choosing to adopt a social constructionist perspective, which has become increasingly important in recent years in the field of childhood studies (James and Prout 1998). The idea of a universal child, an essential child, a child objectively knowable irrespective of time or place, context or perspective has been increasingly questioned. What has emerged instead is the idea of many possible childhoods, always constructed within particular social and historical contexts and discourses – in short, childhood as a social institution.

The immaturity of children is a biological fact; the way in which that immaturity is understood and made meaningful is a fact of culture. The facts of culture vary, making childhood a social institution. Childhood is constructed and reconstructed for and by children (ibid.: 7). Similarly, from a social constructionist perspective, the purposes of early childhood institutions are not self-evident, but can be seen as:

> the social construction of a community of human agents, originating through our active interaction with other people and with society . . . and constituted by dominant discourses in our society [embodying] thoughts, conceptions and ethics which prevail at a given moment in a given society.
>
> (Dahlberg *et al.* 1999: 62)

Government publications about early childhood say little about the critical questions outlined above. Everything is self-evident, reflection at a premium. But some idea of the social constructions underlying these publications can be gleaned. For example, *Meeting the Childcare Challenge* contains just two sentences which discuss the purposes of 'child care': 'better outcomes for children, including readiness to learn by the time they reach school and enjoyable, developmental activities out of school hours; and more parents with the chance to take up work, education or training' (DfEE 1998: para. 1.29). This is admittedly a slim basis for drawing conclusions, but these sentences seem to embody a construction of the young child as an empty vessel needing to be 'made ready' to learn and for school; and as a supply-side factor in determining the labour force.

In doing so, they throw light on what has happened to early childhood services since May 1997. There has been no major government project concerned with early childhood services *per se*, or more generally with young children as a social group, no strong agenda concerned with early childhood in its own right. Instead, early childhood services and young children have become items on the agenda of two major and related projects of the new government – improving educational standards in school, and increasing labour market participation and economic competitiveness. Viewed from the perspective of these imperative projects, young children are understood primarily as dependants of their parents, in need of 'child care' to enable their parents' employment, and as 'becoming' schoolchildren and economically active adults.

Of course, there are many other constructions of childhood. An alternative understanding of childhood and children, for example, is being produced in the 'sociology of childhood' (James and Prout 1998). Children are both part of, but also separate from, the family, with their own interests, which may not always coincide with those of parents and other adults. Children have a recognised and independent place in society, with their own rights. Children are considered a social group, with their own network of relationships and their own culture. Childhood is understood not as a preparatory or marginal stage, but as a social institution, and important in its own right as one stage of the life course, no more or less important than other stages. Children are social actors, participating in determining their own lives, as well as the lives of those around them and the societies in which they live. They are active learners from birth, co-constructors of knowledge and identity in relationship with other children and adults. In short, children – including young children – have agency.

This construction of childhood has been productive in the early childhood services of the Italian city of Reggio Emilia, and finds voice in the words of the first head of those services, Loris Malaguzzi, when he said that 'our image of the child is rich in potential, strong, powerful, competent and, most of all, connected with adults and other children' (Malaguzzi 1993: 10). The young child emerges from this construction as a *co-constructor* of knowledge, of culture, of his or her own identity – 'ready to learn' from the very start of life. (For a fuller discussion of different constructions of early childhood and the pedagogical work in Reggio Emilia see Dahlberg *et al.* 1999.)

Similarly, there are alternative understandings of early childhood institutions that could be explored. Early childhood institutions are commonly referred to as 'services', implying the production and delivery of a product (for example, 'care' or 'education') from 'producer' to 'consumer'. This construction of the early childhood institution as producer of outputs brings to mind the metaphor of the factory:

> It seems to me that early childhood programmes are increasingly in danger of being modeled on the corporate/industrial or factory model so pervasive in elementary and secondary levels of education . . . factories are designed to transform raw material into prespecified products by treating it to a sequence of prespecified standard processes.
>
> (Katz 1993: 33–4)

But as just one example of alternative perspectives Dahlberg *et al.* (1999) have explored the possibility of understanding the early childhood institution as *a forum and community institution in civil society where children and adults meet and participate together in projects of cultural, social, political and economic significance*. What those projects are or might be is always provisional and contestable, a proper subject of democratic debate, both nationally and locally. But this construction offers the possibility of going beyond dualistic 'education'/'care' thinking, to a more complex and multi-faceted understanding of the possibilities of early childhood institutions – whose purposes can never be taken for granted or assumed to be self-evident.

Conclusion

For old hands in the field of early childhood, the Labour government has brought about an unparalleled and invigorating change of climate, with a recognition of the importance of early years and a willingness to act and spend money. Yet renewed hope mingles with an uneasy sense that an opportunity to transform early childhood services has been slipping away as the imperatives of other projects force hurried responses. What has been missing is a process of collective reflection about early childhood, early childhood institutions, pedagogical work and early childhood workers, a process that is sensitive to other political projects – but concerned centrally with young children and early childhood as important in their own right. Instead of a transformed early childhood service firmly located within the education system, but also challenging that system through asking questions about knowledge and learning and the other projects of the early childhood institution, we seem to be moving to an employment-led child care system, with educational purposes bolted on.

Having waited many years for change, we could have waited a bit longer, perhaps for the production of a White Paper setting out the vision of a transformed early childhood service and the steps needed to achieve that vision over the next five to ten years. That would have required technical and structural change, indeed going far beyond what is currently envisaged. (For further discussion of such changes see EC Childcare Network 1996b; Moss and Penn 1996). But it would also have required a willingness to recognise, make visible and engage with issues of value, purpose and understanding.

Note

1 By 'early childhood services' I mean the whole range of 'education' and 'child care' services for children below compulsory school age. The chapter also deals primarily with England, and does not do justice to the variations in Scotland, Wales or Northern Ireland.

References

Ball, C. (1994) *Start Right: The Importance of Early Learning*, London: Royal Society of Arts.

Cameron, C., Owen, C. and Moss, P. (forthcoming) *Entry, Retention and Loss: A Study of Childcare Students and Workers*.

Dahlberg, G., Moss, P. and Pence, A. (1999) *Beyond Quality in Early Childhood Education and Care: Postmodern Perspectives*, London: Falmer Press.

Department for Education and Employment (1998) *Meeting the Childcare Strategy*, London: Stationery Office.

Department for Education and Employment (1999) *Tomorrow's Children: The Review of Pre-schools and Playgroups, and the Government's Response*, London: Department for Education and Science.

Department of Health (1991) *Children Act 1989 Guidance and Regulations II, Family Support, Day Care and Educational Provision for Young Children*, London: HMSO.

European Commission Childcare Network (1996a) *A Review of Services for Young Children in the European Union, 1990–1995*, Brussels: European Commission Equal Opportunities Unit.

European Commission Childcare Network (1996b) *Quality Targets in Services for Young Children*, Brussels: European Commission Equal Opportunities Unit.

Gandini, L. (1993) 'Fundamentals of the Reggio Emilia approach to early childhood education', *Young Children* 11/93, 4–8.

Ginsburg, C. (1989) *Ledtrådar. Essäer om konst, förbjuden kunskap och dold historia* (Threads: essays on art, forbidden knowledge and hidden history), Stockholm: Häften för Kritiska Studier.

James, A. and Prout, A. (eds) (1998) *Constructing and Deconstructing Childhood: Contemporary Issues in the Sociological Study of Childhood*, second edition, London: Falmer Press.

Katz, L. (1993) 'What can we learn from Reggio Emilia?' in G. Edwards, L. Gandini and G. Forman (eds) *The Hundred Languages of Children*, Norwood NJ: Ablex.

Labour Party (1997) *Early Excellence: A Head Start for Every Child*, London: Labour Party.

Malaguzzi, L. (1993) 'For an education based on relationships', *Young Children* 11/93, 9–13.

Moss, P. (1992a) 'Employee childcare – or services for children, carers and employers', *Employee Relations* 14 (1), 20–32.

Moss, P. (1992b) 'Introductory essay: EC perspectives', in C. Hogg and L. Harker (eds) *The Family-friendly Employer: Examples from Europe*, London: Day Care Trust.

Moss, P. (2000) 'Training of early childhood education and care staff', *International Journal of Educational Research* 33 (1), 31–53.

Moss, P. and Penn, H. (1996) *Transforming Nursery Education*, London: Paul Chapman.

Qualifications and Curriculum Authority (1999a) *Early Learning Goals*, London: Qualifications and Curriculum Authority.

Qualifications and Curriculum Authority (1999b) *Early Years Education, Childcare and Playwork: A Framework of Nationally Accredited Qualifications*, London: Qualifications and Curriculum Authority.

Qualifications and Curriculum Authority (2000) *Curriculum Guidance for the Foundation Stage*, London: Qualifications and Curriculum Authority.

6 The impact of New Labour's educational policy on primary schools

Peter Woods, Bob Jeffrey and Geoff Troman

The shift in emphasis in official policy from the liberal and egalitarian view of the 1960s and 1970s to one dominated by economic considerations, focusing on the need for a highly skilled work force to enable the country to compete successfully in the global economy, brought a more instrumental, technicist approach on the part of government to primary teaching in the 1980s and 1990s (Woods *et al.* 1997). Primary teachers have a broader conception of educational aims embracing the whole child, and many have felt a conflict of values in implementing government policy (Jeffrey and Woods 1998). Nonetheless, Webb and Vulliamy (1996), writing about the first five years of the new order following the Education Act of 1988 introducing the National Curriculum, concluded that, despite overwork and stress, 'Many [primary teachers] have come through . . . clearer about their educational beliefs, recognising what is worth fighting for in primary education and what needs to change, more politically aware of how to go about this at the micro and macro.' Does this continue to be the case under New Labour? Are primary teachers being re- or deprofessionalised? Are primary schools, and the standards of education within them, 'improving' – the declared aim of government policy?

In addressing these questions we shall consider some of the issues connected with curriculum, pedagogy, assessment, school culture, and the ongoing monitoring of schools. We shall do this through case studies of two prominent New Labour initiatives: first, the strategy for improving levels of literacy, the key contribution so far of New Labour to the curriculum (together with numeracy, just introduced), and, second, the strategy for improving schools.

Improving literacy?

Technicism

The National Literacy Strategy, launched in September 1998, is designed to raise standards of literacy in all primary schools in England. The official definition of literacy lays heavy emphasis on skills (DfEE 1998a: 3). The model, as with the National Curriculum in general, is based on 'performance', with fixed goals, task analysis and testing, and the exclusion of any alternative view (Ball 1998a; Broadfoot 1998). This warrants a high level of prescription. The underlying philosophy has been challenged (for example, Cox 1998). There is little in the official documents about the creative uses of literacy or of 'critical awareness', of meaning and understanding. Dadds's (1999) teachers considered that literacy should 'serve a wide variety of purposes' and that there are 'multiple literacies that grow from, and work for, effective communication in different cultural and social circumstances' (p. 13). The DfEE (1998b) training video, however, 'shows the dominance of preset objectives' and 'may be promoting a convergent, monocultural perspective' (p. 13). This promotes a 'getting done' (Apple 1986) mentality, and works against the needs of the individual child and of learning and understanding, and of the promotion of 'personal literacies'.

Even where skills alone are concerned, evidence is beginning to come through that children learn best through a child-centred framework. Medwell *et al.* (1998), for example, found that effective teachers of literacy 'placed a greater emphasis on children's recognition of the purposes and functions of reading and writing and of the structures used to enable these processes'. Teachers 'owned' the literacy knowledge in the sense that 'they appeared to know and understand the material in the form in which they taught it to the children, which was usually as material which helped these children to read and write' (p. 76). Their pupils were 'much more heavily involved in problem-solving and theorising about language for themselves rather than simply being given "facts" to learn' (p. 77). To these teachers the creation of meaning in literacy was crucial. They did not ignore technical skills, but sought to embed them within a meaningful framework. Fisher and Lewis (1999) draw the contrast between teaching as a technical activity, where pedagogy is specified, and teaching as a professional activity, where teachers have pedagogical flexibility among a broad repertoire of methods. The latter has strong support in general as a feature of effective teaching (see, for example, Alexander 1992; Alexander *et al.* 1995).

This does not mean a return to polarities. With regard to literacy, for example, it is not a matter of either literacy techniques or creativity. Both would seem to be required – the techniques within a creative framework. Some teachers seem dismayed at the further prescription and what they see as another assault on their professionalism. Others have managed to appropriate the literacy hour, as they have the National Curriculum.

Appropriation

In general, in recent years, there is less time and space for teacher experimentation, more prescriptive curricula and assessment, and pressure for more whole-class teaching. In teaching methods the trend is towards traditionalism (Galton *et al.* 1999). Teachers today feel obliged to 'deliver' a curriculum and consequently they still maintain a low level of pupil participation (see also Francis and Grindle 1998). Is this inevitable?

We have used the Coombes County Infant and Nursery School at Arborfield in Berkshire as a test case of the possibilities of teachers' appropriation capacities in these increasingly prescriptive times. This school has a high national and international reputation for its creative approach to teaching. Its teachers identify strongly with the same kinds of values articulated in the Dadds research. They were dismayed with those aspects of the National Curriculum and especially national assessment which threatened to inhibit creativity and force an education of what they regarded as a very narrow and limited kind. 'Things are so well tailored that the spontaneous gets neglected. The magic cocktail of the children's reaction is missing' (Head-teacher). Also, while the National Curriculum is strongly compartmentalised, Coombes has weaker boundaries around subjects in their quest to integrate knowledge. However, in time the Coombes teachers managed to reconcile their own values with those of the National Curriculum. They did so through the cultivation of their own political awareness, the refinement of their own philosophies, and engagement with the National Curriculum 'as a baseline from which to grow' (Woods 1995).

Our latest research suggests that this is being sustained under New Labour, but not easily. Coombes's teachers continue in their creative use of space, bringing the community to the school and nourishing a 'learning community' (Woods 1999), and including 'grand topics' as part of their pedagogical armoury. These are similar to 'critical events', which the teachers of Woods's 1993 research thought would not be possible under the new order. They can last a term, have a hands-on element for children, permeate the subject-centred 'contents', forge links across subject divisions, and carry an air of excitement (see Jeffrey 2001). In general the Coombes approach seems an interesting example of 'reconstructed progressivism' (Sugrue 1997: 227) more suitable for the current age than the child-centredness of the 1960s and 1970s so roundly condemned by government and others (see, for example, Alexander 1992; Alexander *et al.* 1992). It is even approved of by OfStEd. Following their inspection, they reported, 'The school provides an exceptional standard of education, which not only pushes the boundaries of imaginative teaching but ensures pupils achieve well in all areas of learning' (1997: 1).

In these ways, then, it may be claimed that Coombes has appropriated the National Curriculum. They have found a way, it seems, of reconciling two apparently opposing discourses (see also Wood 1999). How, then, are they coping with the Literacy Strategy, operationalised within a daily 'literacy hour', which is presenting such problems for Dadds's teachers and others?

Coombes and literacy

Coombes teachers saw the literacy hour as a 'Challenge . . . but we did it our way. We did it within the school's value system, and put the school's stamp on it, and made it ours.' They observed the strict prescriptive divisions of the literacy hour on some days and not on others, always trying to ensure that the children were actively involved, and that learning was fun. They sent the children on 'detective' hunts for a set of 'initial sounds' that they had secreted around the grounds, which, when rearranged correctly, spelt a relevant phrase; they composed a variety of songs with actions that related to phonemes and digraphs: 'I write songs driving back from Sainsbury's. They get into the syllabus very quickly'; they employed a 'Joseph's coat of many colours' to investigate words with an 'oa' sound; they made hand puppets and represented particular digraphs, for example a frog; they regularly brought in something for the children to eat related to that week's 'sound', for example, Maltesers and brown bread with bramble jelly, and they encouraged the children to write letter sounds and words in coloured chalk on the playground. They maintained their holistic approach to children and to knowledge. They tried to involve all the children's senses. Opportunities were taken to reinforce this work during the school's allied activities involving visits by community artisans and performers, environmental activities and during their other curriculum subject work in an attempt to integrate the literacy hour subject matter across the children's experiences.

Constructing a working timetable for a first school that valued mixed age class 'family' groups was also a challenge, for the literacy hour is programmed for age groups. Nevertheless, the teachers perceived advantages for the children in that they were exposed to a varied diet of experiences, and gained more independence and ownership as they took themselves off to their respective cohort classes for literacy every morning. Furthermore, a programme focusing on the same curriculum for each parallel year group encouraged the teachers to work even closer than they had done previously. This, in turn, promoted teacher development. You 'bounce off each other' and 'learn so much'. The children also are 'sometimes able to choose between us, which is good for them'.

The Coombes approach was commended by evaluators – though they saw more of the structure of the literacy hour as prescribed, albeit creatively used. However, despite these successful aspects of appropriation, teachers did have some concerns. The Literacy Strategy is based on a theory of like individuals and like systems, and 'is such a rigid one, delineating what you teach in each half-term'. It did limit their teaching: 'If I have wings then I fly and, sometimes I think, they want to withhold my rights and the children's rights to fly and to think, to swim, to float around.' The teachers' commitment to creative pedagogy, necessary because the literacy hour 'is a massive amount of time in one chunk for a 5 year old', takes its toll: 'There has been on enormous drain on energy in the making of resources and trying to think of inventive ways of delivering it, making it better and exciting, so that it isn't a "bottoms on seat" experience.'

The characteristics of time, pace, intensity, opening and closing, meeting deadlines, 'getting done' (Apple 1986) become prioritised. They have consequently lost some valuable methods and curriculum areas, such as children hearing each other read, sharing news, reading and writing, parents helping with reading, creative art. One teacher reported herself 'running from an hour of literacy to an hour of numeracy, to an hour of science, and then to curriculum groups. There is no in-between.' 'We have lost sight of the child in education.'

On the whole, then, while Coombes teachers have appropriated the literacy strategy to some degree, they are perturbed by its prescriptive nature, unlike the looser framed National Curriculum, which they managed to absorb more easily. They are finding their child-centred principles increasingly squeezed, and there seems little likelihood of this easing in the foreseeable future – rather the reverse, as the numeracy hour fills more of the day.

Improving schools?

New Labour's chief agency for raising standards generally is the Office for Standards in Education (OfStEd), established in 1992 under the Conservative government, and charged with the oversight of national arrangements for the inspection of schools. We demonstrated in previous research how the values that informed OfStEd's conception of a good education and their mode of operation contrasted sharply with the prevailing child-centred discourse preferred by primary school teachers (Jeffrey and Woods 1998). During inspections, teachers were conscious of a deep and damaging value clash in areas of knowledge, pedagogy, assessment and culture. Inspectors used a technicist, managerialist approach which impacted against the holistic and humanistic values of the teachers, producing a high degree of trauma among them. No advice or guidance was offered. They were simply 'inspected'. At the more traumatic moments of the inspection itself, teachers felt deprofessionalised. Yet all six schools of our research emerged with good or satisfactory reports. Teachers asked, 'Was it worth it?' and one opined, 'There has to be a better way.'

Despite a number of criticisms of this nature, New Labour endorsed OfStEd, and the drive for improvement along narrow, managerialist lines has continued. A parliamentary select committee examined OfStEd in 1999, and made certain recommendations, the impact of which remains to be seen. Up to the time of writing OfStEd has continued along the same lines, most notably through the development of the policy for naming, blaming and shaming 'failing' schools. If a school is judged to be failing it is made subject to special measures (OfStEd 1999: 1). These include an action plan that has to be approved by the DfEE and regular monitoring inspections by HMI until the school is deemed to be providing an acceptable standard of education.

Schools that have been through this process do improve in some ways – unsurprisingly, given the extra resources that are made available or a key change in management that occurs (Scanlon 1999). The question is – at what cost? Do the ends justify the means? Is there a better way? In a survey of schools that have been placed under special measures, a majority of which were primary, compared with a similar number that have not, Scanlon reports resentment, tension and divisions among the staffs as some were seen to 'pass' and others 'fail', and worsening relation between Heads and their staffs. There was a marked deterioration in staff morale among teachers in both groups. Some schools had problems of recruitment and retention. Most of Scanlon's teachers, while acknowledging improvements, felt that 'There were better and more cost-effective ways of achieving the same ends. . . . It had also created new problems or aggravated existing ones.' We draw on a study of one such school from our general research on teacher stress (see Troman and Woods 2001) to highlight some of the issues. Gladstone Street Primary School (a pseudonym) was cited in 1996 as a failing school, and spent two years in special measures. Of the fourteen full-time teachers in post in 1996, eight left during this period, including the headteacher and deputy headteacher.

As with Scanlon's schools in general, Gladstone might have seen 'improvement' at a technicist level, as judged by measurable tests, so that, as one teacher commented, 'pupil sausages would be popping out at the other end as neatly as Wall's could do it in their real sausage factory'. This would be at a cost to other aspects of what some consider a full education, such as developing the individuality of children. Another teacher identified multiculturalism, emotional development and caring as important aspects of the school's ethos. Teachers spoke of 'much more tolerance of children with difficult home backgrounds' and the school's determination to face and deal with difficult social problems.

Indeed, OfStEd acknowledged these caring and sharing aspects as strengths of the school in its inspection report. However, the school was judged to be failing because of poor leadership and management, poor financial management (including a budget deficit and not providing value for money), poor pupil behaviour, teachers' low expectations of the pupils, and poor teaching quality. The task would appear to be, therefore, how to improve the school in these respects while preserving its existing strengths. How successful in this were the 'special measures', other than in a limited, technicist sense?

The teachers experienced considerable trauma during the inspection week when they realised they were failing. Joan explained that it was 'a total shock nobody had expected – it just hit me – my whole life was affected – it was a horrible time'. Richard said, 'The atmosphere was hysterical – people were crushed – everyone was stripped raw – the teachers were crumbling.' Frances said, 'The foundations of the school had been kicked hard.' It may be argued that the school needed a 'shock' as the first stage in its transformation. But inducing these profound emotions, it may equally be argued, goes far beyond the bounds of professionalism, striking at the teachers' innermost selves. In cutting the ground from under their feet the inspection induced a state of *anomie* with the only direction being given a narrow technicist path. The broader aspects of teachers' expertise were put at risk.

Though most of the teachers received good individual reports, they felt collectively condemned by the judgement on the school. At a time when the media were searching for the 'worst school in Britain' and headlines were appearing such as 'Failing school named: incompetent teachers to be sacked' (Ball 1998b: 78), teachers had strong feelings of guilt and shame. The teachers questioned their accumulated knowledge and experience of schools and teachers. Sean felt that the school's failing had 'brought everything into question'. Joan thought 'It was that total confusion because people couldn't believe that some of their colleagues had been criticised. People they thought were good teachers. It was just a total muddle really.' Edith felt her 'judgement had all gone wrong' and 'found it difficult to evaluate if [she] was a good teacher or not'. Ann, who had considerable experience as a support teacher and had worked in the classrooms of many colleagues over the years, was 'shocked because I thought I knew what teaching was. It made me question if I knew anything about teaching at all even though I had a lot of experience to judge.' Richard wondered whether he had 'chosen the wrong career'. Teachers who had managed to find out OfStEd's evaluation of them started comparing themselves with their colleagues, and, for some, this tended to lower their already low self-esteem.

Shame involves experiencing feelings of inadequacy. Sean said that before the inspection he used to 'feel quite a good teacher'. The experience of failure had resulted in what he felt was an 'erosion of personal skills'. OfStEd had found 'skills missing' in Richard's practice and he felt 'a complete failure – I didn't think I had a future in teaching.' Rita was made to feel 'such a useless lump; you're not a good teacher. You're a waste of time and space. And it feeds on itself, really. So your confidence is just hacked away.' Even some of those teachers judged to be successful felt acutely inadequate. Vanessa, who achieved a '1' rating, found the process leading up to it 'utterly stressful'. Some of the teachers with good personal reports felt a strong collegiate responsibility and experienced collective inadequacy. Edith, for example, 'found the inspection so awful. I think it was because there was this strong feeling here of being part of a team. . . . I identified with the school sufficiently to feel criticised by the general criticism of the school.' Joan had been anxious lest her potential personal failure would 'let everybody down'. Anthony was concerned in case the 'succeeding' teachers were 'dragged down' by the failing ones.

Some teachers, though not experiencing stress-related illness, became 'stressed at seeing colleagues go under and extremely angry at seeing what the system has done to others' (Sean). Frances became stressed because a colleague with whom she worked collaboratively and who was also a close friend was absent from school owing to a nervous breakdown. Alan was on his 'knees physically and emotionally and ground down by it all'. Anthony said many teachers were 'exhausted and couldn't keep working at that pace; they were on a stress-ridden downward path; and stress levels were high and morale was low'. Sean experienced sleeplessness prior to the termly inspections. Throughout the special measures Frances 'couldn't stop crying'. Richard got 'more and more depressed, and tireder and tireder'. Four of the eight teachers who left the school during special measures were diagnosed as suffering from clinical depression. The problem in such circumstances is that where a teacher becomes subject to competence procedures 'you couldn't tell if she couldn't cope with it because she couldn't adapt or if she couldn't cope with it because she was very stressed' (Rita).

It was not all negative trauma. Some of the teachers passed through what Anthony described as a 'cleansing' or 'healing' period. In this phase they regained confidence and a sense of self-worth. Colin said that some had found it necessary to 'reinvent themselves to re-establish self-esteem'. Some teachers were 'girded' into action and saw special measures as a 'new starting point'. Richard was 'galvanised into action' and 'excited by all the changes that could be made'. Sean thought his confidence 'will come back hopefully as I work with a team'. Richard 'wouldn't let the bastards grind him down' and Joan said: 'No, no. I wouldn't give in. I was determined, even if I stayed here till I was 65, to get out of special measures. Because I felt I couldn't have left and got another job. Some people did. But I felt, for me, I had to stay and prove something.' For some, being in special measures had been a 'learning experience'. One teacher gained promotion on the strength of it.

On balance, though, most of the teachers argued that, save for the improved SAT scores, the school was no better after leaving special measures than it was when entering. Indeed, in some respects it could be considered to be worse. Half-way through special measures a group of middle class parents complained to Anthony about the school's increasing concentration on increasing 'standards' in the children's academic work. This group explained at a school meeting that they had chosen the school for their children because of its multicultural ethos and curriculum. They were objecting to the decision to reduce time spent on celebrating and learning about customs and festivals in a wide range of cultures. This time was to be devoted to preparation for increasing pupil performance in the National Curriculum. As for the teachers, they felt deprofessionalised, in the same way as those featuring in the school studied by Jeffrey and Woods (1998: chapter 4).

Conclusion

New Labour has continued the education policies introduced by the New Right Thatcherite administration, bringing creative and child-centred teaching in primary schools under greater strain. This has to be seen within the context of the 'low-trust society' (Giddens 1990; Troman and Woods 2001). Teachers are no longer trusted to implement reform, and must be directed and monitored. The 1999 Green Paper aimed at increasing teacher motivation, job satisfaction and morale and making teaching a more attractive and 'modern' profession by the introduction of performance-related pay and firmer appraisal. However, in our analysis, as illustrated by our case study, it is likely to bring about the opposite effects, increasing divisiveness and leading to further erosion of trust among the participants in primary schooling. As for the curriculum, it was the overload of prescriptive work that brought most complaints, and despite the rationalisation by Dearing (1994) the introduction of the literacy and numeracy hours is introducing new pressures.

There have been some, what many regard as, good effects of the reforms. The National Curriculum itself is generally accepted in principle among primary teachers (Webb and Vulliamy 1996) as providing a useful framework and improving teaching in certain key areas, such as science. Some teachers feel enhanced and reskilled by the reforms, particularly in areas of management and assessment (Gipps *et al.* 1995; Woods *et al.* 1997). As far as our case studies here are concerned, there are some not unpromising signs. For example, the government set up a National Advisory Committee on Creative and Cultural Education which reported in 1999. The report was welcomed by the Education Secretary of State, David Blunkett, who said he had set up the committee because:

> I was concerned that pupils should not only be equipped with the basic skills of literacy and numeracy, but should also have opportunities to develop their creative potential . . . The Government wants to develop young people's capacity for original ideas . . . The revised curriculum [i.e. the National Curriculum currently under review for the year 2000] will offer teachers more flexibility in their delivery of the curriculum, with more opportunities for pupils to explore their creative potential. The increased emphasis which will be placed on thinking skills in the revised curriculum will also enable pupils to focus more on their creative talents.

Kenneth Robinson, the chair of the committee, felt 'the government's plan would not be enough to restore creative energy to the classroom' (*Guardian*, 15 May 1999), and since then the report has become marginalised. It remains to be seen whether the revision of the National Curriculum in 2000 bears out the Minister's promise.

OfStEd, too, is evolving. Schools identified as 'improving' will now be subject only to 'light touch' inspections, with much less paperwork, less stark confrontation, more collegiality and trust, less pressure on staff. One headteacher commented, 'This is a new relationship with OfStEd. I felt as though we were being treated in a grown-up way' (Hoare 2000: 4). Other schools will still have full inspections. For these, also, OfStEd has a new code of conduct, aimed at lessening teacher stress, cutting down paperwork, giving feedback and explanation – in other words, treating teachers more as professionals. However, an inspector comments, 'I can see a stigma being attached to a full inspection. It makes parents believe a school is not first rank. It's a clearer message than the league tables. It's the difference between Premier League and First Division' (ibid.). The new code also has to be put to the test.

We still have, therefore, a hierarchical framework and a calculated divisiveness. There is still, in practice, a narrowness and exclusiveness of vision and a homogeneity of practices based on performativity. There is a unilinear and simplistic conception of learning and a socially decontextualised view of school effectiveness (Pollard 1999). These are the parameters of 'success' and 'improvement' as measured by standardised tests. Teachers are still not trusted, and are seen in a managerial rather than developmental context (Batteson 1999). We still have league tables of schools, and summaries of OfStEd findings on individual schools are still published in local and national press. There is still continuing media and 'policy hysteria' about low standards and international competitiveness (Stronach and Morris, 1999). New Labour has made noises suggesting a broadening of view. It remains to be seen whether this broadening will be concretised in policy and practice or whether, as many feel about the rest of New Labour's activity so far, it remains at the level of rhetoric.

References

Alexander, R. (1992) *Policy and Practice in Primary Education*, London: Routledge.

Alexander, R., Willcocks, J. and Nelson, N. (1995) 'Discourse, pedagogy and the National Curriculum: change and continuity in primary schools', *Research Papers in Education* 11 (1) 81–120.

Apple, M. W. (1986) *Teachers and Texts: A Political Economy of Class and Gender Relations in Education*, New York: Routledge.

Ball, S. (1998a) 'Performativity and fragmentation in "Postmodern Schooling"', in J. Carter (ed.) *Postmodernity and Fragmentation of Welfare*, London: Routledge.

Ball, S. (1998b) 'Educational studies, policy entrepreneurship and social theory', in R. Slee and G. Weiner, with S. Tomlinson (eds) *School Effectiveness for Whom? Challenges to the School Effectiveness and School Improvement Movements*, London: Falmer Press.

Batteson, C. (1999) 'The changing politics of primary education', *Education 3 to 13*, October, pp. 61–5.

Bernstein, B. (1975), *Class, Codes and Control* III, *Towards a Theory of Educational Transmissions*, London: Routledge.

Broadfoot, P. (1998) 'Quality standards and control in higher education: what price lifelong learning?' *International Studies in Sociology of Education* 8 (2), 155–81.

Cox, B. (ed.) (1998) *Literacy is not Enough: Essays on the Importance of Reading*, Manchester: Manchester University Press and Book Trust

Crace, J. (1999) 'Stressed out at the age of seven', *Guardian Education*, 20 July, p. 2.

Dadds, M. (1999) 'Teachers' values and the literacy hour', *Cambridge Journal of Education* 29 (1), 7–19.

Dearing, R. (1994) *The National Curriculum and its Assessment: Final Report*, London: SCAA.

Department for Education and Employment (1998a) *The National Strategy: Framework for Teaching*, London: DfEE.

Department for Education and Employment (1998b) *The National Literacy Strategy: Literacy Training Pack*, London: DfEE.

Fisher, R. and Lewis, M. (1999) 'Implementation of the National Literacy Strategy: Indications of Change', paper presented to ESRC Research Seminar 1 on Raising Standards in Literacy, University of Plymouth, May.

Francis, L. J and Grindle, Z. (1998) 'Whatever happened to progressive education? A comparison of primary school teachers' attitudes in 1982 and 1996', *Educational Studies* 24 (3), 269–79.

Galton, M., Hargreaves, L., Comber, C., Wall, D. and Pell, T. (1999) 'Changes in patterns of teacher interaction in primary classrooms, 1976–96', *British Educational Research Journal* 25 (1), 23–37.

Giddens, A. (1990) *The Consequences of Modernity*, Cambridge: Polity.

Gipps, C., Brown, M., McCallum, B. and McAllister, S. (1995) *Intuition or Evidence? Teachers and National Assessment of Seven-year-olds*, Buckingham: Open University Press.

Hoare, S. (2000) 'The long and short of OfStEd', *Guardian Education*, 25 January, p. 4.

Jeffrey, B. (2001) 'Reconstructing child-centred education: curriculum eventing at Coombes first school' in J. Collins, K. Insley and A. Craft (eds) (forthcoming) *Understanding Pedagogy*, London: Falmer.

Jeffrey, B. and Woods, P. (1998) *Testing Teachers: The Impact of School Inspections on Primary Teachers*, London: Falmer.

Medwell, J., Wray, D., Poulson, L. and Fox, R. (1998) *Effective Teachers of Literacy: A Report of a Research Project commissioned by the Teacher Training Agency*, Exeter: University of Exeter.

Office for Standards in Education (1997) Inspection Report on Coombes Infant and Nursery School, Reading, Berkshire, 1–4 December.

Office for Standards in Education (1999) *Lessons learned from Special Measures: A Report from the Office of HM Chief Inspector of Schools*, London: OfStEd.

Pollard, A. (1999) 'Towards a new perspective on children's learning?' *Education 3 to 13*, October, pp. 56–60.

Scanlon, M. (1999) *The Impact of OfStEd Inspections*, Reading: NFER.

Standards and Effectiveness Unit (1998) *The National Literacy Strategy: Framework for Teaching*, London: DfEE.

Stronach, I. and Morris, B. (1999) 'Polemical notes on educational evaluation in the age of "policy hysteria"', *Evaluation and Research in Education* 8 (1–2), 5–19.

Sugrue, C. (1997) *Complexities of Teaching: Child-centred Perspectives*, London: Falmer Press.

Troman, G. and Woods, P. (2001) *The Social Construction of Teacher Stress*, London: Routledge.

Webb, R. and Vulliamy, G. (1996) *Roles and Responsibilities in the Primary School: Changing Demands, Changing Practices*, Buckingham: Open University Press.

Wood, E. (1999) 'The impact of the National Curriculum on play in reception classes', *Educational Research*, 41 (1), 11–22.

Woods, P. (1993) *Critical Events in Teaching and Learning*, London: Falmer Press.

Woods, P. (1995) *Creative Teachers in Primary Schools*, Buckingham: Open University Press.

Woods, P. (1999) 'Talking about Coombes: features of a learning community', in J. Retallick, B. Cocklin and K. Coombe (eds) *Learning Communities in Education: Issues and Contexts*, London: Routledge.

Woods, P. Jeffrey, B., Troman, G. and Boyle, M. (1997) *Restructuring Schools, Reconstructing Teachers: Responding to Change in the Primary School*, Buckingham: Open University Press.

7 Will the curriculum caterpillar ever learn to fly?

Mike Davies and Gwyn Edwards

Adding wings to caterpillars does not create butterflies – it creates awkward and dysfunctional caterpillars. Butterflies are created through transformation.

Stephanie Pace Marshall (1996)

Any evaluation of New Labour's curriculum policies since assuming office in May 1997 has to be set within the wider context of the cultural politics of the last thirty years and against a backdrop of significant socio-economic transformations that we have witnessed during this period. Indeed, it was partly in response to the gathering momentum of these transformations that the previous Labour government (1971–9), under the leadership of James Callaghan, launched the Great Debate on education, the outcomes of which are clearly manifest in the curriculum today. Moreover, it could be argued that Callaghan's Ruskin speech in 1976, together with the Green Paper that followed (DES 1977), established the discursive boundaries within which all subsequent curriculum debate and policy making at government level have been framed. The speech highlighted a number of concerns about schools which the government and public shared and, it was argued, had a legitimate right to air. Particular attention was drawn to complaints from industry that new recruits lacked the required skills and to parental unease about new informal teaching methods. To address the concerns raised in the speech, the government Green Paper (ibid.) proposed a review of curricular arrangements and, in the light of the review, to establish broad agreement on a framework for the curriculum with the possibility of a 'core' or 'protected part'.

Over the next ten years numerous frameworks for a 'core' or 'common' curriculum were put forward (DES 1976, 1980, 1981, 1984, 1985; Schools Council 1981) but a statutory national curriculum was never formally proposed, and there was no apparent support for any form of national testing. On the contrary, emphasis was given to arriving at a consensus on a broad framework for the curriculum without seriously undermining the professional autonomy that schools had always enjoyed in curriculum decision making (DES 1980, 1984, 1986).

By 1987, however, the mood had dramatically changed. With a general election on the horizon, the Conservative government announced its intention to legislate for a national curriculum should it be returned to power. In fulfilment of this election pledge, the Education Act 1988 legislated for 'a balanced and broadly based curriculum which: (a) promotes the spiritual, moral, cultural, mental and physical development of pupils at the school and of society; (b) prepares such pupils for the opportunities, responsibilities and experiences of adult life' (DES 1988). As a general statement of intent, few would take issue with these broad aims. But their translation into a defensible and workable curriculum is a more contentious matter. What the 1988 Act failed to provide was a coherent rationale whereby its broad aims could be translated into a national curriculum which could be adapted to meet the needs of schools operating a variety of contexts and circumstances.

In essence, the National Curriculum was constructed from a collection of existing school subjects on the assumption that a coherent whole would emerge from the sum of the parts. Predictably, it did not. Moreover, to comply with the model of assessment proposed by the Task Group on Assessment and Testing (DES 1987), the subjects were broken down into programmes of study and these, in turn, were further fragmented into attainment targets organised hierarchically into ten levels.

Subsequently the National Curriculum Council endeavoured to address what were seen as serious shortcomings by bolting on a framework of cross-curricular components designed to 'tie together the broad education of the individual subjects and augment what comes from the basic curriculum' (National Curriculum Council, 1990: 2). But this only compounded the problem by imposing an additional burden on an already overloaded curriculum. Not surprisingly, the cross-curricular themes have been marginalised to such an extent that their recovery is unlikely without a substantial revision of the National Curriculum subject orders (Whitty *et al.* 1994).

Running alongside the demand for greater curriculum uniformity (culminating in the National Curriculum) – and to some extent in tension with it – there was also from the mid-1970s onwards a concerted effort to align the school curriculum more explicitly to the perceived needs of the economy, especially in the 14–19 phase. The Green Paper (DES 1977) that followed Callaghan's speech highlighted 'the feeling that the educational system was out of touch with the fundamental need for Britain to survive economically in a highly competitive world through the efficiency of its industry and commerce' (p. 2). Young people, it was argued, were not 'sufficiently aware of the importance of industry to our society' and they were 'not taught much about it' (p. 2). Consequently they left school 'with little or no understanding of the workings, or importance, of the wealth-producing sector of our economy' (p. 34). Henceforth, it was envisaged, education would 'contribute as much as possible to improving industrial performance and thereby increasing the national wealth' (p. 6).

The view that schools were out of touch with the needs of industry was reiterated in subsequent official government statements on the curriculum. *The School Curriculum* (DES 1981: 18), for example, asserted that 'pupils need to be given a better understanding of the economic base of our society and the importance to Britain of the wealth creating process'. In a similar vein, the White Paper *Better Schools* (DES 1986: 16) advocated a curriculum that brought education and training 'into closer relation in a variety of ways' and had 'preparation for employment as one of its principal functions'.

The most significant response to the demands for a more economically oriented curriculum was the Technical and Vocational Education Initiative (TVEI), established by the Conservative government in 1982 to meet 'a growing concern about existing arrangements for technical and vocational provision for young people' (Thatcher, quoted in Dale 1989: 147). Despite its predominantly instrumental intent, in the hands of educational practitioners TVEI contributed significantly to a form of 'vocational progressivism' (Ball 1990) which fostered new approaches to teaching and learning and went some way to bridging the traditional academic–vocational divide (Young 1998). The innovative practices of TVEI, however, were strategically marginalised by the National Curriculum, which was configured and developed in compliance with a neo-conservative 'cultural restorationist' agenda (Ball 1994).

In April 1993, in response to growing concern about content overload, John Patten, the Secretary of State for Education, invited Sir Ron Dearing to review the National Curriculum, albeit within the somewhat narrow remit of slimming down the curriculum, improving the central administration, simplifying the testing arrangements and reviewing the ten-level scale for recognising children's attainment. Dearing's final report (SCAA 1994), submitted in December 1993, recommended a substantial slimming down of curriculum content in Key Stages 1–3, and a reduction in the number of compulsory subjects at Key Stage 4 to create space for a vocational pathway. Not surprisingly, the casualties at Key Stage 4 were the arts and humanities subjects.

It could be argued that the general approval these recommendations received from the educational community was misplaced in that the underlying assumptions of the National Curriculum were never questioned – for it was not in the remit to do so – and its underlying structure survived virtually intact. Moreover, the changes at Key Stage 4 seriously undermined the principle of a broad and balanced entitlement during the years of compulsory schooling which almost universally has been accepted as one of the redeeming features of the National Curriculum legislation.

This, then, was the curriculum legacy inherited by New Labour in May 1997. Moreover, it was a legacy that was now firmly embedded, both discursively and structurally, in the educational system and, consequently, set strategic limitations on curriculum possibilities for the immediate future. Therefore, a useful way of analysing the subsequent curriculum policies of the New Labour government is in terms of the continuities and disjunctures with those of its predecessor. Perhaps the most obvious observation to make is that so far there appears to be no radical departure from the curriculum policies of the previous Conservative government. The post-Dearing settlement continues more or less intact in that revisions of the National Curriculum in 2000 were confined to a cosmetic tweaking of subject content with the overall structure remaining essentially the same, except for the statutory inclusion of citizenship education at Key Stages 3 and 4 from 2002. Indeed, David Blunkett, the Secretary of State, instructed the Qualifications and Curriculum Authority (QCA), albeit in response to advice given to him by that body, that the revision of the National Curriculum should 'avoid excessive disruption and upheaval in the curriculum' and 'must be limited to addressing what needs to be changed to allow schools to concentrate on raising standards' (quoted in QCA 1999: 2).

This endorsement of the curriculum *status quo* does not square with pre-election promises of an alternative curriculum framework 'which values local flexibility and the professional discretion of teachers' (Labour Party 1994: 15), provides, 'in terms of areas of experience' (Labour Party 1993: 28), 'a broad . . . entitlement to all children without stifling a teacher's creativity and ability to respond to pupils' needs' (Labour Party 1995: 24) and recognises that 'development and innovation is essential if the curriculum is to be relevant in a modern and progressive society' (ibid.). So, for the foreseeable future, schools will continue to work within the confines of a 'prescriptive', 'content-specific', 'over-assessed', 'conceptually arid' (Labour Party 1993) National Curriculum that, arguably, serves neither the personal needs of pupils nor the social, political and economic needs of the society in which they live.

Closer examination, however, reveals a number of distinctive features to New Labour curriculum policy that represent a significant departure from what went before. Most notably, under New Labour 'standards' have replaced 'curriculum' as the discursive hub of educational policy making. And this discursive reorientation has legitimated the obsessive setting and pursuit of pre-specified targets. The stated educational priority is to 'ensure that every child is taught to read, write and add up' (DfEE 1997: 9). This involves the setting of 'ambitious and challenging' (p. 19) literacy and numeracy targets for 11 year olds to be achieved by the year 2002.

While no one would seriously dispute the desirability of raising standards in literacy and numeracy – although many would object to this being seen as the predominant purpose of education – it seems reasonable to suggest that there will inevitably be a degree of contestation as to how it is best achieved. Not so for the New Labour government, which, despite criticisms and setbacks, is dogmatically committed to both the appropriateness and the feasibility of its targets. Moreover, it simplistically assumes that the targets can be met by the application of what is taken to be 'proven best practice' (ibid.). Underpinning this assumption is a discourse which perpetuates the view that teaching is a techno-rational activity and that once its underlying mechanics have been revealed through appropriate research they then can be universally applied in classrooms.

What the discourse avoids is any engagement with deeper questions relating to the complex, and inevitably contentious, relationship between educational purposes and the school curriculum and, in turn, the implications of this for what constitute educational standards. There is an assumption that educational standards are unproblematic, and, furthermore, that they can be raised without any consideration of curriculum content and pedagogical practice. Within a pre-given, taken-for-granted curriculum framework, raising standards is seen as simply a matter of adopting the 'proven way' (ibid: 12). And for New Labour there is only one way. So the claim that the National Curriculum and its assessment, together with regular OFSTED inspections and the publication of league tables, are raising educational standards needs to be treated with a degree of scepticism in that it is premised on unquestioned assumptions about the nature and purpose of education.

Consistent with this discourse are attempts to exert greater control over pedagogical practice in schools by imposing on teachers tightly prescribed curriculum packages which are considered to be consistent with 'best proven practice' (ibid.: 13). The most obvious examples are the literacy and numeracy hours. But of equal significance are the exemplar schemes of work that have been produced by the Qualifications and Curriculum Authority for other national curriculum subjects at all Key Stages.

Thus, whereas the Conservative government established tight control over the content of the curriculum and sought to influence pedagogy indirectly, it seems that New Labour may allow schools greater freedom over content but is adopting a more interventionist stance in relation to pedagogy. What both approaches share, however, is a profound mistrust of teachers: the former in relation to their ideological commitments; the latter in relation to their professional competence. And they also share a fundamentally distorted understanding of curriculum by permitting content and pedagogy to be separated and determined independently of each other.

Some teachers, of course, will 'read' government edicts and injunctions as open texts and reinterpret them in light of their own values, understanding, experience and circumstances. The danger is, however, that others – possibly the majority – will find it difficult to contest the new pedagogic identity being prescribed for them. Consequently, they will become little more than 'operatives' whose professional expertise is reduced to a command of the technical aspects of teaching and classroom management necessary to the pursuance of state-sanctioned standards. Teachers, Stenhouse (1983: 189) argues, 'must be educated to develop their art, not master it'. For him, 'close control of curricula and teaching methods in school is to be likened to the totalitarian control of art' (1984: 68). If we extend this analogy further, the literacy and numeracy hours and the exemplar schemes of work could be seen as the pedagogical equivalent of painting by numbers.

A second area where New Labour has sought greater control over educational practices concerns the grouping of pupils in the secondary phase of schooling. Its unequivocal position is that 'we are no longer prepared to ... defend the failings of across-the-board mixed-ability teaching' and, henceforth, the presumption will be 'that setting should be the norm in secondary schools' and 'in some cases, is worth considering in primary schools' (DfEE 1997: 37). Again, it appears that New Labour is prepared to intervene more directly in areas of educational organisation and practice that have previously been considered to be the professional responsibility of educational practitioners. What is significant here is that New Labour policy appears to be at odds with research, which suggests that for a considerable number of pupils in some schools setting may not be the most appropriate form of grouping for enhancing their educational achievement (Boaler 1997).

Further compromises and contradictions in New Labour's curriculum policies are evident in the recently established Education Action Zones. Here, local partnerships are being invited 'to put forward their own radical ideas and imaginative proposals to raise standards' (DfEE 1998a). Moreover, 'innovation and flexibility in curriculum organization and delivery' (ibid.) are encouraged, including the possibility of 'adapting the National Curriculum – or radically redesigning parts of it – to meet local needs' (DfEE 1998b). Thus, for the majority of schools, standards will be raised through prescription, standardisation and central control; in others it requires flexibility, experimentation and local autonomy. Moreover, there is also the implication that in predominantly middle class suburban and rural areas entitlement to a broad and balanced curriculum is maintained, in working class inner city areas it can be disapplied. Whether Education Action Zones will be catalysts of radical curriculum innovation remains to be seen. Evidence based on an examination of the 'first wave' of Education Action Zones applications suggests that so far the response has been 'safe' rather than 'radical' (Riley *et al.* 1998). And the main emphasis has been on structure and provision rather than curriculum and learning.

For New Labour 'education is the key to personal fulfilment for the individual, to economic success for the Nation, and to the creation of a more just and cohesive society' (Labour Party 1994: 3). What is lacking, however, is any appreciation of the complexities, tensions and contestations that are endemic in the realisation of curriculum consistent with these three goals. Certainly there should be no serious obstacle, at least in theory, to the creation of a curriculum that facilitates the pursuit of personal fulfilment of individuals and that contributes to the development of a more cohesive and just society. But creating a curriculum that achieves these two aims and, at the same time, ensures the economic success of the nation is far more problematical. Indeed, there are those who argue that there is an inevitable tension between educating young people for personal fulfilment and democratic empowerment and preparing them for the world of work (Brosio 1991; Jones and Hatcher 1994; MacIntyre 1987). And it is a tension that cannot be conveniently wished away. Thus, while in New Labour policy documents we get rhetorical gestures to the value of learning for its own sake and for democratic empowerment, it is clear that the overwhelming imperative is to recast education primarily, if not exclusively, as an instrumental means of ensuring economic success in an increasingly competitive global market.

It is beyond the scope of this chapter to pursue this issue further. Suffice it to say that at the present juncture there might potentially be greater compatibility between New Labour's three goals. However, the realisation of this in practice would require a radical reordering of the epistemological, pedagogical and organisational assumptions that underpin the school curriculum. Such an undertaking is unlikely to come about if schools are not given the necessary freedom, incentive and expertise to do so.

Research indicates that for a significant number of young people the school curriculum, in terms of both content and pedagogy, is not a pathway to enlightenment and empowerment but a source of alienation and failure, especially so in the later years of compulsory schooling and in inner city areas (Carlen *et al.* 1992; Kinder 1997). Viewed from this perspective, current government policies are, ironically, causing the educational problems they are supposedly designed to address. Reassuringly, there is at least some official acknowledgement of the causes of disaffection and its consequences for the lives of young people. Douglas Osler, the Senior Chief Inspector of Schools in Scotland, for example, points out:

> There are an increasing number of young people who find school to be an uncomfortable learning environment. We cannot write these people off and say that they got it wrong. Young people can often be disaffected from school rather than from learning. Sometimes we speak as if the big idea is school. It is not. The big idea is learning and schools are just economical, collective ways of providing it.
>
> (Quoted in Munro 1997)

In what follows we offer some tentative suggestions for a more holistic view of the curriculum which advances the view that 'the big idea is learning'. We seek a more sophisticated curriculum framework based upon a better understanding of the relationship between content and pedagogy and on a recognition that educational standards are realised in and through the teaching–learning process itself, as well as being its extrinsic products. As Stenhouuse (1967: 89) argues, 'A good curriculum is one which makes worthwhile standards possible.' Of particular concern to us is the degree of control learners have over the content and/or methods of their learning and how these may relate to what are considered worthwhile areas and forms of enquiry.

Within the traditional subject-based curriculum the norm is for students to be inducted into the various fields of knowledge and the conceptual structures that comprise each field. The learners are the recipients of the knowledge and have very little control over what they learn or how they go about learning. Prescription, regulation and testing stemming from the end of the last century have been the dominant features of this conception of curriculum.

In recognition of the fragmentation of experience embodied in such a curriculum various attempts have been made over time to combine subjects into integrated areas. But, within this format, the learner is still required to deal with thoughts and ideas mediated through a teacher, a text or, increasingly, a computer program. The content, materials and methods of the curriculum remain external to the learner.

Looking back to an era when teachers were much more involved in curriculum making there was a strong disposition to view the curriculum more holistically. Indeed, this was very much the view that underpinned post-Plowden primary practice. And a good example in the secondary phase of schooling was Lawrence Stenhouse's Humanities Curriculum Project (HCP). But even within this project, what counted as worthwhile content for study and debate was very much set externally to the learner. There was, nevertheless, a commitment to making the curriculum more relevant by reducing the gap between the lived experiences of the student at school and in the rest of their lives.

A variant of HCP could be seen in some of the developments that came from TVEI, where the emphasis was placed more firmly on authentic experiences (often in a work placement) coupled with emphasis on the acquisition and development of core generic skills (such as team work and problem solving). This approach was evident in the work of pioneers such as Eric Midwinter who, in Educational Priority Areas, sought to bring schools alive by using the local community as a resource and stimulus to learning. And there is a well established practice in some Scandinavian schools to involve students themselves in defining both the area of study and the method by which the study is undertaken.

These initiatives, and others like them, were imaginative responses to questions posed by the educational concerns and the socio-economic context at the time. What then are the questions the educational system should now be asking of itself in response to the social, cultural, political and economic transformations we are currently experiencing – or anticipate in the future – and in the light of new understandings about the nature of intelligence and learning? In relation to a number of 'sites' of educational organisation and practice we suggest the following.

- *Teams.* Is it possible to view the curriculum as large swathes which represent areas of common interest and complementary expertise between groups of teachers? Could the arts or the humanities, for example, be seen as a whole? And could the teacher be seen as both a resource and a coach and, additionally, as someone who continues to practise and research in his or her own field for part of the week as well as teach?

- *Time.* Is it necessary to bound learning by predetermined slots of time that are set on an annual basis irrespective of whether they meet the needs of learning and learners at a particular moment? How can we encourage greater flexibility over the use of time and effect greater collaboration between teachers?

- *Place.* With exponential developments in information and communication technology do we really need to have young people in school all the time or could we find greater flexibility in both the where and the when of learning? Would there be merit in all young people being involved in learning which took them 'beyond the classroom' (Bentley 1998) on a more regular basis?

- *Pedagogy.* What are the implications of recognising that any group of people represents a broad range of human ability, motivation and need? How can we respond more creatively to all that we know about the multiplicity of human intelligence (Gardner 1983), including emotional intelligence (Goleman 1995) and the diversity of learning and thinking styles (Sternberg 1997)?

- *Resources.* What are the curricular implications of ICT for the ways that we organise learning? How do we ensure that students engage critically with the knowledge made available to them through ICT? How can we use resources to increase motivation and a sense of esteem and human flourishing?

- *Relationships.* How can we encourage and strengthen warm, persistent and learning-focused relationships between different people? How can we break out of the stranglehold by which parents view themselves as possessive individuals interested only in what a school has to offer their child rather than as partners intent on getting the best education they can for all children? How can we mobilise local authorities, higher education institutions, businesses and schools to act as partners in a common struggle to improve learning for all?

- *Audience.* How can we develop more 'authentic' (Perrone 1991) forms of assessment where the outcomes and products of students' work can be appreciated and celebrated rather than marked and graded and where the audience is seen not as an anonymous assessor but as peers, the wider community or even the self?

- *Authorship.* How can we reconceptualise and reconstruct the curriculum in such a way that pupils, at least for part of the time, have an opportunity for fashioning some time for themselves so that they can pursue their own ideas and studies?

In conclusion, it is our contention that the school curriculum is predicated on a seriously flawed logic that renders it ill equipped to meet the challenges of the twenty-first century. Whether we like it or not, education is caught up in the turbulence of exponential change the outcomes of which are beyond prediction. Therefore the principal purpose of education should be helping young people acquire the dispositions, skills, understandings and values that will enable them to live their lives intelligently, meaningfully, constructively and cooperatively in the midst of the complexity, uncertainty and instability they will increasingly encounter. There is no sense in a curriculum designed to predict and control in a world that is in a state of constant flux. What is required is a curriculum rationale that seeks to rediscover the intrinsic purposes and principles of education, and that gives schools the freedom and incentive to respond flexibly, creatively and responsibly to the needs of their pupils in an uncertain and rapidly changing world. If our aim is to create butterflies rather than dysfunctional caterpillars then nothing less will do.

References

Ball, S. J. (1990) *Politics and Policy Making in Education: Explorations in Policy Sociology*, London: Routledge.

Ball, S. J. (1994) *Education Reform: A Critical and Post-structuralist Approach*, Buckingham: Open University Press.

Bentley, T. (1998) *Learning beyond the Classroom: Education for a Changing World*, London: Routledge.

Boaler, J. (1997) 'Setting, social class and survival of the fittest', *British Educational Research Journal* 23 (5), 575–95.

Brosio, R. A. (1991) 'The continuing conflict between capitalism and democracy: ramifications for schooling–education', *Educational Philosophy and Theory* 23 (2), 30–45.

Carlen, P., Gleeson, D. and Wardhaugh, J. (1992) *Truancy: The Politics of Compulsory Schooling*, Buckingham: Open University Press.

Dale, R. (1989) *The State and Education Policy*, Milton Keynes: Open University Press.

Department for Education and Employment (1997) *Excellence in Schools*, London: DfEE.

Department for Education and Employment (1998a) *The Learning Age: A Renaissance for a new Britain*, London: DfEE.

Department for Education and Employment (1998b) *The National Literacy Strategy: Framework for Teaching*, London: DfEE.

Department of Education and Science (1976) *The Curriculum 11 to 16*, London: HMSO.

Department of Education and Science (1977) *Education in Schools: A Consultative Document*, London: HMSO.

Department of Education and Science (1980) *A View of the Curriculum*, London: HMSO.

Department of Education and Science (1981) *The School Curriculum*, London: HMSO.

Department of Education and Science (1984) *The Organization and Content of the 5–16 Curriculum*, London: HMSO.

Department of Education and Science (1985) *The Curriculum from 5 to 16*, London: HMSO.

Department of Education and Science (1986) *Better Schools*, London: HMSO.

Department of Education and Science (1987) *National Curriculum: Task Group on Assessment and Testing: A Report*, London: HMSO.

Department of Education and Science (1988) *The Education Reform Act*, London: HMSO.

Gardner, H. (1983) *Frames of Mind: the Theory of Multiple Intelligences*, London: Heinemann.

Goleman, D. (1995) *Emotional Intelligence: Why it can Matter more than IQ*, New York: Bantam.

Jones, K. and Hatcher, R. (1994) 'Educational progress and economic change: notes on some recent proposals', *British Journal of Educational Studies* 42 (3), 245–60.

Kinder, K. (1997) 'Causes of disaffection: the views of pupils and educational professionals', *EERA Bulletin* 3 (1), 3–11.

Labour Party (1994) *Opening Doors to a Learning Society: A Policy Statement on Education*, London: Labour Party.

Labour Party (1995) *Excellence for Everyone: Labour's Crusade to raise Standards*, London: Labour Party.

Labour Party (1996) *Aiming High: Labour's Plans for Reform of the 14–19+ Curriculum*, London: Labour Party.

MacIntyre, A. (1987) 'The idea of an educated public', in G. Haydon (ed.) *Education and Values: The Richard Peters Lectures*, London: Institute of Education, University of London.

Marshall, S. P. (1996) 'How chaos and complexity theory can inform leadership in transition', *Education 2000 News*, Letchworth: Education 2000.

Munro, N. (1997) 'No "radical surgery" 5–14', *Times Educational Supplement for Scotland*, 3 October.

National Curriculum Council (1990) *The Whole Curriculum*, Curriculum Guidance 3, York: NCC.

Perrone, V. (1991) (ed.) *Expanding Student Assessment*, Alexandria VA: Association for Supervision and Curriculum Development.

Qualifications and Curriculum Authority (1999) *QCA's Work in Progress to Develop the School Curriculum: Materials for Conferences, Seminars and Meetings, Booklet A*, London: QCA.

Riley, K., Walting, R., Rowles, D. and Hopkins, D. (1998) *Education Action Zones: Some Lessons learned from First Wave of Applications*, London: Education Network.

School Curriculum and Assessment Authority (1994) *The National Curriculum and its Assessment: Final Report*, London: SCAA.

Schools Council (1981) *The Practical Curriculum*, Schools Council Working Paper 70, London: Methuen.

Stenhouse, L. (1967) *Culture and Education*, London: Nelson.

Stenhouse, L. (1983) *Authority, Education and Emancipation*, London: Heinemann.

Stenhouse, L. (1984) 'Artistry and teaching: the teacher as focus of research and development', in D. Hopkins and M. Wideen (eds) *Alternative Perspectives on School Improvement*, London: Falmer Press.

Sternberg, R. J. (1997) *Thinking Styles*, Cambridge: Cambridge University Press.

Whitty, G., Rowe, G. and Aggleton, P. (1994) 'Discourse in cross-curricular contexts: limits to empowerment', *International Studies in Sociology of Education* 4 (1), 25–42.

Young, M. F. D. (1998) *The Curriculum of the Future: From the new 'Sociology of Education' to a Critical Theory of Learning*, London: Falmer Press.

8 Further education under New Labour

Translating the language of aspiration into a springboard for achievement

Ann Limb

At a meeting of some of the most senior figures from industry and education in November 1998 at the Council for Industry and Higher Education (CIHE), Baroness Tessa Blackstone, Minister for Further and Higher Education, vigorously stressed the government's unequivocal commitment to putting into practice the vision of lifelong learning outlined so passionately by the Secretary of State, David Blunkett, in his introduction to one of the key educational policy documents to emerge from the Labour government – the Green Paper *The Learning Age: a renaissance for a new Britain* (Secretary of State for Education and Employment 1998). Her arguments were persuasive, her case was convincing and, in my opinion, her commitment genuine. She acknowledged, too, the media's persistent indifference or imperviousness to this particular aspect of the government's education message, thus reinforcing the impression that the Prime Minister's now legendary mantra, 'Education, education, education,' is still widely interpreted as meaning in practice 'schools, schools, schools' or, at most, 'early years, primary, secondary'.

The origins of this lack of understanding may in part derive from the persistent failure of previous governments to develop a coherent policy framework for adult, continuing and further education – something which the Green Paper on lifelong learning begins to address. The complexity, diversity and fragmentation of further education – wherein lies some of its considerable strength – has at the same time militated against its cohesion as a recognisable sector in the wider learning spectrum. The concept of lifelong learning, initially crafted under the Conservative administration as lifetime learning (DfEE 1996), represents a conscious attempt to begin the process of changing perception, attitude and practice. This chapter explores the adult, continuing and further education dimensions of the debate about lifelong learning.

In her discussions with members of the CIHE Tessa Blackstone did not, however, go on to draw attention to another influential segment of society – her parliamentary colleagues of all parties, for whom there is also evidence of equal lack of interest in the importance of lifelong learning policies and in the role of adult, continuing and further education in their implementation. It is a matter of record that in the House of Commons debate in June 1998 on the report of the Select Committee on Education and Employment (Education and Employment Committee 1998), another milestone along the road to the development of a coherent strategy for further education, no more than a handful of MPs were present in the Chamber to debate some of the most positive and radical proposals for the sector since incorporation in 1993.

These two random events illustrate the central problem faced by the government and by those of us working in adult, continuing and further education: widespread lack of acknowledgement of our distinct identity and poor recognition of our authentic voice amid the clamour of compelling cries from competing sectors of education.

The crucial question which must be examined is whether the policies announced and the actions taken in 1999–2000 by the Department for Education and Employment (DfEE) will enable further education to flourish and to fulfil its role as one of the key engines of economic, social, cultural and personal change in the lifelong learning revolution. This is a belief self-evidently held by David Blunkett and Tessa Blackstone as well as George Mudie and Malcolm Wicks, who have followed Kim Howells, the first occupant of the newly created post of Parliamentary Under Secretary of State for Lifelong Learning.

Use of the term 'lifelong learning' has become *de rigueur* and widespread under New Labour. It permeates and colours much of the strategic thinking and policy formulation of David Blunkett's ministerial team and reflects the assumption that everyone now knows what lifelong learning is and what it is for – both in the United Kingdom and worldwide.

This chapter aims to contribute to the debate about the nature and purposes of lifelong learning. It highlights some of the main themes of the new government's policies for adult, continuing and further education and outlines some of the reasons why my own answer to the question I raised is 'Yes' – albeit with qualification. My central argument is that the responsibility for bringing about the lifelong learning revolution lies both with government and the sector and that it is the strength of this partnership and particularly its ability to convince a host of other stakeholders – students, parents, employers, politicians and the population as a whole – of its value which in future years will determine the success or failure of the government's mission. I conclude with a look towards the future, presenting a case for the sustainability of the lifelong revolution. This can be achieved only through further radical changes to the structure, system and management of adult, continuing and further education and by parity of esteem being given to the personal as well as the economic imperatives for transformation.

The main themes of the government's policies for further education can be linked with two seminal reports which were set up under the Conservative administration and are usually referred to as the Dearing (NCIHE 1997a, b) and Kennedy (Kennedy 1997; Further Education Funding Council 1997a, b) reports. The new Labour government made two separate responses to these reports (DfEE 1998a, b) and published them with their Green Paper *The Learning Age* in March 1998. At the same time a consultation document, *Accountability in Further Education* (DfEE 1998d), containing proposals for changes in the structure and membership of governing bodies was also produced. In all these documents can be found the origins of much of the research and many of the ideas which have shaped the government's thinking on further education. Five broad themes emerge. These are:

- social inclusion and coherence;
- quality improvement;
- partnership working;
- regionalisation;
- accountability.

Additionally, the report of the National Advisory Group on Continuing Education and Lifelong Learning, *Learning for the Twenty-first Century*, chaired by Professor Bob Fryer (1997), a committee set up by David Blunkett within the first few weeks of the new government, and the FEFC's own reports by Professors Tomlinson (1996) and Higginson (1996), provide further theoretical and practical underpinning to the government's vision of 'a transformation in our learning culture'. All these documents, and the many detailed responses to them from individuals, colleges, employers and organisations working in adult, continuing and further education, constitute a huge body of literature from which practitioners in the field are left to distil something tangible, focused and pragmatic. Given the new government's commitment to maintaining spending in the first two years of its administration at levels agreed by the former government, it was not surprising that, during the first two years of the government's life, staff in colleges had, in David Blunkett's own words, their 'souls nourished' and their intellects inspired by his radical vision of a lifelong learning society but did not see it turned into hard cash for college budgets. Looking back over the actions of the Labour government since May 1997, it is clear that we have in place the foundations for reform – a clear vision, mission and purpose which give rise to the five strategic priorities already referred to. It was Sir Christopher Ball who coined the phrase 'resources follow coherent purpose'. It is my view that much of the activity of the first two years of the new Labour government has been concerned to focus and consult on the coherent purpose of further education. Now this has been established, the funding can flow.

The publication of the report from the House of Commons Select Committee on Education and Employment in June 1998 (Education and Employment Committee 1998), followed by the Chancellor of the Exchequer's announcement of the results of the Comprehensive Spending Review, signalled the watershed in the move towards turning vision into reality. In November 1998, at the Association of Colleges national conference, David Blunkett revealed that he had secured a very positive settlement from the Comprehensive

Spending Review and announced the largest ever investment in the further education sector – £725 million between 1999 and 2001. This funding was subsequently outlined in detail as part of the government's full response to the Education and Employment Select Committee's report in which David Blunkett also set the twin key objectives for the sector – to raise standards and to widen participation.

Have David Blunkett and his team succeeded at last in establishing and funding a coherent strategic framework within which there are clear priorities for the development of further education in the third millennium? Evidence to date suggests that a positive step in that direction has been taken. Few in the sector have argued against the main thrust of his lifelong learning vision and overall strategy – in fact, as detailed by Ainley and Bailey (1997) in their book *The Business of Learning*, most claim to have held such views themselves for a long time!

Now the funding has been committed, a clearer picture of what the government expects further education to do has emerged. It is a challenging and, some argue, an unrealistic agenda. It has echoes of the 'zero tolerance of failure' culture which runs through other areas of government policy. The deal is unambiguous and beguilingly simple. In return for affirmation and validation of many of our long held educational values, accompanied by real 'cash injections' into the sector, we have a responsibility to deliver and meet the government's targets on standards, a 'something for something' agreement in which raising standards is non-negotiable.

To underpin the drive to raise standards a Further Education Standards Fund of £115 million has been created for the period 1999–2001. This development is accompanied by another non-negotiable strand in the government's policies for further education, one which turns on its head the arguments traditionally used by the sector to defend poor student performance in course completion and examination achievement. It is no longer a case of 'access to learning for all with (possibly) achievement' but rather 'access to learning for all *and* achievement for all'.

The message, then, for those of us working in further education is that *we* must serve *more* students and *they* must do better. There is no doubt that further education is central to the achievement of the government's vision of a lifelong learning society. We are not, however, the only players and we enjoy no special privileges. Funding *is* being made available to us to enable us to achieve specified targets, and if we fail we can expect government to intervene – as elsewhere in the education system.

Will further education rise to this challenge? Have we realised that, by placing an emphasis throughout *The Learning Age* on human capital as the key to competitiveness in the global economy, those of us working in further education are accepting not just that we all need to learn continually to keep pace with change but also that, in the post-Thatcherite consumer-driven society, learners as customers expect to get what they want, when and where they want it and with no fuss. Can further education really respond to this imperative and implement the government's agenda? I believe the majority in the sector want to succeed and will have a determined go. After so long in the wilderness, now we have moved nearer the 'sunlit uplands' we cannot afford to pass up the opportunity we have been given. Success will depend on the leadership given across the sector by individual college principals. Overall success, however, will ultimately depend on the strength of the partnership between the government and the sector as a whole, and here there is still much work to be done on both sides. This 'New Deal' for further education is not a one-sided pact with Mephistopheles – the something-for-something agenda cuts both ways. For the government's part, consistency of policy, equity of approach, transparency in behaviour and accessibility of information and personnel are fundamental. For our part, colleges must accept accountability, act coherently and with integrity, and organise ourselves collectively. The appointment of two experienced college principals to head the further education sector's two major national agencies, the Further Education Development Agency (FEDA) and the Association of Colleges (AOC), is an encouraging start in this direction. The extent to which the sector can play its part in the partnership with government rests significantly in the hands of these two people and the way in which they are able to encourage their colleagues in the colleges to work effectively with government, the FEFC, the Higher Education Funding Council (HEFCE), the National Institute of Adult and Continuing Education (NIACE), and other key national partners. If these partnerships work, there is now a real opportunity for further education to emerge from the doldrums and to eradicate its 'second-chance inevitably means second-rate' image which hangs like an albatross around its neck.

Improved professionalism by the sector must be matched by political action on the part of the government. This means a much higher profile for adult, continuing and further education in the life of the nation. Government must convince the media, employers and the population at large that 'education, education, education' is not merely 'schools, schools, schools'. To put it another way, if the Prime Minister's mantra really meant 'standards, standards, standards' – and it is clear from recent policy implementation that further education is *included* in this – then further education would not expect to be *excluded* from other aspects of government thinking. It is regrettable, therefore, that other actions taken in the first throes of government to raise the status of teaching as a profession, such as the establishment of the General Teaching Council and the Teaching Awards Trust or the formation of an Institute of Teaching and Learning for Higher Education, have tended to reinforce segregation in the education service. Although a welcome recent development, the setting up of a national training organisation for further education, Further Education National Training Organisation (FENTO), is hardly a move on a par with these other initiatives. The government's priorities for 'inclusion' have clearly not yet extended to the education system itself. There is still much the Prime Minister and his Cabinet colleagues could do to support David Blunkett and his team in their promotion of adult, continuing and further education. A higher regard and better rewards for further education teaching as a profession, recognition of the teacher recruitment and retention problem in the sector, visits by Cabinet members to further education sector colleges and active support by senior members of government for the all-party parliamentary group are possible future areas which the government could explore. The Further Education Standards Fund is intended to boost performance by improving teaching, updating subject skills and improving management training, as well as providing targeted intervention in failing colleges and funding for excellent colleges to spread their good practice. The creation of this fund also provides a real opportunity to refocus on pedagogy and leadership and to reassert the importance of curriculum research and development. Although FEDA and FENTO have a role to play in taking this forward, I believe that high-profile action by government similar to that taken in the school and university sector is required. The raising of standards of achievement throughout a mass market of lifelong learners calls for the creation of a national body or institution, such as an Academy of Leadership, Teaching and Learning in Further Education, equal to the organisations being set up in the secondary and higher education fields.

Government is the catalyst of sustainable change nationally and must take a lead in helping stimulate mass demand for lifelong learning. Further education will support such actions and, since incorporation, has proved it can respond efficiently and effectively on the supply side provided that fair funding is forthcoming. The years 2001–3 will see the implementation throughout the sector of specific initiatives related to the government's key priorities. Individual Learning Accounts have been introduced and the University for Industry (DfEE 1998c) was launched as 'Learndirect' in autumn 2000. These are both mechanisms by which the government hopes to generate greater (even mass) demand for learning and achievement. In practice, both will also be infused with messages about tackling the social inclusion agenda and will give encouragement to further education providers and others to work with government on this. However, we cannot have an effective knowledge-driven economy capable of competing globally without an appropriately skilled work force. The reports on the National Skills Task Force *Towards a National Skills Agenda* (Reports 1–3, Humphries 1998, 1999, 2000), the Moser report *A Fresh Start: Improving Literacy and Numeracy* (DfEE 1999c), the report from the Social Exclusion Unit, *Bridging the Gap: new opportunities for 16–18 year olds not in education, employment or training* (DfEE 1999d), the introduction of the New Deal, the creation of the Youth Support Strategy and Service (ConneXions), the development of an Investing in Young People scheme, the creation of the Training Standards Council to oversee the raising of standards in government-funded training, the consultation paper on the future of Training and Enterprise Councils *Meeting the Challenge of the Millennium* (DfEE 1998e) and the creation of Regional Development Agencies, all indicate that, as far as the lifelong learning revolution is concerned, the government is casting its net much wider than the further education sector.

There is an important message about networking and partnership for us here – which strengthens the case for further education to get its act together fast. It is one of the contradictions of the new government that, despite the rhetoric of collaboration, when it comes to bidding for badged funds, no one has yet devised a creative or fair alternative to old-fashioned, straight-forward competition. It is to be hoped that someone somewhere is keeping an eye on the national picture which is beginning to emerge from the honeypot economy of the last two years, which has resulted in some areas gorged with new work and funds whilst others are starved. Such unequal practice creates the impression of a lack of explicit and consistent strategy which is at odds with the apparent emerging coherence of government policy. It would be ironic if, in its attempts to deal with social cohesion by redressing the legacy of neglect experienced by some sections of society, the government's actions resulted in the creation of *different* groups of people feeling deprived and alienated.

Further education colleges have certainly thrown their weight behind the proposals set out in the Lane committee's report on student support and behind the challenge to government made by the select committee to replace Child Benefit with a learning allowance for 16–19 year olds. In his response to the Select Committee Report on Further Education, David Blunkett indicates that he has planned a new comprehensive package of student support for the period 1999/2001, providing £183 million for further education students and those in school sixth forms towards transport, child care and other costs. This includes the new Education Maintenance Allowance pilots for low income 16–19 year olds.

However, it is no good trying to ease the pressure at one point in the system if it is just transferred further along the line. Given the government's decision to introduce tuition fees and to phase out maintenance grants in higher education, it will need to keep a watchful eye on the way its attempts to implement the social inclusion agenda in further education has an impact in higher education. This is certainly one of the biggest challenges of the lifelong learning revolution – both for the government and for the education service. Although generally well received by staff in colleges and universities, claims made by the Secretary of State that 'we will more than deliver the Prime Minister's target of 500,000 more people in further and higher education by 2002, and that, compared to the 1997/98 academic year, we will be supporting an additional 700,000 students in further education alone by 2001/02' may prove in time to be both overoptimistic and ill judged.

Government is also the architect of sustainable change nationally and there is one piece of its design for the building of the learning age about which it has said remarkably little – a credit-based qualification system. The Kennedy report recommended a credit framework for further education within five years and there is now an urgent need for a new national register to pull together all post-16 qualifications. Radical measures are needed to give new forms of credit for units, modules and whole courses, taking in everything from A levels and vocational courses to basic skills and adult and community education. There will be debate about exactly how this should be achieved but the fact that it needs doing is unequivocal and must be high on the government's agenda, as it is the only means by which adult, continuing and further education can help the government ensure that there is 'access to lifelong learning for all *and* achievement for all'. To this end, it is interesting to note recent innovations in a number of large general further education colleges UK-wide which are working together to develop an overarching award for post-19 students – the Advanced College Diploma.

If the partnership between the government and the further education sector works, we can begin to take real strides in the achievement of the lifelong learning vision. If we are successful by 2002 we will need to measure ourselves against some of the following criteria.

- Does the further education sector have a strong identity clearly under-stood by the population at large?
- Has lifelong learning become lifestyle learning, i.e. a part of everyday life as natural as going to the shops or the doctor's?
- Are there as many 'learning centres' in colleges, companies and the community as there are public houses, parish churches, mosques and synagogues?
- Are more people achieving more qualifications and to higher levels?
- Is there evidence of real financial commitment from employers and businesses to match the funding channelled through the public purse?
- Do further education teachers feel valued by society and have they regained their financial status to a point where many more people, including at least 10 per cent of the sector students, aspire to join the profession?
- Have strategic lifelong learning partnerships reduced bureaucracy and created more effective ways of working?

With no substantial evidence of success in most of the above measures, and with disarming guile, summer 1999 saw the government respond to the consultation paper on the future of the TECs with an announcement of major radical reform of the post-16 system of education and training. Changes in the structure and management of adult, continuing and further education are highlighted in the White Paper *Learning to Succeed: a new framework for post-16 learning* (DfEE, 1999b) and constitute the substance of the Learning and Skills Bill (December 1999) considered by Parliament in the first months of the new century. These changes in the organisation and management of vocational education and training in the United Kingdom present significant challenges and opportunities to all affected. Although largely overlooked by the media in their reaction to the last Queen's Speech of the twentieth century, it is clear that measures to change the post-16 landscape contained in the new legislation are ground-breaking and far-reaching. The creation of a single body, the National Learning and Skills Council (LSC), to fund all post-16 education and training and a remit for forty-seven local LSCs to plan provision across the board in response to learner demand represent further tangible evidence of the government's unequivocal commitment to implementing radical reform which delivers results and brings about lasting change.

With a new system in place, by 2001/2 the government might begin to engage in further dialogue about what I am sure will be an ongoing debate about the nature and purposes of lifelong learning. Discussion about the learning society and the meaning of lifelong learning has raged through the last decade of the twentieth century, notable commentators being Tight (1998), Macrae *et al.* (1997) and Hughes and Tight (1995). Following the trail of policy development under New Labour it is impossible not to detect the government's clear underlying purpose – lifelong learning in the 'knowledge society' equates with 'a form of capital'. For many, including Frank Coffield, Professor of Education at the University of Newcastle upon Tyne and Director of the Economic and Social Research Council's Learning Society Programme, this means that the government is operating with a 'debased notion of knowledge'. As he says, 'Socrates taught me that knowledge would set me free; Peter Mandelson tells me its modern function is to make employers rich.'

My hope for the third millennium is that principals and teachers in the adult, continuing, further and higher education sectors together with our national professional associations such as NIACE, FEDA, AOC and the Committee of Vice-Chancellors and Principals (CVCP) will initiate and lead this discussion. Policy making must be informed through the experience, pragmatism and idealism of those of us working in the field. As Coffield (1996) says, 'the government rightly insists on a change in culture in education and business, but it must take the lead in becoming a model of learning, and learn from teachers'.

There is not necessarily anything wrong with the fact that lifelong learning, as Maggie Woodrow, Director of the European Access Network at the University of Westminster, has commented, 'is all things to all people: the Holy Grail, a lottery win, a double scotch, Viagra – whatever turns you on'.

Nonetheless, if future government policy is to continue to be based on the concept on lifelong learning the debate about its purposes must be extended beyond the current notion that it is 'part of the rhetoric of individual adaptability to economic imperatives', as Linden West (1999) has explained. If further education delivers on the standards agenda and successfully widens participation, the sector will have a stronger voice with which to present to government the case that a truly revolutionary vision of lifelong learning includes more than ideas of investing in 'human capital' for global competitive advantage. As Socrates reminds us, personal and individual transformation and the impact it has on those around us lie at the heart of all meaningful learning – and it takes a lifetime to achieve!

References

Ainley, P. and Bailey, B. (1997) *The Business of Learning*, London: Cassell.

Coffield, F. (1996) 'A Tale of Three Little Pigs: Building the Learning Society with Straw', paper presented at the ECER, Seville, September.

Department for Education and Employment (1996) *Lifetime Learning: a policy framework*, London: DfEE.

Department for Education and Employment (1998a) *Higher Education for the Twenty-first Century: Response to the Dearing Report*, London: DfEE.

Department for Education and Employment (1998b) *Further Education for the New Millennium: Response to the Kennedy Report*, London: DfEE.

Department for Education and Employment (1998c) *University for Industry: Engaging People in Learning for Life*, London: DfEE.

Department for Education and Employment (1998d) *Accountability in Further Education*, London: DfEE.

Department for Education and Employment (1998e) *TECs: Meeting the Challenge of the Millennium*, London: DfEE.

Department for Education and Employment (1999a) *The Learning and Skills Council Prospectus: Learning to Succeed*, London: DfEE.

Department for Education and Employment (1999b) *Learning to Succeed: A new Framework for post-16 Learning*, London: DfEE.

Department for Education and Employment (1999c) *A Fresh Start: Improving Literacy and Numeracy*, London: DfEE.

Department for Education and Employment (1999d) *Bridging the Gap: New Opportunities for 16–18 year olds not in Education, Employment or Training*, London: DfEE.

Education and Employment Committee (1998) *Further Education*, Sixth Report, Vols I–II, London: HMSO.

Fryer, R. (1997) *Learning for the Twenty-first Century: First Report of the National Advisory Group for Continuing Education and Lifelong Learning*, London: National Advisory Group for Continuing Education and Lifelong Learning.

Further Education Funding Council (1997a) *How to Widen Participation: A Guide to Good Practice*, London: HMSO.

Further Education Funding Council (1997b) *Widening Participation in Further Education: Statistical Evidence*, London: HMSO.

Higginson, G. (1996) *Report of the Learning Technology Committee*, Coventry: Further Education Funding Council.

Hughes, C. and Tight, M. (1995) 'The myth of the learning society', *British Journal of Educational Studies* 43, 290–304.

Humphries, C. (1998) *Towards a National Skills Agenda: Report 1*, London: DfEE.

Humphries, C. (1999) *Towards a National Skills Agenda: Report 2*, London: DfEE.

Humphries, C. (2000) *'Skills for All': National Skills Task Force Final Report*, London: DfEE.

Kennedy, H. (1997) *Learning Works: Widening Participation in Further Education*, Coventry: Further Education Funding Council.

Macrae, S., Maguire, M. and Ball, S. (1997) 'Whose learning society? A tentative deconstruction', *Education Policy* 12, 499–509.

National Committee of Inquiry into Higher Education (1997a) *Higher Education in the Learning Society: Summary Report*, London: National Committee of Inquiry into Higher Education.

National Committee of Inquiry into Higher Education (1997b) *Higher Education in the Learning Society: Report of the National Committee*, London: National Committee of Inquiry into Higher Education.

Secretary of State for Education and Employment (1998) *The Learning Age: A Renaissance for a new Britain*, London: HMSO.

Tight, M. (1998) 'Education, education, education! The vision of lifelong learning in the Kennedy, Dearing and Fryer reports', *Oxford Review of Education* 24, 473–85.

Tomlinson, J. (1996) *Inclusive Learning*, Coventry: Further Education Funding Council.

West, L. (1999) in the *Times Educational Supplement*, 5 March.

Woodrow, M. (1999) 'More second chances, fewer second helpings', *Times Educational Supplement*, 5 March.

9 'It lifted my sights'

Revaluing higher education in an age of new technology

Richard Smith and Paul Standish

For nearly three years after Labour's victory in May, 1997 it was hard to imagine that the new government was particularly interested in higher education. Its focus was firmly on the 'standards' agenda in primary and secondary schools, on early years, on literacy and numeracy. In higher education, as in so many other things, Labour seemed to be carrying on Conservative business as usual, with the proviso that Labour clearly wanted more of it – committing itself, for example, to increasing participation still further. If Tony Blair's priority was 'Education, education, education' then this certainly seemed to mean that there would be more of it, but with no evident thought devoted to what *it* precisely was.

And in this absence of serious thinking about the point of education, about what in the context of higher education was once called 'the idea of the university', New Labour seemed wholly in accord with the spirit of the times. The Dearing report of 1997 is almost entirely innocent of any real reflection on the aims or point of university education. We have written elsewhere (Blake *et al.* 1998) of how proper discussion of such aims is replaced by vapid talk of the 'learning society', which in turn is conceived in primarily instrumental and economic terms. We quote here again Dearing, para. 1.10:

> The expansion of higher education in the last ten years has contributed greatly to the creation of a learning society, that is, a society in which people in all walks of life recognise the need to continue in education and training throughout their working lives and who see learning as enhancing the quality of life throughout all its stages. But, looking twenty years ahead, the UK must progress further and faster in the creation of such a society to sustain a competitive economy.

Here higher education is justified in terms of the creation of a 'learning society': this, in turn, despite passing mention of enhancement of the quality of life, apparently needs to come about primarily in order to sustain a competitive economy. What kind of world we need that competitive economy *for* is not indicated.

It seemed wholly of a piece with this inability or refusal to engage in discussion of educational values that the only real debate that Dearing stimulated concerned the funding of higher education and the question of student fees (a debate only slightly widened during the last year by the case of the comprehensive school pupil, Laura Spence, supposedly denied an Oxford University place by 'elitist dons'). This is hardly a trivial issue. Yet a vacuum has opened at the heart of things when questions can be asked only about *how*, and not about *what* or *why*; when the only language that can be spoken is the language of economics; and when the status of this as the only proper, grown-up language in which to talk about education is quite taken for granted.

Higher education business as usual for New Labour, then, was inseparable from the dominance of the economic genre of discourse. It was a prevailing technicism which talked in terms of the delivery of a curriculum and the accountability of those who delivered it, very much in the spirit of the old-fashioned housewife counting the sacks which the coalman emptied into the cellar. A basic lack of trust characterised the way government regarded teachers at all levels: the 'discourse of derision' of the 1980s and 1990s had by no means finally been silenced. And there was no willingness to talk about educational ends and *values*, most disappointing of all in an administration replacing a Conservative government which careered between leaving everything to market forces and desperately trying to bolt values back on (as in the 'Back to basics' educational initiative) when from time to time it noticed that values had, mysteriously, gone missing.

Those of us who have had experience of primary and secondary schooling recently – of its chronic underfunding, the collapse of morale among teachers, the oppressive regime of inspection and much more – do not criticise Labour for not making higher education its first priority, even if we may be unconvinced by some of its solutions to the problems of schools. It is not that higher education did not need addressing, rather that the urgent issues manifestly lay elsewhere. Still, the university sector did not lack its own problems: the drift to uniformity of mission following the collapse of the binary divide between the polytechnic and university sectors in the early 1990s; continuing inequity of access to higher education; lack of will to confront the quality of teaching, together with the descent of 'subject review', the assessment of teaching quality, into an exercise in the management of bureaucracy; the tendency of the RAE, the assessment of research, to reward conservatism, depress creativity and ossify existing subject structures; the relative lack of incentive for universities to develop links with their local communities; the arid and instrumental nature of much of the new discourse of 'lifelong learning'; the serious and unreversed decline in funding.

Later we shall suggest that attitudes to new technology in higher education are revealing in the context of these issues and problems. An unrestrained and uncritical worshipping of Information and Communication Technology (ICT) threatens to enter into the vacuum left by the disappearance of values.

It is typical of our nihilistic culture[1] that a kind of digital boosterism seems to operate as the perfect substitute for asking the basic question of what universities are *for*. First, however, let us ponder how far change may now be in the air.

Raising expectations

David Blunkett's 'landmark speech on higher education and the challenges it faces in the 21st century' (as it is described on the DfEE website), made on 15 February 2000 at the University of Greenwich, is of considerable significance, in the light of what we have written above, in setting out policy for higher education at the beginning of the new millennium. The setting for this speech, we are reminded, was the very location where Tony Crosland gave an important address about the polytechnics in 1966 – the former Woolwich Polytechnic, now the University of Greenwich; clearly Blunkett intends his own speech to be seen as equally fundamental in signalling new directions for higher education. The headline issues are the introduction of a new two-year foundation degree to serve as a vocationally focused route into higher education, and the development of a consortium of universities ('e-universities') to exploit information and communication technologies in order to share approaches to enhancing quality. But these are not to be seen as additions to an existing system which will otherwise remain unchanged. What is contemplated here is 'a step change which lifts our higher education system onto a new development path' (para. 31). At the heart of it is the move from uniformity to diversity (paras 29, 30), with universities developing distinctive strengths and doing so collaboratively instead of attempting to do the same sorts of things in competition with one another.

It is of course early days to begin to analyse the new policy. Much depends on detail still to be developed, particularly in the case of the new foundation degree. There is, however, enough in the 101 paragraphs (nearly twenty pages when the text is printed from the Web) to make comment worthwhile even at this stage. First we wish to welcome the strong note of vision, the commitment to a distinctive 'idea of the university', even if this note is postponed until the conclusion. There we read about the role of higher education in helping government and society 'to respond to globalisation without abandoning wealth creation and social justice', about its embodiment of values such as truth and freedom 'and collective engagement in the improvement of the human condition'. It would be easy to see these as ritual and rather hollow phrases. Perhaps what should strike us is rather how seldom we have heard this kind of language – a nascent philosophy of educational values – in recent years. The sense of commitment here is unmistakable in the powerful, and indeed moving, last paragraph of the speech:

> Higher education has also meant a great deal to me personally. In the community in which I grew up, it was unheard of for anybody to enter

> higher education, and in too many communities that remains the case.
> It is one of the reasons why I take the widening participation agenda so
> seriously. Higher education opened up significant new opportunities
> for me. It lifted my sights and raised my expectations. The learning
> I undertook, and the friendships I formed at university, have been of
> enduring value to me.

The vision of *what education can do for a life* is not developed to any extent.
One can only do so much, even in a landmark speech. What is significant is
that Blunkett is prepared to describe higher education in these terms. It
enriches the life of individual persons, and is not valuable simply in so far
as it helps them to contribute to 'society' or 'the economy' by equipping
them with the relevant skills or competences. But – the reply can be imagined
– however would you establish whether a university education had lifted
someone's sights and raised their expectations? Here are outcomes that *cannot*
be measured, a shining acknowledgement that not everything that higher
education does (and does at its very best) can be calibrated by the new army
of quality assurers, institutional facilitators and compilers of league tables.

University education, then, is not only an economic good, and is not to be
discussed and understood only in the economic genre of language. Of course,
it is an economic good, for all that. 'Learning has become big business' (para.
12); higher education 'endows people with creative and moral capacities,
thinking skills and depth knowledge that underpin our economic competitiveness and our wider quality of life' (para. 10). These things must be said,
for there is the taxpayer to convince, and perhaps the Treasury too; and it is
regrettable that para. 69 implies that those benefiting from higher education
are solely those who gain access to it, rather than the wider society that is
served by doctors, teachers, social workers and in general people with better
rather than worse creative and moral capacities. Here Blunkett becomes
enmired in that apology for a philosophy of higher education, the debate
about justifying tuition fees. We catch too an unfortunate echo of the neo-
liberal argument that the good of higher education consists essentially in the
increased earning power of the graduate, no doubt with its trickle-down effect.

However, because he achieves something of a balance between seeing
university education as on the one hand an intrinsic good, a good-in-itself,
and on the other a service with direct and quantifiable extrinsic, economic
benefits ('The global market for higher education is already estimated to stand
at £300 billion per year', para. 12), Blunkett is able to make other important
points that the exclusively technicist thinking we have heard recently – the
thinking that embraces only measurable outcomes – has forgotten. In
particular he is able to insist on the need for university research which has
value even though there is no quick pay-off or indeed any pay-off at all. 'We
need to sustain this creativity, not stifle it' (para. 46). Here again, though,
the perceived necessity of reassuring those whose imaginations do not extend
beyond the quantifiable threatens to undercut the point he is making. 'There

must be room for research with no immediate short-term value – but which may lead to significant economic and cultural benefits in the long term' (ibid.). This is the kind of language characteristic of the Dearing report: loss of nerve in the face of those who imagine that constant reference to the 'bottom line' establishes them as realists, who think of evidence-based research as the only kind of research and of 'what works' as an uncomplicated criterion of the merit of educational research in particular.

A similar loss of nerve, or perhaps ambivalence, can be seen in a speech made on 2 February 2000 to an ESRC seminar. According to the press release on the DfEE website, Mr Blunkett 'called upon social science researchers to join with policy-makers in breaking down the "seam of anti-intellectualism running through society". He also stressed the importance of sound, relevant and intelligible research.' Here, it would seem, is what the academic community has been waiting for these last twenty years or so: a true dialogue, the opportunity to influence the policy makers, and an end to the 'discourse of derision' in which universities were routinely caricatured as ivory towers and academics as out of touch with the 'real world'. At last, we may imagine, those bottom-line realists have been rumbled. Yet the press release bears studying in some depth. The 'seam of anti-intellectualism' is alluded to at the beginning and the end, in the first instance said to be running through society and in the second through government, where 'the policy process itself also has to undergo a radical change'. There are remarks about politicians and civil servants becoming 'more relaxed about welcoming radical thinking' and about the need for academics to think the unthinkable, since if they don't no one else will.

But in among this lies an unmistakable undertone of wariness and instrumentalism. The title to this press release should have given us pause. It is 'Blunkett rejects anti-intellectualism and welcomes sound ideas'. This has something of the flavour of 'Mosely rejects antisemitism and welcomes Aryan immigrants'. It suggests that only certain sorts of ideas are going to receive the seal of approval. And so it turns out to be. The ideas required are those which the politicians require. 'We need social scientists to help to determine what works and why, and what types of policy initiative are likely to be most effective.' We need to ensure that the information generated by this sound research is more readily available, so that those who want it can 'get it easily and quickly'. Social scientists, then, are to fall in line (no doubt the bottom line) behind government priorities, seeking the answers (the most effective answers, of course, and those that are easiest to understand) to questions asked by others.

We suggest, then, that in policy on higher education matters stand at a watershed. There is a cautious willingness to break out of the exclusively economic dimension of debate which is one of Labour's legacies from its market-obsessed predecessors. There is a readiness to stand back from 'business as usual' and risk the kind of thinking that – and opponents of academic elitism should ponder the point – brought us university education for more than an elite in the first place. But at the same time a quiet and apparently commonsensical instrumentalism, linked perhaps with an increasing tendency to see universities as an arm of the state (or even of the party – a confusion consequent on Labour's massive majority), feeds the anti-intellectualism which David Blunkett claims to deplore.

Anti-intellectualism has its cruder manifestations in British society but it is its subtler forms that are ultimately more damaging for higher education, for these undermine the very *raison d'être* of that education. Instrumentalism has spawned a discourse of efficiency and effectiveness, and we suggest that all the hallmarks of an ideology are there. A vocabulary and sets of procedures become orthodox, and this empowers anyone willing to speak in its terms. The only innovation that is then tolerated must be of such a kind as to reinforce the ideology. The language and practices may be adopted cynically and opportunistically, or innocently where we are simply in their grip. This is anti-intellectual because of its suppression of any point of view that is not expressed in its terms and of any practice that is not measurable by its criteria. The mark of intellectual enquiry, in contrast – and, that is to say, of higher education – must be readiness not to rule out what cannot be simply 'taken on board', as that revealing phrase puts it. Intellectual enquiry means the challenge of criticism and the spark of creativity and invention. It is only with this that any traditions of enquiry worth their name are developed and sustained.

There are powerful rhetorics operating here – of quality assurance, assessment and accountability, skills and competences, international competitiveness and excellence, and the management of teaching and learning. One characteristic of these ways of speaking is their pretence to a form of objectivity. Of course, objectivity is desirable, but the sense of objectivity here derives less from the cogency of particular practices than from the colour of particular vocabularies. They become *de rigueur* among certain kinds of educational practitioners. Not to use them is effectively to exclude oneself from the practice, or at least from being perceived as a serious player in the game. Be like this or fade from the picture, they seem to say. They harbour values that are not explicit – concerning, for example, the nature of the learner as a detached individual acquiring a portfolio of skills. Part of the power of these assumptions has to do with their obvious democratic appeal, especially where this is understood in terms of choice and the availability of consumer goods. The dominance of these powerful rhetorics in education over the past twenty years means that there is a generation of teachers, administrators and managers who have known little different, and who perhaps have been rewarded for adopting them, a generation that perhaps has lacked the acumen to view critically the tide of change that performativity has brought, or that has merely been glad, often for laudable reasons, to embrace its instrumental opportunities.

New Labour, new technology

The manner in which Information and Communication Technology (ICT) is adopted in higher education can be seen, as we noted above, as a critical test here. The rise of the rhetoric of effectiveness and objectivity and so on has without doubt been aided by the rise of new technology. In the management and accounting of institutions it encourages reliance on quantifiable data. In teaching and learning it encourages a reduction of knowledge to information with the emphasis on the developments of skills for accessing it. This is the way that computers operate and it is the way we then come to think. And this is well attuned to the separation of means and ends that is characteristic of instrumentalism. Broader and deeper pictures of what is learned, the sense of importance in the content of what is learned, the inherent mystery in human enquiry are all but eroded, and the proper account that might be made of this activity is reduced to a kind of book-keeping.

Of course, we are well aware that even to raise doubts about ICT is to risk a number of charges: to be called Luddite in our views, and blind not just to the extraordinary potential that ICT offers for higher education but, worse, to the fact that its rapid development is essential if the 'digital divide' is to be overcome and social exclusion reduced. To enter any note of reservation is to risk being thought unrealistic and nostalgic for the kind of higher education that was enjoyed by an earlier generation, when a university education was the experience of an elite. So we emphasise that we, the authors of this chapter, are in numerous respects *enthusiasts* for ICT, particularly in higher education. We use it constantly in our teaching, and are excited by its enormous practical potential as well as by the theoretical issues it raises (Blake and Standish 2000). Our reservations are prompted very largely by fears that *uncritical* adulation of ICT will prevent that potential being realised, or bring costs that offset the benefits.

It is worth beginning with some more general remarks about the difficulty people typically have with any change that technology brings. New Labour is not silent on these matters. In *The Times* Michael Wills (1999) has written:

> Technology transforms societies but the relationship is an unwitting one: the 18th century mill-owner believed his spinning jennies would make him money. He never intended them to undermine and change his comfortably ordered world – but they did. And every new technology has a seed of revolution planted within it. To avoid being overwhelmed by change, societies must recognise its inevitability, the better to profit from its opportunities and avoid its dangers.
>
> This is all the more difficult today when we are living through change unprecedented in human history. The convergence of information and communications technologies, epitomised by the growth of the Internet, is creating greater changes faster than ever before. Broadcast television

in the US took 13 years to reach an audience of 50 million. PCs took 16 years. The Internet did it in just four years.

The term 'technology' is, of course, used across a vast range and this can cover over some of the factors in its development that most repay consideration. If there is an acknowledgement of danger here, questions remain about the nature and effects of this particular technology, and more generally about how this 'seed of revolution' is to be understood.

Many see the advent of the technology as having its own natural logic. Evangelists, on the one hand, preach about the Internet's power to transform education, motivated in part by an understandable conviction that many teachers and parents are unbelievers and have yet to hear the word. On the other side there are those who fear the reduction of knowledge to information, the displacement of classroom interaction, the fragmentation and deperson-alisation of learning and the increase in commercial involvement in education that the Internet will bring. Both sides are inclined, it seems, to think that there is an inevitability to the technology, for good or ill. A more balanced attitude is the view that the technology itself is neutral, that it is *we* who decide how to use it, and we decide in the light of *our* values. But this does not get things quite right either. Let us try to see why.

Such a view fails to recognise the way that technological development always occurs against and as a result of such a social and cultural background, which already has values built into it. Seeing human purposes as some-how separate from the pure machine, these assumptions fail adequately to acknowledge the ways that technological developments always incorporate values that have already been espoused. Failure to recognise this goes hand-in-glove with what is really a kind of bad faith: failure to accept responsibility for the values already incorporated into the machine. Technology is part of the inexorable logic of Progress itself. And, worse, the technological starts to acquire something of the aura of 'scientific facts' which only the most ivory-towered of academics or Luddite of practitioners will fail to acknowledge.

The social and cultural background into which modern ICT is introduced needs to be understood in terms of the kinds of computers that have been part of our daily lives, and familiar in education, for the past twenty years or so. It is clear that the comparatively crude programmed learning that has been typical of education via computers is vastly different from what new ICT can offer. Nevertheless, such a way of thinking about learning is part of the background against which new curriculum planning will take place. And we should recall here that programmed learning dovetails neatly with the dominant regimes of accounting and planning, themselves inspired in part by the facility of these machines. The rhetorics of efficiency and effectiveness require no less. *But in the absence of a challenge to these embedded values and practices the huge potential of ICT will be lost.* (For some account of that potential see Blake and Standish 2000.)

We take heart here from Blunkett's remark that 'on-line learning is still in its infancy, particularly in pedagogic and learner support' (2000, para. 19). What must be realised is that there are critical decisions to be made in curriculum planning, questions that require painstaking attention to the content of what is to be learned, questions that are inseparable from the quality of the learning experience. This is where the model of information plus skills of access is so hopelessly inadequate. In higher education, especially, it is crucial that these are addressed by those who have a commitment to that content, the subject specialists. Of course, they will need technical help and they will need to be given examples to show the kind of thing that is possible. But there must be wariness of any constricting effects of the programming and of the distortions caused by the dominant rhetorics of efficiency and effectiveness.

In speaking of the dangers of entrenchment of the 'digital divide' Michael Wills goes so far as to say that 'Familiarity with information and communication technologies is the indispensable grammar of modern life. Those not empowered by it are disenfranchised: job prospects and security depend on it' (ibid.). It is, he suggests, a key to lifelong learning. It is difficult to resist the broad good sense of this, but so much depends on how phrases such as 'indispensable grammar' are fleshed out.

One thing we can be sure is that we can get things wrong here. In the early 1980s schools invested heavily in providing courses in computing for children, strongly encouraged by politicians and parents. It was not long before it was realised that the elementary programming skills that pupils might hope to acquire were in fact neither the rewarding experience nor the secure route to employment that the advocates of the courses had envisaged, and the courses were soon quietly dropped. We can also be reasonably sure that many of the elementary skills that the use of a computer now commonly requires, and that now pass for computer literacy, will become obsolete. Not so long ago the critical first steps involved memorising elementary Wordstar commands (for example, CONTROL – KD). What use is that knowledge to anyone now? In short, being comfortable with a computer is important, but the particular skills and bits of knowledge that are acquired are characteristically obsolescent. Such a conception of computer literacy, however, touted as the key to opportunity, can have an attractiveness to a populist politician in spite of its modest educational value. Social inclusion then becomes reduced to a kind of tokenism and lifelong learning a parody of what it might otherwise become. Skills such as these are useful but we cannot regard *them* as the indispensable 'grammar' of modern life, still less of higher education.

The problem we identify here regarding the inflated claims that are sometimes made for computer literacy presents in miniature the broader danger that persists in current policy. The past twenty years have seen an undermining of higher education in such a way that there has developed a surreptitious loss of confidence. The indications of a new departure in policy suggested by Blunkett's speech will undoubtedly require existing institutions to change and develop, and in this much will depend on the way they incorporate and adapt to new technology – but much will depend too on their ability to respond critically and creatively to the digital age.

That criticism and creativity will not occur in the absence of the kinds of structures through which they are fostered and supported. It is clear that, with the endorsement of diversification, the set of institutions that we now have will not look the same. On the other hand, there is another sense in which institutions must be preserved. And here we are not thinking of Oxbridge colleges or functional glass towers or virtual universities or anywhere in particular, but rather of traditions of enquiry – that is, of sustained practices of teaching, learning and research engaged in by communities of people in which a strong element of trust is allowed to develop around shared commitment to the addressing of particular sets of problems. Blunkett expects that the teaching and learning in the universities of the twenty-first century are likely not to be solely electronic but rather to be mixed-mode. This is a fitting approach to the problem of exploiting new technology in aid of a higher education that, without abandoning its proper academic goals, helps in the creation of a better and more inclusive civic life, for it rightly recognises the essentially social nature of both these ends. Criticism and creativity are indispensable to that civic life.

The new technology has the potential, if we approach it in the right way, to help us lift our sights from the keyboards and technical manuals to which digital boosterism threatens to confine us. It can problematise the 'idea of a university' anew – but only where it is taken to recontextualise, and not replace, fundamental thinking about the nature and purpose of higher education.

Note

1   Cf. Blake *et al.* (2000). There we argue that 'nihilism' is the dominant characteristic of our educational times. Compare also Sir John Drummond, former controller of Radio 3: 'The real low point for me was a few months ago when the greatest artists and writers in the country were invited to Downing Street to be told by some prat from Wolverhampton that information technology is culture. On the contrary, it is a delivery system like a telephone. It has bugger-all to do with culture. Yet this chap was introduced to us by Tony Blair himself and then thanked by Cherie . . . We were all of us, Salman Rushdie, Richard Eyre and Trevor Nunn included, put in a room and told that we are inflexible and incompetent and have achieved nothing in our lives'. (*Guardian*, 14 August 2000.)

References

Blake, N. and Standish, P. (eds) (2000) *Enquiries at the Interface: Philosophical Problems of Online Education*, Oxford: Blackwell (and *Journal of Philosophy of Education* 34 (1), special issue).

Blake, N., Smith, R. and Standish, P. (1998) *The Universities We Need: Higher Education after Dearing*, London: Kogan Page.

Blake, N., Smeyers, P., Smith, R. and Standish, P. (2000) *Education in an Age of Nihilism*, London: RoutledgeFalmer.

Blunkett, D. (2000) Speech on higher education, http://cms1.gre.ac.uk/dfee/

Wills, Michael (1999) 'Bridging the digital divide', *Times*, 2 November.

10 The creative society

Reuniting schools and lifelong learning

Tom Bentley

For the last hundred years education reform in the United Kingdom has followed a clear and predictable path. Since the Balfour Act of 1902, which instituted a national system of schooling in England and Wales, the major thrust of reform has been to extend and refine the reach and impact of a particular kind of institution – the school or college (Green 1990). This chapter argues that, despite the pace and scale of policy change over the 1990s, we are on the threshold of a deeper and further-reaching period of transition. Government policies show partial recognition of the depth of this change, but are not yet producing a coherent, radical or long-term approach to the challenges of educational innovation and restructuring.

The two most important changes in the *context* for education policy are: first, a transformation in the status and role of knowledge in society, leading to a very different set of demands and challenges for individual learners; second, a related change in the structure and operation of organisations across society, which poses a major challenge to the basic constitution of schools and colleges (Mulgan 1997).

The challenge is best summed up in the idea that individuals must become effective *lifelong learners* in order to thrive. This matters not just for our economic prospects in future labour markets, but also for our roles as parents and citizens, and our capacity to achieve fulfilment and personal autonomy. However, lifelong learning, as it applies to individuals, is not enough to explain or inform the necessary transformations in the infrastructure of learning. The idea of the skilled, flexible, individual learner, adept at identifying and accessing those learning opportunities needed to keep up with the pace of external change, does not tell us enough about the social and institutional contexts which underpin learning. To achieve a learning society we must also transform these contexts.

Two concepts are integral to understanding and achieving the kind of education system which enables twenty-first century societies to thrive: creativity and community (Seltzer and Bentley 1999). Creativity matters because possessing knowledge in the information age is not enough, for individuals or for organisations: only those who are able to apply it in new and valued ways will be able to respond effectively to the demands and opportunities of the era. Community is central for different reasons. Learning is an activity embedded in social relationships and values. To be meaningful, it must fit a surrounding context of norms and standards. The recently developed national infrastructure for testing and inspection presents standards as an objective, technocratic domain (see various OfStEd annual reports). But learning, in the broadest sense, is evaluated according to standards which are rooted in the structures of society. Communities therefore matter for two reasons: first, they provide a wider context from which learners can draw guidance, motivation and meaning for what they are trying to learn. Second, the communities surrounding schools and colleges can provide resources for learning which are frequently untapped, for reasons which I will explore below (Bentley 1998).

Institutions out of place

Twentieth century education reform is a story of institutions. From the Balfour Act of 1902 to the Butler Act of 1944 and the expansion of school, college and university places in the 1960s, 1970s and 1980s, the underlying thrust has been to broaden participation in the formal education system, and to increase the time spent in it by younger generations. The current government's policies to increase nursery and early years places, and to encourage participation beyond age 18, are the culmination of this trend. At the turn of the last century you could start school at 7 and finish again at 12 or 14: extended participation was for a narrow elite. At the start of the twenty-first century you can enter the public education system at 3 and stay in it until 23.

This story is one of enormous social progress, and is mirrored in many other countries. Too often, however, it escapes our notice that the basic form and structure of the institutions have hardly changed. Schools retain dominant organisational characteristics which heavily influence the character and quality of learning within them. These characteristics are increasingly at odds with the organisations and environments which learners will encounter in the world beyond. Schools, almost without exception, are:

- hierarchical;
- operate standardised routines and draw on standardised measures of performance;
- information sparse (they ration and control the flow of information and knowledge to learners);
- designed to transmit knowledge from expert to learner, with limited scope for collaboration between the two;
- subject to centralised control;
- custodial;
- vertically integrated (that is, they organise teaching and administration around a vertical division of departments and subjects).

In contrast, they seek to prepare students to thrive in an environment which is increasingly:

- complex;
- unpredictable;
- network-based;
- changing rapidly, with innovation and adaptation becoming essential skills;
- horizontally integrated (that is, projects and team-based collaboration are becoming central forms of organisation; partnerships and alliances between organisations are becoming essential);
- open;
- information-rich;
- out of control.

Public policies in creative tension

This contrast helps to illuminate current approaches to education reform. One broad swathe of policies, initiated during the 1980s and continued by the current UK government, aims to improve the performance and productivity of the existing institutional infrastructure. In the short term, it is working to raise conventional standards of attainment by improving motivation, attendance, teacher effectiveness and exam results. Under this heading we could include the Numeracy and Literacy Strategies for primary schools, the capital works programme to rebuild and repair schools' fabric, league tables, the OfStEd regime, the Fresh Start programme and performance-linked pay for teachers. All these initiatives work the existing institutions harder, seeking to produce better outputs from the same basic set of resources and structures.

A second, intertwined cluster of policies seem to aim at a different kind of target – although improving the attainment of current students is their primary short term objective, they also impact on the structure of educational institutions, and the channels through which content, instruction and guidance are accessed. These might include Excellence in Cities, in its attempt to build new urban learning networks, the National Grid for Learning, the new Leadership College, and the National Framework for Study Support. These initiatives experiment with new technologies and with network forms of organisation, and seek to draw on a wider range of resources to support learning, from online content to out-of-school time and community volunteers. Education Action Zones, as an explicit attempt to stimulate and learn from innovation, may also fall in this cluster, although their outcomes are still uncertain.

These latter policies are more in tune with the government's approach to lifelong learning in the adult world. Here, through the UFI (or LearnDirect), Individual Learning Accounts, and attempts to increase employer support for learning, we see a different implicit model of provision: learning activity is individualised and flexible, and takes place in a wide range of contexts. Financial investment is shared, and attempts to change learners' behaviour are based on persuasion and incentive rather than on compulsion and direction.

The vision which supports these moves – of a society of motivated, responsible and productive adult learners – is compelling. But it is clear that the policies so far are modest, incomplete steps towards such a scenario. While the concept of lifelong learning has become familiar in policy circles, it has yet to penetrate the vocabulary or aspirations of most people. In many areas of provision the change is rhetorical, and has not radically changed the forms or patterns of educational provision.

That said, however, we are beginning to see unprecedented levels of innovation in learning, across every sphere of society. Organisations in every sector are busy inventing new ways of organising learning. There are two or three basic reasons for this. One is cultural – the more 'educated' a society becomes, the greater the demand for learning. Basic education leads to a thirst for knowledge which sustains itself over time. The second is economic – as knowledge and skills become more important as commodities, demand for qualifications rises, fuelling innovation and expansion in their provision (Leadbeater, 1999). The third is technological. The development of a new communications infrastructure enables new ways of developing and delivering learning services. This partly means online access to course content, other relevant information, and guidance or assessment services. More important, in the long run, it means new ways of coordinating learning activity. The new technologies mean that learners can collaborate or compete through networks which are geographically unrestricted. They enable 'real time' learning – forms of problem solving and collaboration which are embedded in the challenges and routines of other activities, rather than being conducted at one remove, within education institutions, and then applied later on to 'real life' situations.

These changes will mean an ongoing increase in the levels of innovation associated with education. Perhaps most important, they also imply that this innovation will take place far beyond the bounds of the formal education sector. Inventing new ways to organise and evaluate learning has become an imperative for any organisation which wants to thrive. Learning is a test of its success.

A glance at the 'vanguard' sectors of the economy helps to substantiate this claim. Businesses which depend most heavily on 'pure' knowledge work – communications and media companies, for example, and management consultancies – are investing more and more in forms of learning which increase the creative potential of their employees. Even the traditional manufacturing sector is increasingly dependent on team-based learning and systematic innovation to improve the quality of products and the efficiency of production, an emphasis which places new demands on employees to contribute to the innovative capacity of the whole enterprise. The service industries, likewise, increasingly demand that employees continuously develop personal qualities and interpersonal skills which make them more responsive to customer demand and preference. The growth of corporate 'universities' is evidence of the growing need of such companies to draw on their own learning infrastructures. For all such organisations, strategies to increase and improve innovation mean strategies to develop and refine various forms of learning. In a whole series of fields the most successful knowledge workers are developing and modelling their own forms of learning behaviour.

Reuniting schooling and lifelong learning

What does this mean for education policy? The basic challenge seems clear. Schooling should be the foundation of an ongoing lifelong learning career, the first episode in a much longer series of encounters with learning. This role is in striking contrast with that of a century ago, when for most of the population school was the only encounter one could expect with formal education.

The great danger, however, is that the new forms of learning organisation, as they evolve in the private, voluntary and community sectors, will have little to do with the form or nature of core public education services. As a result, learners and students will have to rely on resources and support other than that provided through the school system to adapt to the environments which they encounter elsewhere.

The conventional response to changing demands on schools is to adjust the priorities and content of the curriculum. For example, as numeracy and literacy took higher priority during the late 1990s their prominence in the primary curriculum increased. Similarly, as new 'key skills' such as communication and problem-solving were identified as important, they were added (with little success) to curriculum requirements for most courses in secondary and vocational education. Our instinctive reaction is to attempt a specification of the knowledge needed which can be incorporated into the formal expectation of what school students will learn. Schools and teachers can then be organised, pressured and incentivised to provide the outcomes specified by our collective priorities.

But this response misses the underlying thrust of the analysis. While curriculum content is important, it is only one dimension of the way in which learning is organised, assessed and modelled by education institutions. Two other dimensions are crucially important, even though they are often taken for granted in the education debate.

The first is the set of attributes, disciplines and virtues which a successful learner should develop and display. Schooling, with its emphasis on obedience, punctuality, attendance to routine, linear progress and identifying 'correct' answers, encourages a set of attributes which are less and less applicable to the challenges of our external environment. Of course, there is much that good schools do to develop underlying attributes and attitudes to learning which is positive: we should not throw the baby out with the bath water. But it is clear that schools, as institutions, remain fixed in routines and behaviour from which most other sectors are moving away.

Second, and perhaps even more influential, is the impact of the school's basic organisational structure and ethos on its ability to innovate radically in the provision of learning opportunities and experiences. The argument here is that basic aspects of the school's institutional identity – the fact, for example, that all activity is governed by a centralised timetable which no longer corresponds with the routines or rhythms of any other major organisation, or the division of learning activities into a vertically separated curriculum which places formidable barriers in the way of effective cross-disciplinary learning – will hold back the school's capacity to access and make use of new opportunities and resources for learning.

This matters for two reasons. The first is that the scope for continuous improvement in output and productivity within the existing infrastructure is limited. In the long run it is not possible to maintain the momentum for improvement simply through incremental innovation and modest increases in public spending. The demand for education services, and for a growing range of outcomes for schools, will continue to increase faster than the capacity of government to finance it through taxation, for the reasons set out above. Moreover, if the institutional characteristics of the education infrastructure remain out of kilter with changes in the wider society it will be increasingly difficult to maintain it at current levels of performance. The crisis in teacher recruitment is perhaps the most glaring illustration of this problem.

The second reason is that current forms of organisation impose an opportunity cost on schools. The resources potentially available to support education extend far beyond the categories we are used to debating, which usually revolve around sums of public money and the contracted skills of educational professionals. They include the financial and organisational resources of other sectors, knowledge and information which exists beyond the world of formal education, social, cultural and human resources which reside in the communities surrounding schools. New technologies, in particular, open up the channels of communication and coordination which could tap such resources for the benefit of learners and teachers. But to do so, we must look for ways to experiment more radically with the organisational characteristics of schooling.

Learning for a creative age

This analysis opens up a challenging agenda for educational practitioners and policy makers. But a simple increase in innovation for its own sake would produce chaos. A sustained transformation of the education system needs a guiding purpose. I have suggested that this goal should be creativity, at the individual, organisational and societal level.

This requires a shift in our definition of creativity: rather than equating it with particular groups of people, such as artists, or with natural talent or intuitive qualities, creativity should be defined as a set of capacities which *can be learned*. As such, creativity has as much to do with what people do *not* know as with what they do. It requires the ability to solve problems progressively over time, and apply previous knowledge to new situations. Creativity is also bound up with context – it can be defined and assessed only in relation to the situation in which it is achieved. It must be developed through the interaction of the learner, her underlying goals and motivations, and the resources and context in which she operates (Csikzsentmihalyi 1996).

Our definition is relatively simple: creativity is the application of knowledge and skills in new ways to achieve a valued goal. Four main characteristics define the creative, or progressive, problem-solver:

- The ability to formulate new problems, rather than depending on others to define them.
- The ability to transfer what one learns across different contexts.
- The ability to recognise that learning is incremental and involves making mistakes.
- The capacity to focus one's attention in pursuit of a goal.

These characteristics, it is worth noting, are not specific to any particular social or age group, or to a particular kind of organisation or institution. They are generic. As such, they can help to form a foundation for a lifelong learning agenda which cuts across our existing institutional and conceptual boundaries.

Creative learning environments

But creativity does not take place in a vacuum. Because it is not a fixed individual characteristic, it cannot be understood without reference to the context in which it takes place. Context plays a significant role in determining whether one makes use of existing skills and knowledge and seeks out creative ways to build on what they already know. Case studies and other evidence point to a number of factors which help to make an organisational environment creative:

- *Trust.* Secure, trusting relationships are essential to environments in which people are prepared to take risks and are able to learn from failure.
- *Freedom of action.* Creative application of knowledge is possible only where people are able to make real choices over what they do and how they try to do it.
- *Variation of context.* Learners need experience applying their skills in a range of contexts in order to make connections between them.

- *The right balance between skills and challenge.* Creativity emerges in environments where people are engaged in challenging activities and have the right level of skill to meet them.
- *Interactive exchange of knowledge and ideas.* Creativity is fostered in environments where ideas, feedback and evaluation are constantly exchanged, and where learners can draw on diverse sources of information and expertise.
- *Real world outcomes.* Creative ability and motivation are reinforced by the experience of making an impact – achieving concrete outcomes, changing the way that things are done.

Again, these factors are generic – they can be found in schools, companies or families. It is worth noting, though, how many of dominant institutional characteristics of the school system seem to run against our list. A system based on routine-based learning, within a heavily standardised context, using individualised, abstract forms of assessment, and removing much of the choice from the hands of the student, does not seem well suited to developing creative potential.

Strategies for change

Elegant diagnoses are all very well. Could this kind of agenda be a basis for sustained, radical change? Schools, after all, are among the most resilient of all institutions. Accelerated reform has been achieved by the current government only at the cost of further centralisation of control. This shift, in the long run, diminishes the capacity of the whole system to innovate and generate new practical solutions. To understand and enhance the possibility of change, we have to adopt a particular view of how knowledge is created at the level of practice. My view is that radical change is possible through a combination of bold structural changes at the national level, a shift in the political climate to encourage judicious risk taking among innovative practitioners, and a shift towards more systematic innovation at the level of school and local community.

Such a strategy is very different from either the policy blueprint model, in which change is mapped out and imposed by central decision makers, and the traditional 'local autonomy' model, beloved of many in the education sector, in which professional integrity is interpreted as a prohibition on intervention, and a thousand flowers are left to bloom unseen. Three priorities stand out.

The first is to reduce curriculum content. We must recognise that the scope, not just for innovation, but also for depth of understanding, is inhibited by the crowding of the National Curriculum. Rigour and depth of understanding become more, not less, important for learners in a knowledge-based society. If such depth is to be accompanied by increased breadth of application, the 'coverage' of many different topics and programmes of study within curriculum subjects becomes an enemy of true understanding. Reducing National Curriculum content by half, over a period of ten years, as part of a rolling programme of curriculum development and experimentation, is therefore a reasonable, if controversial, goal.

The second is to increase opportunities for learning beyond the classroom. Between birth and the age of 16 the average child spends only 20 per cent of her waking hours in school. Connecting what happens in school with opportunities for learning outside is therefore vital for creating a new foundation for a system of lifelong learning. New technologies play an important part here. Even more important, however, is the development of learning opportunities in other contexts: museums, workplaces, public spaces, community organisations and families. Some of this infrastructure already exists, or is being developed. Pioneering examples, such as the University of the First Age in the United Kingdom or Citizens' Schools in Boston, Massachusetts, are showing how new forms of provision can be developed in concert with existing school routines. Excellence in Cities provides an important opportunity, in this context, to develop new learning networks. These new forms of learning activity are an important generator of social capital, and the networks in question are as much social, or human, as physical or electronic. This development creates the potential for schools to become hubs of community learning, accessing a far wider range of resources, and offering learning opportunities to many different client groups.

The third priority is to transform the nature of teaching. An ambitious programme to restructure and re-energise the teaching profession is already under way in England and Wales. In the long term, however, it is not enough. The impact of online technologies on teachers will be profound, because they undermine their historical role as the sole gatekeeper of knowledge. Teachers will retain a central role in the coordination and assessment of learning, but their ability to control and channel the flow of information to students will be drastically undermined. The analysis also suggests that the range of people directly involved in teaching and learning should increase dramatically, to include specialist contributors, providers of learning placements, mentors, community learning coordinators and so on. Government plans to develop a new category of teaching assistant are only the first step in this respect. The implications of such change are manifold, but one in particular stands out: teachers will need to model the kinds of learning behaviour which they are seeking to develop among students, and be able to apply their professional knowledge in contexts other than the classroom. It seems obvious that staying in touch with the changing worlds of work and organisation in other sectors are a precondition for such modelling, and teacher sabbaticals are already encouraged by public policy. A longer-term, and more radical, possibility is that the practice of teaching in schools should become part-time, and be linked with a learning specialism in another field of organisation or enquiry. Such a structural shift might also provide part of the solution to current recruitment and retention problems.

These three basic changes, though they go far beyond the scope of current policy, would provide a stimulus to far-reaching change. They could all be licensed and encouraged by central policy makers, but to bear fruit they would depend on innovation at the local level. A host of other changes are also necessary, from new models of interdisciplinary teaching and learning to new forms of assessment and evaluation and new systems for managing and monitoring student attendance in a more individualised, multi-site model of schooling. New standards and safety measures for involving employers and community partners in the provision of learning opportunities would also be needed.

Creating a learning society through learning communities

Such a strategy, of course, is a tall order. The idea that we must develop a coherent, holistic overview of change across society in order to act effectively in one sphere of it is daunting. It goes against the grain of many of our habits and institutional assumptions – that knowledge and action can be subdivided, specialised and professionalised. We also often assume that the institutions and *mores* of adult society should be capable of designing solutions for educating younger, less developed minds. The problem is that, too often, this assumption leads us to think within too narrow a range of possibilities and solutions.

It would be possible to continue for decades with modest, incremental forms of policy innovation which tinker at the edges of the institutional core. But such a strategy would produce diminishing returns, and would only postpone the reinvention which is clearly needed.

It is time for far-sighted political leaders, and for thinkers, practitioners and observers of the educational scene, to begin work on a long-term vision which is sufficiently compelling to mobilise the resources and support which are needed to make a start. Such a vision does not need to provide comprehensive details of the final outcome – part of the point is that we need a strategy for change which will enable us to learn as we go. But without fixing our perspective on the long-term possibilities, the potential for far-reaching change will be wasted.

Such a vision has to be rooted in down-to-earth, everyday reality, as well as in grand ambition. That is why community is so central. Schools can become the new hubs of local communities, building social capital and renewing collective life through the process of offering new learning opportunities. Education can become part of society's central nervous system, underpinning many other forms of activity and institutional life, in particular the civic sphere. But it can do so only if schools and colleges are able to turn themselves inside out, reconnecting with the communities that surround them, and forging new relationships with learners, parents, employers and others. This, at root, is a practical, local challenge, which must be achieved at human scale. But it is also the foundation of a movement which could transform whole systems of provision, and revolutionise our prospects for the future.

References

Bentley, T. (1998) *Learning beond the Classroom: Education for a Changing World*, London: Routledge.

Csikzsentmihalyi, M. (1988) 'Society, culture and person: a systems view of creativity', in R. Sternberg (ed.) *The Nature of Creativity*, New York: Cambridge University Press.

Csikzsentmihalyi, M. (1996) *Creativity: Flow and the Psychology of Discovery and Invention*, New York: HarperCollins.

Green, A. (1990) *Education and State Formation: The Rise of Education Systems in England, France and the USA*, London: Macmillan.

Leadbeater, C. (1999) *Living on Thin Air: The new Economy*, London: Viking.

Mulgan, G. (1997) *Connexity: How to Live in a Connected World*, London: Chatto & Windus.

Seltzer, K., and Bentley, T. (1999) *The Creative Age: Knowledge and Skills for the new Economy*, London: Demos.

Part IV
Levers of change

11 Target setting, policy pathology and student perspectives

Learning to labour in new times

Michael Fielding

In an ever busier, constantly changing world the capacity to pin down some identifiable aspect of our work or our lives and through concerted, focused activity to be able actually to demonstrate that things have changed for the better has enormous psychological as well as practical and political appeal. Indeed, the fervour with which target setting is embraced across such a wide expanse of occupational and personal settings, combined with the doubtful quality of its evidence base, suggests that its appeal has as much to do with our psychological needs as our economic aspirations. It is, in one sense, the Viagra of economic and educational underperformance: set some targets and you'll feel better, be seen to get something done and satisfy the prurience of an increasingly promiscuous accountability.

The playfulness of the metaphors is not accidental here: we are in grave danger of taking ourselves too seriously and, as a result, forgoing the humility and openness which are the *sine qua non* of responsive and successful policy. The hard-edged, real-world timbre of contemporary talk hides an intellectual fragility beneath the no-nonsense *machismo* of products and outcomes. It is time we took stock and in a way which looks more carefully and more imaginatively at different kinds of evidence base and from standpoints other than those to which we are accustomed.

In attempting just such a task the chosen methodology of this chapter is primarily, though not exclusively, philosophical and the standpoint of its interrogation that of students in schools, rather than the teachers, parents and politicians who so often take it upon themselves to speak with such alacrity and confidence on their behalf. Recourse to philosophy is particularly important here. Target setting has accrued such a substantial, self-evident appeal that the philosophical task of delving beneath the surface of clear charts, crisp paragraphs and confident cameos and asking fundamental questions disruptive of the ubiquitous appeal to 'what works' becomes more than usually desirable. Recourse to the perspective of students is important too, and for similar reasons. The presumption of policy is too often that careful thought, rigorous planning and a degree of consultation are adequate guarantors of success. Whilst all these things are, without doubt, important, the major failing of such a list is its conspicuous lack of engagement with the very people who are the objects of policy change and for whom the actual experience of its implementation constitutes the new reality which is so fervently desired (Thiessen, 1997).

The case for target setting

What, then, provides target setting with its multi-faceted appeal? Central to any viable case for target setting are likely to be at least five intrinsic and three extrinsic considerations. The intrinsic considerations are often captured by the now familiar SMART (specific, measurable, attainable, relevant, time-related) acronym. Thus, first, in identifying a process that incorporates specific steps or clearly identifiable actions the student, teacher or institution whose targets are under consideration is clear about what it is that needs to be done. Target setting thus stands in stark contrast to general, if worthy, exhortations to do better or work harder that so often seem convincing at the time but leave us floundering when we come to translate the conviction into action. Second, not only are we clear about what specific actions we are committing ourselves to, we are also clear about how we may measure the extent to which they have actually been achieved. This takes us beyond a general feeling about a quantifiable evidence base for the accomplishment of what we have set out to do. Furthermore, this quantifiable evidence base informs considerations involved in the construction of the targets themselves, not just the demonstration of their realisation. Third, a target differs from a more general aspiration or overarching commitment in its insistence that we are actually able to accomplish what we wish to do. There is no point in having a target that is beyond our reach, however desirable it may be. Fourth, if target setting is to motivate us as well as provide us with an enabling structure, it is important for the target to be seen as relevant or meaningful by those involved. Fifth, if the specificity, measurability, attainability and relevance of targets are to bear fruit in ways which are productive and useful in our daily work they also need to be time-related.

The three main extrinsic considerations which comprise such a strong contemporary case for target setting are, unsurprisingly, linked with its pragmatic, outcomes-driven approach and concern its apparent transparency, potential accessibility and ready amenability to the context of accountability at both an individual and an institutional level. The virtually hegemonic appeal of target setting lies as much in its contextual insistence on developing ways of working that, first, clearly demonstrate what it is we have been doing, second, open up our work to external scrutiny in ways which are easily understood and, third, fit sympathetically within a rigorous framework of audit and control, as it does to its internal virtues of substantive achievement. At its best, then, target setting is potentially and pre-eminently a means of helping us actually achieve what we aspire to, holding us to account to ourselves and others, and doing so in a way that is entirely consistent with democratic values: it democratises achievement in the sense that it makes achievement possible for all and visible to all.

The tyranny of targets: the making of a modern superstition

The fact that it is difficult to find even cautionary, let alone oppositional, voices articulating alternative perspectives from an increasing impatient insistence on 'what works' says a great deal about the strength of the incorporation of target setting into our national psyche. There are, nonetheless, a number of reservations and counter-arguments which, whilst not necessarily anti-target setting, serve as appropriate correctives to the kind of target mania that currently confronts us all.

The confusion of clarity

Whilst advocacy of specific, clearly identifiable steps seems eminently sensible, the elevation of clarity to something akin to canonical status within the litany of target setting is much more problematical. It is not that clarity is, of itself, objectionable; rather it is that if too much is asked of it – or, indeed any other virtue – it becomes predatory in its inclinations and complacent in its self-regard. To be clear about the next steps in a course of action may tell you something important about efficacy but precious little about legitimacy.

The broader, more profound point here is that there are real dangers that distorting the importance of clarity within a strongly instrumental process like target setting runs the risk of severely weakening its essential links with the larger undertaking which it is designed to serve. Target setting is a means to a wider educational end, not an end in itself. Thus, whilst its pragmatic virtues may include an apparent capacity to raise test scores, questions about (1) *how* those test scores are raised, e.g. through an increasing incidence of teaching to the test (Carvel 1998; Reay and Wiliam 1999), greater competition (Coward 1999) and substantial individual and group pressure (Reay and Wiliam 1999), and (2) *whose* test scores are raised, e.g. those on the C/D or level 3/4 borderline at the expense of those whose attainment is seen to be significantly lower, give rise to concern about the moral integrity of its application under conditions of substantial external pressure. As Stephen Ball (in press) has observed, 'Efficiency is asserted over ethics. The humanistic commitments of the substantive professional – the service ethic – are replaced by the teleological promiscuity of the technical professional – the manager'. More fundamental still, (3) overemphasis on what works (in this case the raising of test scores) forces prior questions of purpose, i.e. what test scores are *for*, from the centre to the periphery of our attention and, in so doing, runs the risk of marginalising education in favour of a more l   ⁻tion of schooling. As Reay and Wiliam remark, 'The more specific t' is about what it is that schools are to achieve, the more like' but the less likely it is to mean anything' (1999: 353).

The idolatry of measurement

A similar set of concerns centre round its second intrinsic virtue of measurability. Here, as before, the objection is not to measurability *per se*, but rather to the idolatry of measurement, which is both more likely and more necessary within a context that sets its standards and rests its future on the attainment of publicly accessible, readily understandable outcomes. The worry here is that strength of conviction about the necessity of measurement blinds its proponents to the limitations of current instruments and we all end up not only mismeasuring the measurable but misrepresenting the immeasurable or elusive aspects of education which so often turn out to be central to our deeper purposes and more profound aspirations. Hence the tenacity with which, for example, proponents of SATs cling on to the wreckage of its reputation and the fervour with which, for example, the arts are reduced from an expansive, unpredictable, creative encounter to a brightly instrumental set of saleable skills.

Even if fears about the vaulting ambition of measurement are not realised there remains the concern that the legitimacy of and delight in those relationships and undertakings which are not amenable to target setting become increasingly less convincing, more problematical and doubtfully worthy of precious time and effort in a highly pressured world. How many teachers, particularly those of younger children, are now able to listen openly, attentively and in a non-instrumental, exploratory way to their children/ students without feeling guilty, stressed or vaguely uncomfortable about the absence of criteria or the insistence of a target tugging at their sleeve?

Control or creativity?

Whilst the emphasis on realism as the third intrinsic component within target setting is generally to be applauded, it, too, is not without its dangers and difficulties. Realism can too readily become a mental and practical barrier to creativity, risk taking and the more exploratory dimensions of learning. In our quite proper desire to ensure progress and success we need to be vigilant about overemphasis on caution and control. Just as Michael Fullan argues that 'bureaucratic reforms may be able to guarantee minimal performance, but not excellence, in teaching' (Fullan 1992: 121), so I would suggest that, generally speaking, target setting has little to do with creativity and a great deal to do with basic competence. Of course, there is nothing the matter with competence, but competence is not enough.

Realism can also run real risks of being prematurely agreed and externally cajoled. If waves of pressure and substantial fear of failure roll through each layer of encounter from government to local education authority (LEA), to school, to department/team, to class teacher, to student, the likelihood is that realism will retreat to security and predictability. Frightened children revert to the safety of habit or the mimicry of learning; frightened teachers revert to the atavistic pedagogy of a half remembered past, the 'curriculum of the dead' (Ball, 1993) or the security of a purely technical proficiency. As Reay and Wiliam observe, the 'narrowing of the focus of assessment, together with an emphasis on achieving the highest scores possible produces a situation in which unjustifiable educational practices are not only possible, but encouraged' (1999: 352–3).

Whose relevance? Whose meaning?

The fourth intrinsic argument for target setting is vulnerable to similar reservations. In emphasising that targets should be both 'meaningful' and 'relevant' it is also important, first, to ask sharp questions about what is meant by these terms and, second, enquire as to whose version of these desiderata ultimately holds sway. With regard to what is meant by a target being meaningful and relevant it is worth reminding ourselves that there is a world of difference between, on the one hand, meaning and relevance as products of a thinly conceived and insistently driven response to immediate, instrumental, often external pressures and, on the other hand, meaning and relevance as qualities which have their origins in a deeper, more enduring energy that springs from the agency and awareness of learners themselves. Second, asking whose version of meaning and relevance sets the agenda and informs the process that is to be followed inevitably requires us to face up to concerns about issues of power and control in ways which merely invoking the managerial mantra of ownership does absolutely nothing to assuage. Just as LEAs are experiencing the meaning and relevance of government targets in ways which make these points abundantly clear, so too headteachers, teachers and students in schools will in turn feel the weight of a reality defined largely by others, albeit for what is judged to be their own good.

Responsiveness or predictability?

The counter-considerations with regard to the last of the intrinsic justifications for target setting, namely that the process should be bounded by time constraints which help us to both get things done and demonstrate to significant others that they have been done, echo many of the points made thus far. There is also the worry that target setting's premium on clarity, measurement, realism and relevance tends to carry with it a burden of caution and control that stands in significant tension with flexibility and responsiveness to change that we are increasingly urged to consider in our efforts to improve what we do. Singleness of purpose, which provides target setting with its most sustainable and significant dynamic, can also be its most significant limitation: despite our best intentions, firmness can become dogma and intensity of conviction harden into the fixed gaze of myopia. Less dramatically, in concentrating so hard on the target we ignore or sideline unpredictable and unpredicted events and interpretations which are important and potentially helpful. In the words of Hesse's Siddhartha, 'When someone is seeking . . . it happens quite easily that he only sees the thing he is seeking; that he is unable to find anything, unable to absorb anything, because he is only thinking of the thing he is seeking, because he has a goal, because he is obsessed with his goal' (Hesse 1982).

The bias of transparency

Many of the intellectual and practical weaknesses of the five internal components of target setting are also echoed by similar flaws in the external case for its legitimacy. Thus the argument for transparency is susceptible to the kind of concerns raised in the case against an overconfident, under-argued, empirically weak valorisation of measurement. This is not to say that transparency is bad; far from it. Rather, it is to say that transparency within the context of a particular kind of performativity runs a substantial risk of becoming prey to reductionism and distortion. The work of scholars like Michael Power (1994) eloquently reminds us that the instruments we use to audit the world of work are far from neutral. Our practices change in anticipation of and in response to the administration of the audit in ways which are often substantial (Troman 1997), as anyone who has either experienced or observed an OfStEd inspection will be quick to point out. Within the context of accountability transparency is always partial; always refracted through a specific, value-laden framework; always managed and presented to us by particular people for particular purposes.

Reinstating the complexity of clarity

The argument for accessibility has similar ambitions and limitations. The worry here is that overemphasis on clarity and common sense obscures the extent to which these notions are themselves deeply imbued with particular meanings that are never neutral, frequently covert and invariably expressive of a common sense that is differentially shared and unevenly sensible. Thus Chris Woodhead's common sense is shared by many, but not by all, and the manner and message of his clarity are shaped by complex interrelation-ships of power, time and place. Pierre Bourdieu's injunction that we should 'reinstate respect for the complexity of the world by untangling confusions that some deliberately maintain' (1998: 91) is an important reminder that clarity and complexity are as likely to be interlinked as unrelated.

'No one knows who or what these measurements are for'

Finally, accountability. What are we to make of this most compelling of imperatives in contemporary British society? Here, it seems to me, we near the heart of the target-setting project and engage with similar sorts of dilemmas to those still current among many teachers with regard to appraisal: is target setting essentially about development or is it about accountability? Is it possible for it to serve both masters equally well or do we need different schemes which may or may not be linked at various points? These are difficult matters to resolve, both theoretically and practically, and yet they must be more satisfactorily addressed than they have been thus far.

At a theoretical level there is little evidence that the nature of the problem as it affects education policy has been adequately understood by the present government, and at the pragmatic level there is mounting evidence that the consequences of this confusion are hitting teachers, parents and students hard. Thus, in a survey carried out for the Association of Teachers and Lecturers '90 per cent of English teachers felt they were under pressure to coach 14-year-olds to pass tests instead of developing their broader understanding of the subject. And 83 per cent admitted that too much lesson time was spent preparing for the tests, thereby narrowing the curriculum' (Carvel 1998: 7) and in the *New Statesman* Suzanne Moore, who is also a columnist in the *Mail on Sunday*, observed, 'One day we read that children are more anxious and depressed than ever before. The next day we get another stupid league table. Parental anxiety is passed on to children, and that makes parents very worried indeed' (1999: 17). More revealing still, she goes on to add:

> No one knows exactly who or what these measurements are for. . . . League tables say more than they should about our education system. It makes a fetish of information at the expense of any real understanding of what to do with it. Debate has been replaced by lists, idealism by aggregated scores on tests that teachers don't know how to mark. As schools are forced to jostle for position, inevitably little children must jostle with each other, their parents grooming them for SATs. Or are they Ph.Ds?
>
> (Ibid.)

Students: targets of schooling or agents of educational transformation?

What I have argued thus far is that target setting, as one particular example of a centrally important plank of the government's education strategy, has considerable educational potential. It can be genuinely enhancing of progress at a whole range of different levels involving students, teachers, schools, parents, LEAs and even governments. Indeed, the current government's future may well rest in part on its capacity to persuade those various partners to meet the targets it so publicly proclaimed in coming to office. I have also argued that target setting has the capacity to be profoundly destructive of our educational well-being. Its clarity can blind as well as reveal, break the bonds of our moral engagement as well as show us the next steps; measurement can reify as well as reward; realism can stunt creativity as well as support progress; relevance can be superficial as well as authentic, imposed as well as authored; time parameters can foster rigidity as well as results; in seeking too hard we may fail to find anything of worth. Furthermore, the context of target setting is equally ambivalent. Transparency can encourage reductionism as well as responsibility; accessibility of information can mask its inevitable partiality as well as enhance the possibility of informed debate; accountability can intimidate and confuse as much as it can stimulate effort and deepen understanding.

The reality of this continuum of possibilities lies, of course, in the classroom, the school, the home and the community. Policy reality is felt, not merely acknowledged; it is lived, not merely contemplated. Table 11.1 presents a series of alternative practices centring round the experience of target setting from the standpoint of students themselves. The two constructs, the Person-centred School and the Effective School, are based upon two quite different philosophical bases, express two quite different sets of anthropological assumptions and thus give rise to two sharply contrasting sets of practices of target setting. The Person-centred School is expressive of education in its wider, more expansive sense, is centrally concerned with the relationship between ends and means and is infused by the reciprocally conditioning values of freedom and equality which are constitutive of schools as learning communities (Fielding 2000a, b). The Effective School is preoccupied with certain kinds of outcomes of schooling, is concerned mainly with the reality of their achievement rather than the rhetoric of their intended processes, and is driven by the necessity of performance and productivity, which are central to schools as learning organisations.

There is a further implicit distinction between the two orientations which needs to be drawn out here, and it is this that engages specifically with student data emerging from current fieldwork. It concerns not only the degree to which the voices of students are heard in the conversations about their own work and aspirations, but also the degree to which their voices are actively engaged in constructing the framework within which conversations take place. It is not just about listening attentively and with interest to students, though it is certainly and importantly about that: as Deborah Meier reminds us, 'Teachers cannot help young people to make sense of things if they do not have time to answer their students' questions – and time to really hear the questions' (1997: 154–5). It is also about the explicit development of students as agents of their own and each others' educational transformation (Fielding 1998: 2001; Weatherill 1994). It moves beyond students as interesting sources of data, as objects of teachers' professional gaze, to students as co-constructors of new meanings and shared understandings rooted in the unpredictability of dialogue rather than the often covert inflexibility of the timetabled tutorial.

As these two constructs suggest, quite different practices and motives inform the experiential reality of target setting. At one extreme students encounter the minutiae of performative paranoia in which their voice is little

Table 11.1 Contrasting practices of target setting

The Person-centred School	The Effective School
Concern for persons • Conversations with students about attainment and aspiration have always been driven by concern for them as individuals • The nature of the questions asked is concerned with action, but not confined to a narrow understanding of its remit • Individual attainment has ipsative rather than comparative significance	*Concern for results* • The impetus for the development of target setting lies primarily in the emergence of league tables and government requirements • The nature of the questions asked is instrumentally conceived • Individual attainment is significant largely through its capacity to improve a comparative picture of the school's attainment
Integrity of ends and means • Achievement is widely conceived • Questions are expressive of an integral concern for and detailed knowledge of the uniqueness of the individual student • The manner of asking is genuinely attentive rather than a disguised form of teacher assertion	*Overriding emphasis on outcomes* • The kinds of things targeted are confined to a narrow notion of what is desirable • Questions are more often generic, detached from or tangential to the real concerns and aspirations of the student • Questions are asked in a way which is inattentive to or ignorant of personal detail
Expressive freedom • Target-setting conversations are informed by the felt concerns of both parties • Understanding emerges from dialogue as often as it precedes it • Both parties have the confidence and the courage to raise difficult issues • The course of the conversation is a genuinely joint endeavour	*Managed freedom* • Target setting conversations are dominated by the teacher's agenda • The presumption is that teachers' perceptions of what needs to be done define the outcome • Difficult issues are often seen as primarily the student's responsibility • The conversation is managed by the teacher
Reciprocal learning • Target setting seen as supportive of the student's learning • In doing so it turns out to be enabling of the teacher's learning too: learning about the student, learning from the student, learning with the student, learning about the process of learning and the teacher's role in it • Target setting is predicated on the teacher's capacity to listen, to be receptive, as much as on the student's capacity to do these things	*Unitary learning* • Target setting is conceived and executed on the assumption that its true purpose is instructional • The learning is unidirectional • The most appropriate manner is thought to be monologic

more than an assenting punctuation mark in an institutionally constructed sentence. At the other end of the continuum there lies the complex reality of a lived partnership. Here an expansive, holistic dialogue gives personal meaning to instrumental preoccupations. Instead of the dislocation of attainment and achievement in which the preoccupation with school performance grants only derivative significance to individual commitment, the interconnectedness of daily work and human encounter creates a personal rigour which is typically more generous, more demanding and, ironically, more productive than the busyness and self-assurance of its performative counterpart.

The poverty of performativity

Whilst recognising that the realities of most schools will be mixed and will depend to a significant degree on particular people in particular circumstances, my concern is that the external context of performativity in which all now work pushes most of us most of the time towards practices typical of what I have called, somewhat contentiously, the Effective School. And yet, both intellectually and experientially, it is a profoundly mistaken model. Work within the field is now beginning to encounter students expressing doubts about the genuineness of their school's interest in their progress and well-being as persons, as distinct from their contribution to their school's league table position (Ball 1999; Fielding 1999; Reay and Wiliam 1999). The overriding instrumentality of conversations makes listening difficult: attentiveness is overdirected; clues to meaning are trodden underfoot in the scramble for performance; dialogue disappears as reciprocity retreats under the sheer weight of external expectation; contract replaces community as the bond of human association.

The fact that the confident instrumentalism of the Effective School continues to gain ground is not an accident. The current mania for performativity enhances and extols the very narrowness inherent in its intellectual make-up. If target setting turns out to be genuinely educative, rather than merely successful, it will be so despite and not because of a largely well-meaning but philosophically flawed government policy. Government's tenacity, its courage and its laudable impatience with persistent complacency, low expectations and substantial underachievement are entirely deserving of support. It now needs to match its political will with an appropriately rigorous and imaginative intellectual drive, at the heart of which must lie a belief in the education of persons in and through community. The trick is not to repeat 'education' more loudly or more often; rather it is to speak of our commitments in a way which does justice to their subtlety, their passion, their ethical integrity and their belief in human agency. It is to speak the nuanced language of education, not the metallic language of the market. It is, as Michael Ignatieff reminds us so beautifully and so urgently, to acknowledge that 'Without a public language to help us find our words, our needs will dry up in silence' (1984: 142).

References

Ball, S. J. (1993) 'Education, Majorism and the "curriculum of the dead"', *Curriculum Studies* 1 (2), 195–214.

Ball S. J. (in press) *Global Trends in Educational Reform and the Struggle for the Soul of the Teacher*, Wei Lun Lecture, Hong Kong Institute of Educational Research Education Policy Papers, Hong Kong: Chinese University of Hong Kong.

Bourdieu, P. (1998) *Acts of Resistance: Against the new Myths of our Time*, Cambridge: Polity Press.

Carvel, J. (1998) 'Scheme for testing at 14 "a waste of money"', *Guardian*, 29 December, p. 7.

Coward, R. (1999) 'Suffering in Year Six', *Guardian*, 19 January.

Fielding, M. (1998) 'Students as Researchers: From Data Source to Significant Voice', paper presented at the International Congress for School Effectiveness and Improvement, University of Manchester.

Fielding, M. (1999) Communities of Learners: myth – schools are communities, in B. O'Hagan (ed.), *Modern Educational Myths*, London: Kogan Page, pp. 64–87.

Fielding, M (2000a) 'Community, philosophy and education policy: against the immiseration of contemporary schooling', *Journal of Education Policy* 15 (4), 397–415.

Fielding, M (2000b) 'The person-centred school', *Forum* 42 (2), 51–4.

Fielding, M. (forthcoming) 'Students as radical agents of change', *Journal of Educational Change* 2 (3).

Fullan, M. (1992) *Successful School Improvement*, Buckingham: Open University Press.

Hesse, H. (1982) *Siddhartha*, New York NY: Bantam.

Ignatieff, M. (1984) *The Needs of Strangers*, London: Chatto & Windus.

Meier, D. (1997) 'How our schools could be', in E. Clinchy (ed.) *Transforming Public Education: A new Course for America's Future*, New York: Teachers' College Press, pp. 145–53.

Moore, S. (1999) 'I'd rather sacrifice my children to my political beliefs than for the sake of an A-level grade or two', *New Statesman*, 26 February, p. 17.

Power, M. (1994) *The Audit Explosion*, London, Demos.

Reay, D. and Wiliam, D. (1999) '"I'll be a nothing": structure, agency and the construction of identity through assessment', *British Education Research Journal* 25 (3), 343–54.

Thiessen, D. (1997) 'Knowing about, acting on behalf of, and working with, primary pupils' perspectives: three levels of engagement with research', in A. Pollard, D. Thiessen and A. Filer (eds) *Children and their Curriculum*, London: Falmer Press, pp. 184–196.

Troman, G. (1997) 'Self-management and school inspection: complementary forms of surveillance and control in the primary school', *Oxford Review of Education* 23, 345–64.

Weatherill, L. (1994) 'The "students as researchers" project at Sharnbrook Upper School and Community College', *Improving Schools* 1 (2), 52–3.

Acknowledgements

My thanks to the following for their conversation, their company, their critique and their commitment to the education of persons in difficult times: Frances Booker, Jan Fielding, Angela Forge, Kevin O'Connell, Diane Reay, Jean Rudduck, Patrick Shevlin, Paul Standish, Andy Thomas and Suzie Webb.

12 Modernising headteachers as leaders

An analysis of the NPQH

Helen M. Gunter

The National Professional Qualification for Headteachers (NPQH) is high-profile training for aspiring headteachers launched in 1997 by the Teacher Training Agency (TTA) based on the National Standards for Headteachers (TTA 1997a), which are 'designed to serve as the basis for planning the professional development of both aspiring and serving headteachers' (TTA 1997a: 1). In awarding the first NPQH certificates David Blunkett stated, 'We are committed to ensuring that all teachers are effective professionals. In future all newly appointed headteachers will have to hold a professional qualification' (DfEE 1998a). The preparation of headteachers has a long and rich history both nationally and internationally (Bolam 1997), and while the role of central agencies is evident in the COSMOS and OTTO courses in the 1970s and 1980s (Creissen and Ellison 1998; Ouston 1998b), the emphasis has been on voluntary and plural provision. The introduction of centrally determined and accredited training for those seeking to move into headship is an attempt to break with the past, and, as Fidler (1998) states, 'there has been a conscious attempt not to use existing qualifications, structures or experiences as the backbone for the new initiative' (p. 314). It seems that locating the development of educational professionals with individuals, unions, higher education institutions, local education authorities, and consultancies is no longer regarded as appropriate.

Ouston (1998b) sees the development of the NPQH as being part of a strong centrist approach to control both the content and the provision of training. Within this context the development, implementation, and evaluation of the NPQH raise some important questions for all those involved in the study and practice of educational leadership. How do we understand the professional practice of the headteacher, and how does it connect with broader changes within the public sector? What are the knowledge claims on which the NPQH structure and curriculum are based, and how do they fit in with research and debates about appropriate professional development? The professional practice of headteachers continues to change, and the NPQH seems to be about integrating new headteachers into the work which site-based management is constructing.

In a performance-driven education system the headteacher must know how to perform and how to produce the data which validate that performance. Underpinning this the headteacher must have the right capabilities to capture, integrate, and deliver teacher, pupil, parent, and community involvement in school performance (Gleeson and Gunter 2001). Through the development of public sector management there has been a shift in power relations (Bottery 1998), and headteachers are being contracted as leaders in which their work is being shaped by rational agency. Within this setting this chapter focuses on what aspiring headteachers are expected to know, understand, and do, combined with the process of how they come to know it through undertaking the learning processes leading to the qualification. I intend to draw on both insider and outsider knowledge of the NPQH: first, my involvement as a trainer for the compulsory module in which I have been involved in the delivery and assessment of the training; and, second, from work within the field of education management which has contributed to debates about how best to understand the location of professional practice within a broader policy context rather than be enabled by an education management industry to make policy work and work better (Gunter 1997). The chapter has two main sections: it begins with an analysis of the restructuring of the public sector in which the NPQH can be described and understood, and goes on to a second section where the NPQH structure and knowledge claims are analysed and critically evaluated.

Contracting teachers, contracting times

Education is being modernised in order to achieve the goal of a 'world class education system' by using funding mechanisms to 'motivate and increase the professionalism of teachers and encourage risk and ambition . . .' (Barber and Sebba 1999: 187). New Labour is concerned to confront what Blair (1999) has called the 'forces of conservatism' that have a 'culture of excuses . . . a culture that tolerates low ambition, rejects excellence, treats poverty as an excuse for failure'. The Green Paper *Teachers: meeting the challenge of change* (DfEE 1998b) presents a package of proposals regarding differentiation within, and assessment of, the profession through performance-related pay, a fast-track route for able entrants, and the formation of a leadership group in schools. Professional development is seen to be crucial, and the government proposes the creation of a National College of School Leadership.

The challenge for the government is in how to attract and retain headteachers, and its approach is to conflate headship with leadership in which the work that Heads have been doing and need to do is about school direction, improvement, and motivation. However, this is a particular form of leadership and has its roots in the neo-liberal version of education as a commodity, in which the headteacher is central to product development and marketing (Grace 1995). Consider some of the changing dimensions within the professional practice of a headteacher over the last ten years:

- bidding for resources from external funding agencies;
- buying in training and consultancy to support staff training and development.
- competitive tendering for cleaning and canteen facilities;
- hiring, firing, promotion and dismissal of staff;
- installation and operation of information systems to measure and report on performance;
- inspection of the school by a privatised team according to the OfStEd framework;
- selection, recruitment, retention, discipline, and exiting of pupils.

It is not suggested that these activities are the sole domain of the headteacher. Strategic and operational decision making is about direct involvement by the headteacher combined with effective delegation, and is underpinned by systems of accountability both to governors and to outside agencies. The legislation of site-based management from 1988 onwards has provided the structures and practices to control work processes within schools, and professional relations are being increasingly controlled through contractual arrangements and compliance mechanisms. The right to manage requires the control of the generation, deployment, and evaluation of resources. Outcomes are targeted, prioritised, and maximised, with a strong utility imperative towards value for money through direct and measurable impact. Educational professionals are being constructed as purchasers or providers, who work in cost centres, and negotiate contracts, and achieve individualised differentials through performance-driven pay.

Familiarity with the word 'contract' comes from a commercial context where it is used to regulate practice and relations in trading, and we enter into an agreement based on free choice and the meeting of agreed obligations. This commodified contract is challenging the underlying assumptions regarding governance and how democracy is constituted and understood as a social contract. Hindess (1997) argues that it is not that a social contract was ever formally made but that we behave as if it was, in order to sustain the legitimacy of the institutions and political culture which have been created from it. In this way, governance is a productive tension between the individual and the collective, and is mediated through institutions in which role, tenure, and public service are valued. The often intangible threads which hold a polity together are a different kind of contract from commercial agreements, and one which has had its legitimacy openly challenged: from the left arguments that governance does not float free from inherited structural injustices, and from the neo-liberal right there have been charges of bureaucratic self-interest. The latter have dominated public sector reforms, and the collective has been presented as a straitjacket which limits the freedom of the individual to exercise choice.

Within education the headteacher is conceptualised as having a 'contractual personhood' in which the emphasis is on the agency of the individual: 'who is sufficiently autonomous as to be regarded as contractually capable, that is, as one who can assume responsibility for his or her own intentions, desire, choice and acts' (Yeatman 1997: 41). The headteacher as leader, or entrepreneur, is regarded as someone who creates and builds a commitment to a vision, and installs commercial contractual processes to enable all stakeholders to be appropriately involved. The legacy of the headmaster tradition remains (Grace 1995) and is being reworked through the individual being willing and able to exercise contractual competences and to secure the dependence of others.

The complexity and speed of change are such that what we know so far about the restructuring of the public sector is both simultaneously clear and blurred as new practices are being overlain on top of others, some have been absorbed, and others are resisted. Positioning from critics and advocates provides a rich area of debate, but confusion for those living and working within the turbulence. For example, the professional practice of headteachers is located in public sector funding structures, but increasingly income streams are becoming less related to service provision and more conditional on bidding and compliance arrangements. While headteachers are being presented with this contractual culture as being empowering and facilitating of their vision for the school, the reality is that it is those with the skills and knowledge to make successful bids who can meet the external requirements of effectiveness.

The language of 'freedom' is seductive and has had electoral success in Western democracies during the 1980s and 1990s, but the connection with underlying structural factors is revealing. Flynn (1994) argues that the restructuring of the public sector has been about saving money, and hence commercial contracting has been made more attractive:

> there will be a continuing emphasis on saving money, to reduce the pressures on spending in the public sector as a whole. This implies stricter rationing, the withdrawal of the state from those responsibilities which it can place on individuals and insurance schemes. It also implies a style of management which emphasizes price and volume control, rather than quality and service development. This control implies detailed control over work process, not least to ensure that the volume and nature of the services is contained within the budgetary and contract constraints.
>
> (Flynn 1994: 223)

While this type of interventionism may be facilitating the fracturing of professional cultures, identities, and allegiances, it does not seem to be overturning them, as headteachers do not come 'freely' to contractual practices. The day-to-day work of the headteacher is full of contradictions and dilemmas (Day *et al.* 2000; Gronn 1996), but the normative models of leadership promoted by government agencies and their collaborators present certainty in the cause-and-effect connection between effective leadership and effective schools. This growth in contractualism requires the recruitment of a particular type of headteacher to undertake contractually based leadership, and the danger lies in the possible closing down of debates about other 'hows' and 'whys' in the preparation of headteachers.

Failing teachers, failing times

In the Green Paper (DfEE 1998b) the government rationalised the incremental developments of the 1990s into a 'Headship Training Framework':

- *Qualification.* NPQH is 'the benchmark for entry to headship'.
- *Induction programme.* HEADLAMP is 'to consolidate and reinforce the skills of new Heads'.
- *Extension programme.* LPSH is 'to give experienced, successful heads the opportunity to stretch their skills' (p. 27).

Central to the preparation, assessment and development of aspiring and serving headteachers are the National Standards (TTA 1997a), a list of eighty-two criteria divided into five sections:

1   Core purpose of Headship.
2   Key outcomes of Headship.
3   Professional knowledge and understanding.
4   Skills and attributes.
5   Key areas of Headship:

   (a) Strategic direction and development of the school.
   (b) Teaching and learning.
   (c) Leading and managing staff.
   (d) Efficient and effective deployment of staff and resources.
   (e) Accountability.

In 1996 contracts were awarded to ten NPQH Training and Development Centres in England and Wales, and Regional Assessment Centres. Alternatively a candidate was able to choose to study through the Supported Open Learning (SOL) programme provided through a partnership between the Open University and the National Association of Headteachers. Training and assessment were undertaken by those selected and appointed by either the Regional Training Centres or the Assessment Centres; Lodge (1998) reports that 695 trainers undertook TTA training and there is a process of trainer accreditation in place.

The NPQH was originally based on the separation of assessment from training, in which the candidates must have:

- undertaken an initial needs assessment designed to help them identify their training needs against the national standards for headteachers, which results in an action plan for training and development;

- completed successfully the complusory strategic leadership and accountability module and any further training and development that is necessary;
- be successfully assessed against all designated national standards during training and in a final assessment designed to guarantee that the candidate has demonstrated overall fitness for headship.

(Ribbins 1999: 79)

So far 'over 7,000 candidates have registered on the programme', and the goal of making the NPQH mandatory for all new headteachers remains (DfEE 2000). Following on from the Green Paper (DfEE 1998b) the establishment of the National College for School Leadership has been set in motion, and it is intended that it will take over responsibility for the NPQH (DfEE 1999). However, changes in the NPQH have already been announced by the government in February 2000:

- a shorter one year programme rather than the existing up to three years;
- an emphasis on school-based assessment rather than assessment tasks;
- greater use of ICT;
- visits to highly successful schools;
- a two day residential hosted by the National College for School Leadership;
- access modules (mainly self-study) to prepare candidates for the NPQH.

(DfEE 2000)

The NPQH now has three stages and can be completed in one year, or in three months for those close to headship:

- *Access stage.* For those who have limited experience there are access modules, tutor-led sessions, self study and online learning.
- *Development stage.* Those who have completed the access stage, or the more experienced candidates, begin here. Candidates are supported by an external tutor who visits school to work with them and their headteacher on development needs and a training plan. The candidate has to undertake a school improvement project, attend training, and undertake self study.
- *Final stage.* There is a two day residential at the National College followed by a day of final assessment before the award is made.

It is very difficult to unravel events and the political processes that underpin the changes in the NPQH structure. Certainly the continuation of the NPQH is based on the clear endorsement that there is a need for aspiring headteachers to be prepared for the job (Select Committee on Education and Employment 1998). The evaluation report by the NFER (2000a, b) is not in the public domain, but its findings have been used to support improvement:

> Centre managers, assessors and trainers have demonstrated a high level of commitment and have found their involvement with the development of the qualification stimulating. Any criticisms and suggestions for improvement have been driven by a concern to get things right within the spirit of the formative evaluation.
>
> (NFER 2000b)

Making the NPQH work better is important for the legitimacy of the qualification and the experiences of candidates who are investing a great deal of their time and professional standing in it. However, it remains to be seen whether the questions raised about the generic nature of the NPQH will be dealt with through the new arrangements, since the National Standards remain in place. For example, Johnson and Castelli (1998) have shown that there is a strong spiritual dimension in leading a Catholic school which is not reflected in the secular National Standards (TTA 1997a).

Bush (1998) in reviewing the original model takes a strategic approach and raises questions about whether the NPQH can 'provide appropriate and sufficient preparation for headship'. In summary Bush argues that:

- The NPQH fits in with the deficit model of 'sorting out' teachers, and is unattractive to senior educational professionals, who see it as another attack on their confidence.
- The National Standards put more emphasis on competence than on support through mentoring systems.
- The National Standards make a false and distorted distinction between leadership and management.
- Drawing on 'best practice from outside of education' is problematic, as the core business of schools is teaching and learning.
- The 'Chinese wall' between assessment and training is distorting learning and undermining the formative process.
- The 'artificial distinction and the pretentious claim that only the NPQH can prepare aspiring heads' (p. 330) has been changed as a result of the Labour policy following the 1997 election. However, the connection between the NPQH and masters' degrees needs more clarification.

Perhaps the most important feature of the new model is the integration of assessment, training, and development, combined with an attempt to support a bespoke approach to the particular candidate's professional context. However, much of Bush's critical evaluation is still valid because what still remains is assessment and measurement against the National Standards. There is a particular interpretation of 'professional leadership' and there is an assumed causal connection between what the Head does and the outcomes from the school such as ethos and teaching quality. The National Standards make no connection between being a headteacher and actually continuing to teach. Professional practice is being restructured around management processes in which 'the headteacher must provide vision, leadership and direction for the school and ensure that it is managed and organised to meet its aims' (TTA 1997: 1). Understanding, acquiring, and implementing these processes are central to the assessment process, and the ability to demonstrate authentic and relevant evidence is regarded as an indicator of potential for headship. Furthermore, while some work has been done on gender (Cubillo 1998) a lot more work needs to be done on social justice issues in relation to access to the learning and assessment processes. Headteachers are being contracted into 'individualistic and individualising' (Hindess 1997: 15) leadership in which professional knowledge and skills are being defined as those that enable the headteacher to both employ and be employed.

The knowledge, understanding and skills within the National Standards are focused on neutral processes, and issues related to power are absent. While Whitty *et al.* (1997) show that studies about the impact of site-based management have found practitioner support for management activities and roles, they go on to argue that there is growing evidence of practitioners being 'differentially privileged' (p. 57) in which there is a growing gap between the managers and managed. Identity is shifted market accountability, as a headteacher 'must provide', 'is responsible', 'secures', and 'is accountable' (TTA 1997a: 1). The way in which leadership is talked about is what the literature identifies as 'transformational leadership' (Gronn 1996) in which the leader has a vision and a mission, builds support through teams, and installs monitoring and evaluation systems. Teachers who were once colleagues are now to be effectively and efficiently deployed, monitored, performance measured, and motivated. While the government is proposing to increase school-based assessments it is unlikely that the fundamental goal of promoting visioning will change. Visioning as a process is almost totemic, and the challenge in reforming the NPQH is in whether there will be opportunities for candidates to problematise it and to be given direct access to research evidence that presents alternatives (such as Fullan 1997, Smyth and Shacklock 1998).

At the development stage the candidate will have to undertake a school improvement project, and in less than a year. There is an assumption that this will actually bring about improvement, but examination of the previous model's school improvement projects shows that the tasks used do not allow the candidate to ask questions about who is defining improvement and for what purposes? The contractual nature of 'improvement' is clear when Assessment Task 1 from the module *Assessment of Key Area of Headship D: Efficient and Effective Deployment of Staff and Resources* is analysed. The aspiring headteacher is asked to:

imagine that you are the headteacher of the school concerned and that for the next financial year your school is likely to have its budget reduced by at least seven per cent. Your task is to draw up a budget for the next financial year, taking account of the reduction. You should also draw up an alternative approach so that you can offer the governors two realistic options.

(TTA 1998: 1)

Perhaps a positive outcome might be for the aspiring headteacher to look to alternative sources of income such as seeking and bidding for contracts with agencies such as the National Lottery. In shifting the focus to school-based assessments the challenge for the NPQH reforms is whether they will continue to position the headteacher as taking a lead responsibility and accountability for the resourcing of public sector education. Retaining this approach is likely, as it enables the party in government to achieve its political goals, and through the operation of short-term employment contracts it will enable the removal of those who do not deliver on the targets linked to those goals.

The summative assessment remains, and the problematic nature of gathering evidence such as obtaining witness statements or using statistics needs to be acknowledged, and it is not clear whether research training will be provided. Without this type of training the award of the NPQH will actually mean that the candidate has shown the ability to construct evidence, from within a particular school context, in a non-headteacher post, at a particular time, according to what is promoted as good practice. In this sense the NPQH is intellectually and emotionally sterile, because it does not provide aspiring Heads with an understanding of the politics of knowledge production and how they are being positioned in a particular way. The potential for aspiring headteachers to position themselves as the 'users and producers of knowledge' (Edwards 2000) through postgraduate study remains, though the intensification of school-based work and the ongoing attack on higher education as irrelevant continues to undermine this type of preparation and support for headteachers. This is consistent with Hargreaves and Evans's (1997) argument that 'educational reform has . . . been anti-intellectual [and] has failed to call upon the professional wisdom of teachers' (p. 4). As long as those registered for the NPQH are candidates to be tested through measurement rather than through intellectual challenge, thinking will be about how best to conform and comply, rather than about professional courage and creativity.

Ouston (1998a) shows that once the rational linear approaches to change have been challenged, and once we recognise that turbulence in educational change is state-directed, 'then values move to centre stage' (p. 125). However, we have been moved radically, and perhaps tragically, from what has traditionally been known as the preparation of headteachers to the training and assessment of headteachers, and all the debates which have gone on both nationally and internationally about pedagogy and purpose are being marginalised. Training faces a contradiction: people have professional educational values which challenge themselves and each other, but at the same time site-based management requires values to be organisational, observable, and measurable facts. Creissen (1997: 118) argues that:

> There are aspects of the head's job which are hard to assess through the NPQH and which have to be measured through confidential references and the interview process. Such issues are about styles of leadership, the individual's notions of 'power' and personal traits. There is also an intuitive nature to headship which is a problematic issue for assessment.

However, it seems to be increasingly the case that what cannot be assessed is at the core of headship. We have known this for a long time, and as Hoyle (1982) argues headteachers engage in micropolitics, but there are moral dilemmas in proactively developing and training political literacy. Perhaps the realities of headship are based more on who dominates professional practice rather than what dominates. The NPQH is based on the latter, in which measurement and assessment sends out the message that headship is about getting things done.

If the starting point is to begin with trying to understand what we do and do not know about the realities of headship then we can access a whole tradition of writing and research which has and continues to inspire those who are, and who work with, educational professionals. Greenfield argues (Greenfield and Ribbins 1993: 112) that the preparation of headteachers (he uses the North American term 'administrators') is complex and requires plural as well as intellectually challenging experiences:

> my solution to the problem of training administrators is to recognise that administrative training is training for life and that only those who have some insight into life – its ironies, joys, and tragedies – are fit to be administrators.

Perhaps this type of approach might enable an aspiring headteacher to engage with their disciplinary background, and ask questions about why and how a mathematician might see the world differently from an historian, and what this means for how we work productively with other professionals. Greenfield (Greenfield and Ribbins 1993) supports this by stating that we cannot certify someone as a decision maker as if they have scientific knowledge which is generic and value-free. He argues in favour of humane management in which 'Values lie beyond rationality. Rationality to *be* rationality must stand upon a value base. Values are asserted, chosen, imposed, or believed. They lie beyond quantification, beyond measurement' (Greenfield and Ribbins 1993: 182–3). There is a rich seam of writing which argues that a school as a unitary entity with tangible goals is a construction, and attempts to formalise one way of understanding are both conceptually weak and dangerous to professional practice (Bush 1995). This is not an issue for the TTA, which is clear in the evaluation from the trials candidates that: 'in a small number of regions, some candidates expressed a concern that the training was too academic and theoretical' (TTA 1997b: 2). The lack of explanation of this statement suggests that the meaning is meant to be obvious, and Ribbins (1999) reports evidence of a definitely untheoretical approach to the training which is supported by centrally assembled materials. This would, in Hoyle's (1986) terms, marginalise 'theory for understanding', where teachers are given access to ideas which challenge how they see the world and the knowledge claims on which thinking is based. For Winkley (1998) having the training does not necessarily mean that you will be an effective headteacher, and he argues that much of the content of the NPQH can be learned quickly, but what is missing and is more essential are deep philosophical questions about working with people and children, and this requires you to think about yourself and your values.

Summary

The section headings of this article have been inspired by the work of Andy Hargreaves (1994), who has a central focus on the work of teachers:

> The British case of multiple, mandated change is perhaps an extreme one. It is extreme in its frantic pace, in the immense scope of its influence, and in the wide sweep of its legislative power. More than anything, however, it is extreme in the disrespect and disregard that reformers have shown for teachers themselves. In the political rush to bring about reform, teachers' voices have been largely neglected, their opinions overridden, and their concerns dismissed. Change has been developed and imposed in a context where teachers have been given little credit or recognition for changing themselves, and for possessing their own wisdom to distinguish between what reasonably can be changed, and what cannot.
>
> (page 6)

Perhaps it is worth stating the obvious, that real people are headteachers, become headteachers, and decide not to become headteachers, and doubts are being raised about the wisdom of making the NPQH mandatory (Revell 1998; Select Committee on Education and Employment 1998). The deputy Head is being conceptualised as an aspiring headteacher in the making, though as Garrett and McGeachie (1999) show there are career deputy Heads who need training and support for that role. James and Whiting (1998) report on research into the decision to become a headteacher, and at a time of a shortage of recruits they argue: 'the notion that there is a large pool of potential heads out there who have the capacity to assume headship and who will, of course, choose to do so in sufficient numbers is unsustainable' (p. 12). They go on to show that the decision not to become a headteacher is related to contextual reasons, from job satisfaction to family commitments, combined with a view of headship as not professionally or personally attractive.

The formal utilitarian aspect of the training and the projected life of a headteacher remains unattractive, and is not helped by the ridiculing of both educational values and those who resist business management. In the development of the NPQH, Creissen (1997) argues, it 'has not been made easy for senior educationalists in schools who hold firm to their educational role. This has prohibited their wholesale acceptance of good management practice outside education' (p. 112). It seems that if NPQH candidates understand and live their professional identity in a different way from the contractual and contracting processes being presented they will either have to succumb or try to resist.

The commitment of the present government to high-quality training is widely acknowledged and supported, and for those about to begin the NPQH the technical improvements are very welcome. However, recent history shows that the preparation of headteachers is more than content and structure, and witness evidence to the House of Commons select committee (Select Committee on Education and Employment 1998) contains views on the reality and importance of varied and plural experiences in preparation for educational leadership. As Yeatman (1994, 1997) and others have theorised, and as the literature on headship (Hall and Southworth 1997) shows, the reality is that the status of the headteacher is being reshaped and it continues to be underpinned by power relations and structures. The promotion of agency through the NPQH is creating a picture of headship which will put a lot of very creative people off, as it denies the broader connection with the social and the moral. As Greenfield has stated: 'To be humane, to escape the fact-driven, calculable world, we must be human, reaching beyond our grasp, towards heaven . . .' (Greenfield and Ribbins 1993: 268).

References

Barber, M. and Sebba, J. (1999) 'Reflections on Progress towards a World Class Education System', *Cambridge Journal of Education* 29 (2), 183–93.

Blair, T. (1999) *Speech to the London Conference for new Headteachers*, London: DfEE.

Bolam, R. (1997) 'Management development for headteachers', *Educational Management and Administration* 25 (3), 265–83.

Bottery, M. (1998) *Professionals and Policy: Management Strategy in a Competitive World*, London: Cassell.

Bush, T. (1995) *Theories of Educational Management*, second edition, London: Paul Chapman.

Bush, T. (1998) 'The National Professional Qualification for Headship: the key to effective leadership?' *School Leadership and Management* 18 (3), 321–33.

Creissen, T. (1997) 'The introduction of the National Professional Qualification for Headship', in H. Tomlinson (ed.) *Managing Continuous Professional Development in Schools*, London: Paul Chapman.

Creissen, T. and Ellison, L. (1998) 'Reinventing school leadership: back to the future in the UK?' *International Journal of Education Management* 12, 28–38.

Cubillo, L. (1998) 'Women and NPQH: An Appropriate Leadership Model?' Paper presented to the British Educational Research Association conference, Queen's University, Belfast, 27–30 August.

Day, C., Harris, A., Hadfield, M., Tolley, H. and Beresford, J. (2000) *Leading Schools in Times of Change*, Buckingham: Open University Press.

Department for Education and Employment (1998a) *First 36 Successful Candidates receive Professional Qualification for Headship*, 364/98.

Department for Education and Employment (1998b) *Teachers: Meeting the Challenge of Change*, London: DfEE.

Department for Education and Employment (1999) *National College for School Leadership: A Prospectus*, London: DfEE.

Department for Education and Employment (2000) *DfEE Headship Training Programmes*, www.dfee.gov.uk/headship/npqh.shtm.

Edwards, A. (2000) 'Evidence-based Practice and the Generation of Knowledge about Pedagogy in Schools: Enhancing Practitioners' Understanding of Pedagogy in School–University Research Partnerships', paper presented at the American Education Research Association conference, New Orleans, April.

Fidler, B. (1998) 'Editorial', *School Leadership and Management* 18 (3), 309–15.

Flynn, N. (1994) 'Control, commitment and contracts', in J. Clarke, A. Cochrane and E. McLaughlin (eds) *Managing Social Policy*, London: Sage.

Fullan, M. (ed.) (1997) *The Challenge of School Change*, Arlington Heights IL: Skylight.

Garrett, V. and McGeachie, B. (1999) 'Preparation for headship? The role of the deputy Head in the primary school', *School Leadership and Management* 19 (1), 67–81.

Gleeson, D. and Gunter, H. (2001) 'The performing school and the modernisation of teachers', in D. Gleeson and C. Husbands (eds) *The Performing School*, London: RoutledgeFalmer Press.

Grace, G. (1995) *School Leadership: Beyond Education Management*, London: Falmer Press.

Greenfield, T. and Ribbins, P. (eds) (1993) *Greenfield on Educational Administration: Towards a Humane Science*, London: Routledge.

Gronn, P. (1996) 'From transactions to transformations', *Educational Management and Administration* 24, 7–30.

Gunter, H. (1997) *Rethinking Education: The Consequences of Jurassic Management*, London: Cassell.

Hall, V. and Southworth, G. (1997) 'Headship', *School Leadership and Management* 17 (2), 151–69.

Hargreaves, A. (1994) *Changing Teachers, Changing Times*, London: Cassell.

Hargreaves, A. and Evans, R. (1997) *Beyond Educational Reform: Bringing Teachers Back In*, Buckingham: Open University Press.

Hindess, B. (1997) 'A society governed by contract?' in G. Davis, B. Sullivan and A. Yeatman (eds) *The New Contractualism*, South Melbourne VCT: Macmillan.

Hoyle, E. (1982) 'Micropolitics of educational organisations', *Educational Management and Administration* 10, 87–98.

Hoyle, E. (1986) 'The management of schools: theory and practice', in E. Hoyle and A. McMahon, *World Yearbook of Education 1986: The Management of Schools*, London: Kogan Page.

James, C. and Whiting, D. (1998) 'Headship? No thanks! A study of factors influencing career progression to headship', *Management in Education* 12, 2–14.

Johnson, H. and Castelli, M. (1998) 'NPQH and Catholic Heads needing something more', *Management in Education* 12, 10–11.

Lodge, C. (1998) 'Training aspiring heads on NPQH: issues and progress', *School Leadership and Management* 18, 347–57.

National Foundation for Educational Research (2000a) *Evaluation of the National Professional Qualification for Headship*, www.nfer.ac.uk/risheets/pdq/htm.

National Foundation for Educational Research (2000b) *Evaluation of the National Professional Qualification for Headship: Phase 2*, www.nfer.ac.uk/risheets/pdk/htm.

Ouston, J. (1998a) 'Managing in turbulent times', in A. Gold and J. Evans, (1998) *Reflecting on School Management*, London: Falmer Press.

Ouston, J. (1998b) 'Introduction', *School Leadership and Management* 18 (3), 317–20.

Revell, P. (1998) 'Help or hurdle for Heads?' *Guardian Education*, 30 June.

Ribbins, P. (1999) 'Understanding leadership: developing headteachers', in T. Bush, L. Bell, R. Bolam, R. Glatter and P. Ribbins (eds) (1999) *Educational Management: Redefining Theory, Policy and Practice*, London: Paul Chapman.

Select Committee on Education and Employment (1998) *Education and Employment: Ninth Report*, 3 November, HC725-1, www.parliament.the-stationery-office.co.uk/pa/cm199798/cmselect/cmedue . . . /72508.ht

Smyth, J. and Shacklock, G. (1998) *Re-making Teaching: Ideology, Policy and Practice*, London: Routledge.

Teacher Training Agency (1997a) *National Standards for Headteachers*, London: TTA.

Teacher Training Agency (1997b) *Report on the Outcomes of the NPQH Trials, 1996–1997*, London: TTA.

Teacher Training Agency (1998) *Information for Candidates: Assessment Tasks for Key Area D*, January 1998, London: TTA.

Whitty, G., Power, S. and Halpin, D. (1997) *Devolution and Choice in Education: The School, the State, and the Market*, Buckingham: Open University Press.

Winkley, D. with Pascal, C. (1998) 'Developing a radical agenda', in C. Pascal and P. Ribbins (eds) (1998) *Understanding Primary Headteachers*, London: Cassell.

Yeatman, A. (1994) 'Interpreting Contemporary Contractualism', inaugural professorial lecture, North Ryde NSW: Macquarie University, 25 October.

Yeatman, A. (1997) 'Contract, status and personhood', in G. Davis, B. Sullivan and A. Yeatman (eds) (1997) *The New Contractualism*, South Melbourne VCT: Macmillan.

Acknowledgements

I would like to acknowledge the professional friendship of the group of Deputy/Acting Heads both Mike Egerton and I worked with during 1997–8. Both Mike and I found the professional courage and commitment of these people to be inspiring and optimistic for the future of schools.

13 Reforming teachers' pay
Crossing the threshold

Mel West

This chapter is organised in four sections. The first section summarises the government's current proposals for the introduction of a performance-related element within teachers' pay as part of a wide series of reforms aimed at establishing performance management schemes in schools. These proposals, though well advanced, have fallen foul of the requirement to engage in appropriate consultation with interested parties before implementation, and were not introduced in September 2000 as planned. However, the Secretary of State for Education has reaffirmed his determination to introduce them as soon as possible and it is likely that they will substantially be implemented in due course. The second section examines the arguments for reform of existing arrangements and salary structures that have emerged in recent years.

Since many of the proposals currently on the table have already been introduced in parts of the United States, the third section briefly reviews the development of performance-related pay (PRP) schemes there over the past fifteen years. It focuses on the advantages and benefits claimed for such schemes, and looks at the contexts in which performance-related pay is said to 'work'. The final section puts forward a critique of such developments, considering some of the anxieties that performance-related pay schemes have created amongst educationalists in the United States, and offers some comments on the prospects of successful implementation in England and Wales.

The proposals for England and Wales

The 1998 Green Paper sets out a strategy for improving standards through 'modernising' the teaching profession. Central to the process of modernisation is a fundamental reform of the teacher pay system: 'a modern pay system should attract and retain sufficient people of the right calibre, reward good performance, improve career progression and enable the best teachers to gain high rewards' (DfEE 1998: Chapter 3: 31). Few would argue with these sentiments. The problems are not new – annual reports of the School Teachers' Review Body from the mid-1980s to the mid-1990s return to the themes of teacher recruitment, teacher retention and teacher motivation. Nor is the desire to reform the pay system, and specifically to incorporate within it an element that is merit or performance-related. In 1993 this body observed that 'It was made clear that, in the Secretary of State's view, performance-related pay should operate in all schools on an individual teacher basis . . .' (School Teachers' Review Body 1993: 43).

However, the proposals set out in the Green Paper, and subsequently enlarged upon in DfEE (1999), offer a much more detailed picture of how reform will be carried out than we had seen previously. And, in detailing its proposals, the government goes beyond the uncontentious – that the salary levels of teachers are an inadequate reward for the skills and commitment of many of those working in our schools and are consequently unlikely to attract into the profession the quality of entrants it looks for in the future – and tackle the controversial – introducing performance-related pay as a remedy.

The proposals outline four main developments in the way teacher salaries are determined, together with the promise that school governing bodies will increasingly be held accountable for ensuring that these developments are implemented in ways that are transparent, consistent and reflect the actual budgets available. The four key proposals begin with the introduction of a performance 'threshold' – determined only indirectly by performance and substantially by years of service (five to seven being the recommended range). However, once this threshold is reached teachers will be able to apply for a 'performance assessment'. Those who successfully come through the assessment procedure – the proposals suggest that the assessment process should be both internal and external, and take account of quality of teaching (to be judged on the basis of pupil outcomes), evidence of continuing commitment to professional development and assessment of the teacher against national standards – will cross the threshold. This would bring an immediate salary increase (up to 10 per cent) and also establish the teacher's eligibility for further increases, 'assigned on a combination of excellent performance and extra responsibility'.

The second major area of reform is teacher appraisal, which is to be made more rigorous and to be drawn on in 'decisions on the pay of individual teachers at all levels'. Dismissing the present appraisal arrangements as a 'pointless additional burden rather than an integral part of the school's management arrangements . . .', the Green Paper proposes new arrangements involving annual appraisals that take into account pupil progress and that lead to individual teacher targets, 'at least one of which should be directly linked to the school's pupil performance targets'. Third, there is the announcement of a School Performance Award Scheme. Unlike threshold and additional merit awards, this would be available on a school rather than an individual basis, though it is proposed that the funds made available through the scheme are distributed amongst staff as non-consolidated bonuses. The Green Paper states that the government hopes that the fund will be able to 'reward a significant number of schools each year' – distributing these according to a series (as yet unidentified) of performance indicators. It is made clear that these indicators will not be based on raw pupil outcomes, so that potentially schools at all current levels of performance could benefit if appropriate improvement is demonstrated. Bonuses to staff will be distributed according to the fourth measure proposed – a performance management scheme at school level.

The proposals for this are enlarged in DfEE (1993). The framework moves forward the proposals set out in the Green Paper, in so far as it implies that the rigorous system of appraisal referred to will become an 'individual annual performance review in the context of the performance management scheme'. Thus the outcome of the performance review will have particular significance for the assessment of whether a teacher should pass the 'threshold', and also whether post-threshold pay points should be awarded.

The case for pay reform

There is general agreement that the current arrangements for teachers' pay are unsatisfactory, though there are different views about what needs to be done to improve them. It is true that teachers, like the majority of public sector workers, found their salary levels depressed during the 1980s and 1990s by the Conservative governments' squeeze on public spending. However, the present government has shown no interest in the kind of 'comparability' or 'catching up' exercise that boosted pay levels in similar circumstances in the 1970s, so a substantial, across-the-board increase can be ruled out. At the same time, it is clear that the recruitment and retention of suitably qualified staff, particularly in some subject areas, are unlikely to improve without significant restructuring of earnings expectations. Nor would across-the-board increases – however welcome to teachers – address the anomalies and contradictions within the present structure.

The Green Paper suggests that the 'main reason why the system has rewarded experience and responsibility but not performance is cultural'. But this is only partly true. Probably the failure to make more general use of the 'excellence' points available within the present arrangements can be attributed to cultural norms and the reluctance of headteachers to infringe them. But the wider problem is structural – it is the salary structures themselves that dictate the pattern of rewards. This pattern, which has at its core 'responsibility' points, reserves the higher salary levels for those teachers who take on managerial (and bureaucratic) roles beyond the classroom. It is simplistic to argue that this scheme has limited incentives to teachers to demonstrate excellence in the classroom – in fact it is precisely by demonstrating such excellence that many teachers have been able to receive managerial roles and the rewards they bring. The problem is rather that the present system tends to 'reward' teaching excellence by removing the teachers from the classroom (in secondary schools) or burdening them with additional roles and responsibilities (primary schools) that compete for time and energy previously devoted to preparing and supporting teaching. Reforming teachers' pay therefore needs to address the structures in which schools make decisions about individual pay levels, as well as the factors that influence the way decisions are made.

Kelley argues that recent years have seen major changes in the organisational needs of schools, and suggests that a new compensation structure is needed if schools are to create internal structures that can meet these needs and fulfil public expectations.

> Today's educational reforms expect teachers to acquire the professional expertise needed to teach a 'world class' curriculum well to the diverse students in schools. Today's teachers also are being asked to take on broader leadership roles in school management, organisation and instruction. And more than ever, today's teachers are being asked to focus on results – student achievement – in addition to education processes.
>
> (Kelley 1996, vol. 15: 22)

She looks at compensation reform in the private sector, pointing out that restructuring, decentralisation and results-orientated performance management initiatives have most often been accompanied by substantial changes in salary arrangements, and identifies three approaches to reward policies that offer potential to the education sector – skill-based pay, group-based performance awards and contingency pay.

Skill-based pay rewards employees for developing the skills needed to do their jobs. Though this could be considered an implicit element in current structures, in that teachers receive increments for additional years of service or 'experience', in practice such payments are only loosely connected with appropriate skill gains. Kelley suggests that a more sensible approach might be to reward teachers for developing particular areas of expertise that have been identified (at system or school level) as necessary to promote increased student achievement. She also distinguishes between skill-based and individual performance-based pay systems; a skill-based system would not create competition between teachers for a fixed level of rewards, but would reward all teachers for 'mastering and demonstrating knowledge and competencies valued by the school' (ibid.).

Group-based performance awards (or collective incentive plans) reward staff for working together towards defined common goals. Kelley argues that there is the potential for such schemes in education to provide 'an important symbolic focus on outcomes while avoiding the divisive aspects of individual performance incentives'. Such schemes could be applied at school level or to groups of teachers, encouraging initiative and creativity. Most often such schemes have been developed around efficiency targets – when groups of employees have found ways to meet goals at lower cost a proportion of the 'saving' is distributed among the group – but, in principle, they could be applied more widely, for example when student achievement targets are exceeded.

Contingency pay schemes also offer some interesting possibilities. Kelley cites the scheme at General Motors, where 10 per cent of employees' pay is 'held back', subject to certain criteria being met. Five per cent is contingent upon all employees spending at least five days of the working year in appropriate training programmes. The other 5 per cent is contingent upon the plant meeting certain quality and production targets. The implication is that an element of the teacher's reward package could be tied to participation in in-service training activities or on the school meeting specified pupil achievement targets.

Kelley puts these ideas forward as alternatives to merit-based approaches. Though each would create tighter links between teacher pay levels and pupil achievement levels, they would not create competition between teachers in the same school, and they are unlikely to promote any greater competitive tensions between schools than those already stimulated by the 1988 reform Act. Certainly they offer the possibility of substantial restructuring without a direct attack on the 'collegiality' that many researchers identify in successful school communities, and demonstrate that teachers' pay could be reformed in important ways without the imposition of simple pay-for-achievement schemes.

The development of performance-related pay schemes in the United States

In the United States a variety of PRP and merit pay schemes have been developed since the mid-1980s, and there are many who feel that such schemes have benefited both students and teachers. Robert Spillane, Superintendent of Fairfax Public Schools, Virginia, where 'Pay for Performance' was introduced in 1986, was an early advocate. Teacher appraisal is at the core of the Fairfax model, with a strong emphasis on the observation and assessment of classroom performance by professional 'curriculum specialists'. The resulting assessments contribute to the 'teacher evaluation' conducted by the school principal, who is responsible for interpreting and determining pay levels.

> This plan seeks a restructured pay scale to raise teachers' salaries across the board substantially, while using a performance evaluation system to reward excellent teachers. . . . The plan also provides special help to, withholds pay increases from, or terminates employment of teachers who do not meet set performance standards.
>
> (Spillane 1987: 38)

Granville County, North Carolina, was another school district early in adopting a 'bonus for performance' plan. The scheme allowed for a 'bonus' equal to 6 per cent of total salary to be awarded for meeting 'individual and school performance goals'. When, in 1991, North Carolina declared that no money was available for the annual teacher pay award, teachers in Granville County voted to retain their six-year-old scheme and the performance-related element, rather than having the bonus consolidated into a general salary payment. Robert Dorman, President of the North Carolina Public Schools Board, hailed this as 'a real cultural change that has taken place'. Perhaps it is just such a shift that the Green Paper has in mind when it expresses determination to create the conditions for cultural change in UK schools. Evaluating this scheme, Gursky (1992: 11) questioned the depth of the shift: 'Granville County's teachers are evaluated and rewarded based on their own goals and results, they are not competing against each other for a limited number of bonuses, as is often the case with merit pay.' But the same conditions could be said to apply, at least in part, to the government's current proposals. And, despite these reservations, Gursky also acknowledged that, during the six years of the scheme's operations, student performance increased steadily, drop-out rates improved and teacher retention had been much less of a problem.

A third early example is the Granite School District, Salt Lake City, which introduced merit pay in 1984. This scheme, based on a teacher assessment instrument known as AIM (Assessing Instructional Methods), was offered to some 3,500 teachers in ninety schools:

> When the AIM program began distributing bonuses based on performance only 900 teachers voluntarily chose to participate. By 1991 that number had increased to 2,100 (60 per cent). The number of teacher complaints about fairness and accuracy decreased from twenty-seven in 1986 to seven in 1990. Such figures indicate that the Granite School District merit pay program is proving to be very successful.
>
> (Farnsworth *et al*. 1991: 342)

Interestingly the Granite scheme did not reward teachers for completing in-service training related to their performance goals within the bonus programme, arguing that research (Wise *et al*. 1984) had shown that the teachers who are paid to engage in in-service training are less likely to develop in the ways called for than those who are not.

All three of these schemes claimed positive results and increases in teacher motivation. Typically, improvements in schooling outcomes were 'explained' through increased levels of professional understanding, peer involvement in review processes, clearer goals and opportunities for progression and decreased staff turnover. But underpinning these is a belief that rewarding 'excellence', defined by or in conjunction with the school system, creates a more reflective, more purposeful and more readily directed teaching force.

Building on these schemes, the 1990s saw performance-related programmes spread both geographically and in scope. The scheme introduced in Douglas County, Colorado, in 1994, for example, claims a number of objectives: achievement of the district's mission/core values for education; attracting, retaining and motivating appropriately qualified and experienced teachers; providing stable but improving teacher salaries; rewarding professional growth and development; assuring continuing teacher participation in the implementation and evaluation of the programme. In 1997 the president of the Colorado Federation of Teachers reported that:

> Our experience leads us to believe that, in fact, compensation systems can be designed and implemented as alternatives to the traditional salary schedule that more effectively reward teachers for various aspects of their performance. What is more, the design of these systems need not create competitive environments that discourage teachers from positive interaction, professional collaboration and cooperation, that benefits both teachers and students.
>
> (Hartman and Weil 1997: 6)

In 1998 the Consortium for Policy Research in Education based at the University of Wisconsin–Madison, which had been conducting research into school-based performance award schemes for several years, sponsored a research programme to take stock of what had been learned. This programme produced case studies of the origins, design and implementation of eight schemes selected to represent both state and district-level initiatives.[1] The case studies also provided details about the student achievement goals selected and how they are measured, the details of the reward systems, and the student achievement and programme evaluation results then available.

In a research report, the consortium identify common features in the programmes, and put forward a list of issues that it felt needed to be addressed before school-based performance rewards (SBPA) were introduced.

> Based on our analysis of the case, whether or not the designers of SBPA programs consciously identified these elements at the outset, it appears that they addressed each of these elements when developing an SBPA program. The design elements are as follows.
>
> 1   The dimensions of school performance: academic achievement and non-academic achievement, including subjects and/or grade levels.
> 2   Measuring the performance dimensions.
> 3   Calculating change or improvement.
> 4   Making the change calculations fair.
> 5   Determining the amount of change required to qualify for an award.
> 6   Setting levels and types of awards.
> 7   Funding the program.
> 8   Enabling conditions/supports for the program.
> 9   Planning for formative and summative evaluation of the program.
> 10 Developing an effective program design process (i.e. one that includes the elements listed above).
>
> (CPRE 1999)

The report discusses each of these elements in more detail. It acknowledges that how 'performance' is defined is the most important single issue, and also that this varies across the schemes. However, all schemes embrace some student achievement measures, though many also embrace non-cognitive 'outcomes', such as attendance, drop-out or continuation rates. Interestingly, little attention seems to be paid to areas of cognitive development – social and personal – that are harder to assess through simple, standardised tests. Student achievements that are measured, with mathematics and English featuring in every scheme, are weighted most heavily in assessing overall performance. The report concludes that the weighting of cognitive to non-cognitive outcomes is, on average, 80 per cent to 20 per cent.

The approaches to measurement also vary, from the simple application of national tests to relatively sophisticated systems for contextualising attendance or tracking students as they switch schools. However, the developing measurement technology seems focused around 'testable' or 'countable' performance, with little progress in relation to the difficult areas for assessment referred to above. Inevitably, the way measurement is approached is strongly influenced by the way performance change is to be calculated. The report suggests that there are essentially three basic approaches here, with some evidence of hybrids that combine elements from at least two approaches.

The basic approaches are comparison with standard, improvement to standard and value-added. *Comparison with standard* means setting performance standards for students in various subject areas and then developing (or identifying) tests that measure student performance against the standard. Typically, the 'change' required is then defined on the percentage of students required to meet or exceed that standard. This is the simplest approach, but it has obvious limitations – for example, the problems of variation in student intake characteristics, and the fact that for some schools/teachers the target may seem so remote that it is more likely to demoralise than to motivate. *Improvement to standard* approaches go some way to dealing with these limitations. Though grounded in the same process of target setting, specific goals are set for individual schools. Thus the progress expected towards the standard can be altered to reflect individual school circumstances, by requiring an improvement on the previous year's achievements or a reduction in the proportion of students not reaching a particular level. Though this model is perceived as offering a fairer and more purposeful context in some respects, it can create problems for schools where students already achieve at high levels – it may be harder to demonstrate continuing improvement, though teachers will feel that their performance is high.

The third approach is to base improvement calculation on a *value-added* model. Though this approach requires complex measurements of student achievement over time, the 'improvement' is calculated not as the difference between achievement levels at different points in time, but rather by looking for improvements beyond what could be 'expected'. Any surplus left over after the expected student gains have been eliminated is the extra 'value' added by the school, and it is this which can be used therefore as a school performance index. Though this approach offers some important advantages over the simple, comparative approaches – it can deal more effectively with differences in school populations, and, because it tracks students cohorts, does not require comparisons across cohorts – again, there are limitations. Tracking can be difficult and expensive; it is necessary to track students across schools; without frequent testing, it is hard to attribute value-added to particular schools or school years. There is also the problem that, when students leave school, whether for further education or employment, it is not how much value their schooling has added, but what levels of achievement have been reached, that is likely to influence their futures.

The report found not just variation in the basic approach to change calculation (four schemes essentially improvement on standard, three with significant value-added components, one comparison with standard), but also considerable variation within the approaches:

> it is clear that even though there are several conceptual models on which to base methods of change calculations, great variation exists even when the same conceptual model is used . . . The variation in the change calculation approach clearly supports the notion that reform efforts must be tailored to the context.
>
> (Odden *et al.* 1999: 54)

This is an interesting observation which may have implications for the development of the scheme in England and Wales. Of course, the United States has a large and decentralised educational system with wide variation in structures and practices. Nevertheless, this does raise questions about whether any one approach to the calculation of improvement in school performance is likely to prove satisfactory across a population of 25,000 schools.

Prospects for reform

Despite the generally positive tone of the Centre's report, there are many who feel that PRP schemes have achieved rather less than is claimed for them. Tharp (1991) found that such schemes were at odds with the collegial environment that schools seek to foster. Drawing on doubts about whether merit pay has actually proved to be a 'motivator', rather than a 'dissatisfier' (Austen and Gamson 1983), he questions whether it is capable of generating sustained commitment. He also echoes scepticism about the evidence supporting the link between pay and performance (Brown 1982), and its impact on individual creativity (Mortimer and McConnell 1988). He argues that it has not worked in educational settings because it is too mechanistic, assumes clarity and consensus of goals where there is none, presumes structures that are not apparent in schools, and is seen as imposing management control on teachers' professional decisions.

Dunwell (1991) highlights five 'myths' which, he argues, pervade studies of merit pay for teachers: that money produces more or better work; that performance-related rewards persuade highly qualified people to enter and stay in teaching; that performance-related pay stimulates constructive competition; that competition stimulates excellence; that teachers are significantly motivated by extrinsic rewards. He questions whether any system of performance-related pay can at best be more than a small part of an effective strategy to attract, sustain and retain talented teachers.

Reviewing the evidence from merit pay schemes and job enlargement schemes, Firestone (1991) finds that job enlargement is likely to be more effective in increasing levels of teacher motivation than performance-related pay. He argues that, in so far as merit pay offers teachers more money to do the same work, it is likely to result in the standardisation of practice. By contrast, job enlargement encourages creativity and enriches practice. However, Firestone also found that merit pay can provide intrinsic rewards if it is given in the form of *time* rather than money, arguing that time is a crucial factor in teacher access to intrinsic rewards. Against this, he also found that the identification of specific tasks with rewards led to non-linked tasks not being done at all.

Poston and Frase (1991) report that research findings are somewhat contradictory, and suggest that the failure of merit schemes may be linked with the way they have been conceived and implemented, rather than due to something inherent in the school system that renders merit schemes *per se* antithetical. They suggest that externally imposed schemes will fail to improve school performance, but that where there is:

- no legislative involvement or restrictive funding limit;
- strong teacher cooperation in planning the scheme;
- clear and realistic targets for teachers;
- freedom to determine locally the form in which rewards are paid;
- sound and accepted measures of teacher performance,

PRP schemes can increase the motivational level and outcomes of teachers.

There is some evidence that both incentive allowances and PRP schemes can improve teacher retention (Straker 1991), but Murnane and Olsen (1990) have argued that, unfortunately, these measures are least effective with those teachers we most want to retain. They found that less committed teachers were more likely to remain in the profession, but that the most lively and talented performers tend to move between jobs anyway.

The available evidence seems therefore rather mixed; some districts clearly felt that their decision to reward teachers according to individual performance had improved pupil achievement and, moreover, had certainly not alienated teachers or reduced morale. At the same time, there remain doubts about whether the outcomes claimed are actually linked with the implementation of PRP schemes or, if they are, whether they are achieved at the expense of other educational outcomes which, though they may be equally valuable, are harder to measure. Both these points are important. The former because there is a danger that gains stemming from restructuring the teaching force may be wrongly attributed to the performance-related element in pay, even though it is often a modest proportion of overall pay levels. The latter because, though declaring which 'outcomes' will be rewarded may indeed focus teacher attention and efforts, we need to be sure that the focus mandated in this way is not diluting the overall quality of pupil experience in more subtle ways that may not become apparent for several years.

These reservations nothwithstanding, there seems to be a consensus that PRP schemes are more likely to work when they are drawn up in close consultation with those (i.e. teachers) they affect, when there is general agreement about what the important outcomes of schooling are, and how they can be measured, when the relationships within schools and between schools and the system are characterised by mutual trust, and when they are seen as part of a wider investment in educational environments and teacher development. The present proposals for performance-related pay in the United Kingdom do not entirely fulfil these criteria but they do represent an imaginative and significant restructuring of teachers' pay arrangements, and there is reason to believe that there may be some level of success despite the way the proposals have been developed.

The threshold payment, for example, seems to meet criteria for acknowledging individual performance without creating unhealthy competition. Potentially, all teachers can qualify (though the number of years necessary before an application seems rather arbitrary), the reward on offer is substantial in relation to overall pay levels, and it is targeted on classroom expertise that all teachers would hope to develop. Despite some opposition from teacher associations to the way the scheme is to be introduced, it is likely to appeal to the majority of teachers as an appropriate acknowledgement of individual contribution within the context of wider collaborative effort. As long as the funding commitment is retained, it will not set teacher against teacher, and the rigour of the assessment process will help to establish its currency as an acknowledgement of teacher expertise.

The School Performance Awards seem unlikely to generate much excitement. The fact that 'performance' will be determined through retrospective judgements using 'criteria' that will inevitably involve subjective assessments about individual school circumstances and rates of improvement suggests that teachers are unlikely to make direct links between their own efforts and achievements and the possibility of 'qualifying' for an award. Consequently, it is unlikely that the existence of such a scheme will motivate teachers on a daily basis; though there may be some sense of 'recognition' generated for those judged to merit an award, the availability of such awards is unlikely to focus efforts before the event and, since the award is retrospective, equally unlikely to provide incentives after the event. Like the present listing of 'most improved schools', it is likely to be viewed as rather arbitrary by those not included, but may provide some satisfaction (or something that can be used to market the school) to those who are. Though there will be those who do not like this way of celebrating the achievements of particular schools, as an 'add-on' its effects are most likely to be neutral and may in some cases and for a short period of time be positive. It is difficult to see how not qualifying for such an award could adversely affect teacher attitudes or performance levels.

The merit awards to be introduced for some teachers above the threshold are likely to prove more controversial. The Green Paper acknowledges that there has been great reluctance to implement existing pay points for teacher excellence, and calls for 'cultural' change, but this may be difficult to achieve. The fact that merit awards can be given for a combination of 'excellent performance and extra responsibility' also leaves open the relative importance to be attached to each. Past experience suggests that schools will continue to be reluctant to associate pay directly with an assessment of teaching contribution, as measured by pupil outcomes, rather than teaching skills or competence, judged by 'professional' standards. Consequently the temptation will be to allocate additional merit increments for contributions to the management or coordination of teaching efforts rather than for teaching itself.

Of course, if the performance management scheme can be made to bite at school level, the resurrection of appraisal as an annual performance review that requires pupil achievement targets to be set and monitored will provide information about individual teacher performance that has not been systematically reviewed previously. However, schools are well aware of pupil achievement levels, and already set targets and monitor for them. And success in the classroom is already one of the major determinants of progression, and hence pay levels, though through a promotion system that perhaps needs to be re-examined. If performance management is to bring about a clearer focus when such decisions are made, all well and good. But the experience from the United States suggests that such a focus will be more constructive only if it is carefully contextualised to reflect the variation within and between schools, and approached sensitively and in a consultative and supportive manner. Any attempt to standardise targets will be construed as unfair, and may militate against the school's capacity to allocate teachers and teaching groups in the overall interests of the school community. This can lead to the unhelpful competition and 'squeezing' and 'creaming' practices that have been observed in some of the US schemes.

Nevertheless, there are some new and exciting elements in the government's proposals, though a second and even third threshold would probably be preferable to the distribution of merit awards to the few. However, while legislation may be needed to kick-start the cultural revolution that the Green Paper seeks to bring about, we need to remember that legislation will not, of itself, improve pupil achievement levels. It is teachers, working with their skills and commitment in the classroom, that increase educational quality. We can look to the government to ensure that teachers are the best recruits, have the best training and support we can provide, and are appropriately rewarded for their efforts. But even the most exciting proposals are only a starting point. Because it is the teachers who must do the job, the legislators need to acknowledge that the framework they are offering is only a beginning and start to develop a closer dialogue with those whose efforts are needed to make it work.

Note

1 The eight schemes selected were those operating in Boston, Charlotte-Mecklenburg, Cincinnati, Dallas, Philadelphia and California, together with the Kentucky and North Carolina State schemes. The case studies are available on the CPRE-UW website at www.wcer.wisc.edu/cpre/teachercomp.

References

Austen, A. E. and Gamson, Z. F. (1983) *Academic Workplace: New Demands, Heightened Tensions*, Report No. 10, Columbia, MO: Association for the Study of Higher Education.

Brown, W. (1982) 'Merit pay in the university environment', *Journal of College and University Personnel* 33.

Department for Education and Employment (1998) *Teachers: Meeting the Challenge of Change*, London: HMSO.

Department for Education and Employment *Performance Management Framework for Teachers*, London: DfEE.

Dunwell, R. (1991) 'Merit, motivation and mythology', *Educational Considerations* 18 (2).

Farnsworth, B., Debenham, J. and Smith, G. (1991) 'Designing and implementing a successful merit pay program for teachers', *Phi Delta Kappan* 73 (4).

Firestone, W. A. (1991) 'Merit pay and job enlargement as reforms', *Educational Evaluation and Policy Analysis* 13 (3).

Gursky, D. (1992) 'Not without merit', *Teacher Magazine* 3 (7).

Hartman, D. B. and Weil, R. (1987) *Developing a Performance Pay Plan for Teachers: A Process, not an Event*, American Federation of Teachers, Washington, DC.

Kelly, C. (1996) 'A new teacher-pay system could better support reform', *Education Week*, 21 February.

Mortimer, C. and McConnell, J. (1988) *Understanding Human Behaviour*, New York: Holt, Rinehart and Winston.

Murnane, R. and Olsen, R. (1990) 'The effects of salaries and opportunity costs on length of stay in teaching', *Journal of Human Resources* 25 (1).

Odden, A. and Kelley, C. (1995) *Reinventing Teacher Compensation Systems*, Madison WI: CPRE, University of Wisconsin–Madison.

Odden, A., Kellor, E., Heneman, H. and Milanowski, A. (1999) *School-based Performance Awards: Redesign and Administration Issues synthesised from Eight Programs*, Madison WI: CPRE, University of Wisconsin–Madison.

Poston, W. and Frase, L. (1991) 'Alternative compensation programs for teachers', *Phi Delta Kappan* 73 (4).

School Teachers' Review Body (1993) *Second Report*, London: HMSO.

Spillane, R. (1987) 'What one school system is doing to professionalize teaching', *School Administrator* 44 (2).

Straker, N. (1991) 'Teacher supply in the 1990s: an analysis of current developments', in G. Grace and M. Lawn (eds) (1991) 'Teacher Supply and Teacher Quality: issues for the 1990s', *Multilingual Matters*, Clevedon.

Tharp, J. (1991) 'When merit pay fails: searching for an alternative', *NAPSA Journal* 29 (1).

14 'Modernising' LEAs

A changing framework of values

Valerie Hannon

In education, as in other areas of social policy, the sense of change and renewed energy as a result of the 1997 election was almost palpable. On 2 May 1997 I opened a training conference for a cluster of Derbyshire schools.The mood among the teachers (many, perhaps most, of whom I am sure were politically unaffiliated) was extraordinary. They clearly felt that, in schools, things really could only get better. The new government took power in an atmosphere of raised expectations and great goodwill.

The energy and drive which New Labour brought to implementing its education agenda were reflected in the language its spokespersons employed. It was to be a 'crusade'. There would be a 'drive' to raise standards. There would be 'zero tolerance' of failure. These metaphors signalled that there would be little time for negotiation, and even less for dissenters – or 'whinging cynics' as they later became. New Labour declared it would 'hit the ground running' in education, and the first of the new government's White Papers was indeed on education. A critical issue for New Labour was what to do with the Local Education Authorities (LEAs): recruit, redeem and reinvent them after the Tory onslaught? Or relegate them to a variety of subservient roles, on strict probation?

Three years into what New Labour clearly plans to be a ten-year programme, it is possible to assess the impact of its policies upon the LEAs. The purpose of doing so is not, yet again, to rehearse the tired will-they-won't-they-survive debate. That is, after all, a secondary issue in comparison with the overall challenge the government has set itself. This is nothing less, according to the rhetoric, than to create a 'world class education service' and a learning society. In contributing to a three-year retrospective from an LEA perspective, what is of most importance is not whether policies thus far will serve in the longer term to aggrandise or eliminate LEAs. Appraisal from an LEA frame of reference suggests that those policies should be evaluated, in part at least, according to the set of values which gave rise to the LEAs in the first place, and which the best have tried to demonstrate and realise in their short history. What are or were those values? Among those which animated the architects of the 1902 Education Act, which created the LEAs, *coherence* and *cohesion* certainly played a major part. The patchy provision and inequalities in education across the country became unacceptable. The LEAs were created to turn the chaotic and random educational provision into something approaching a regulated and coherent service whilst retaining the benefits of a local response. More recently the Widdicombe report (1986) described the three pillars of local government as *pluralism, participation* and local *responsiveness*. In their history LEAs have invented new institutions and methods demonstrating their central concern with advancing and deepening *achievement*. And they have been prominent in identifying the needs of disadvantaged groups and seeking new ways to meet them.

In the space available it is impossible adequately to assess New Labour's programme in respect of all these. I propose to take the three which strike me as the most important and relevant in today's circumstances. These are pluralism, achievement, and equality of opportunity.

New Labour has claimed that it wants to be judged (as it says it will judge the rest of the service) on outcomes. However, it is values that determine which outcomes are to be judged important (and translated into 'targets') and which are not. What gets put in or left out, and why? That depends upon how big the vision is, and who is allowed to contribute to it.

The evolution of policy: from opposition to government

Three slogans, or motifs, will in the future capture Labour's education policy in this period in its history. 'Education, education, education' staked the claim to give it priority. 'Standards, not structures' purported to focus on the important ends, not the means. 'What works' signalled a new pragmatism, which would base decision and action on evidence of success, irrespective of ideological pedigree.

The latter in particular resolved the conflict which the transition from old to New Labour had to deal with. Out of office, Labour had opposed the stripping away of local authority powers, the introduction of the market into education and the fragmentation and differentiation of schools, especially in the policy of grant-maintained status. To occupy the centre ground, New Labour needed to lose its identification with perceived 'producer power'. The shift in emphasis and focus can be traced in its sequence of Green and White Papers concerning schooling (Labour Part 1994; DfEE 1997a, b). Labour sought to identify itself increasingly with 'standards', a concept as difficult to attack as it was slippery to define. This distanced it from the image of a Labour Party in the pockets of the unions and the LEAs. To distinguish it from the Conservatives (since criticism was emerging that their education policies were indistinguishable) New Labour adopted an agnostic view of LEAs and their future. The end ('standards') was all. The means, and the significant players and partners, were immaterial. Later, this would be incorporated into a philosophy of 'the Third Way'.

Ironically, the first major piece of New Labour education legislation was almost entirely concerned with structures. This is not surprising, since the reality is that the right structures are needed to create the conditions for the improvements sought.

Pluralism in retreat?

One casualty of a 'crusading', 'driven' government is pluralism. By this I mean a system in which checks and balances exist, and local diversity is acknowledged and respected. Maurice Kogan (1999: 59) puts it thus:

> The key issue is whether educational policy and practice should be determined according to central norms and values, on the grounds that only central government can read off the needs of society at large and the economy, or by those elected to analyse local wants and needs and convert them into activities, or by the professionals in the schools, or by client groups. If we accept the national, local community, teachers and their clients all have a part to play in value setting and in choice of educational content, we have to look to a negotiated order and exchange, not an imposed order.

Kogan describes New Labour's approach as a kind of 'tone deafness' to the perspectives of other 'prime actors'.

Is this fair? The School Standards and Framework Act 1998 was to express the new settlement through which standards would be 'driven' up. A new duty was laid upon LEAs to improve standards in schools. Some commentators have interpreted this as a formal acknowledgement of a new role. Indeed, the spokesperson for the LEAs was enthusiastic:

> In meetings with Government Ministers and their advisers, I have had confirmed the important role local government has in *implementing their educational agenda*. The Local Government Association has persuaded the government to place a duty on LEAs to raise standards and it is by that ambitious goal that LEAs *will be judged*.
>
> (Lane 1998, my italics)

In his welcome Lane distils the essence of the relationship created by central government with local government. It is that of local delivery agents holding a temporary contract. Tony Blair underlined this message in his pamphlet on modernising local government. Although 'at its best, local government is brilliant', he went on to say, 'there has to be change . . . the current position is not sustainable. It is getting in the way of the government achieving its objectives.' And, addressing local government in general, he said, 'If you accept this challenge . . . you can look forward to an enhanced role and new powers . . . If you are unwilling or unable to work to the modern agenda, then the government will have to look to other partners to take on your role' (1998). Local education authorities in effect now operate under *direction*, *licence* and *scrutiny*.

Direction

The LEAs are the key delivery agents for the government's national education strategies. They are directed to employ the literacy and numeracy consultants who are ensuring these respective strategies are implemented in the schools. Government has set each LEA targets for literacy and numeracy for 2002 which they are expected to achieve (although it is acknowledged that only the schools can do this).

Similarly LEAs have been directed to achieve targets in relation to attendance and exclusion (although a number had already chosen to prioritise this work voluntarily). National and LEA-level targets have now been set for achievement at specified levels at the end of Key Stage 4. It is not yet clear what is to be the consequence of any failure to meet them.

A range of government initiatives is being delivered through the agency of local authorities at the behest of the government, including some which are very large indeed – for example, the National Grid for Learning and the Key Stage 1 Class Size Initiative. So what, if the initiative is good? The KS1 class size example is a perfect illustration of the extent to which the centralist decision to achieve a fixed, predetermined outcome – no child of 7 or under in a class over thirty – is leading to unintended outcomes which a more flexible, locally informed approach might have avoided. These outcomes include many more mixed-age classes, an increase in overcapacity (or 'surplus places') and wasted money on unnecessary capital projects. Had a dialogue been entered into on how to achieve the fundamental objectives of the policy, then it is certain that more creative solutions could have been found.

A further index of the tendency to control is to be found in the growth of hypothecated funding. The Standards Fund which in 1996–7 stood at around £300 million had, by 1999–2000, grown to a planned £900 million.

Perhaps, however, the clearest illustration of the directive approach towards LEAs is the requirement to focus on 'school improvement' – based on a narrow definition of what that constitutes. This must be expressed, under the School Standards and Framework Act, in each LEA's Education Development Plan – in effect, the LEA's licence to operate.

Licence

The requirement to produce, consult upon and submit for approval an Education Development Plan (EDP) underlines the contingent status of LEAs. Most had been using strategic planning techniques for some years. The new Act, however, creates a highly prescriptive framework within which the Education Development Plan is in effect the LEA's School Improvement Plan. The parameters are closely set by the DfEE. The structure is precisely defined: there is a set range for the number of 'priorities'; and these must include the National Strategies. Equally the process by which EDPs are to be produced indicates the nature of the new relationship. The DfEE Standards and

Effectiveness Unit (SEU) created by the new government recruited teams of advisers, managers and 'Regional Directors' (for the Literacy and Numeracy Strategies) whose task it is to oversee the new programmes. In effect, the role of the EDP advisers is to shape the plans in accordance with the required norms.

The LEAs protested that raising standards of achievement entailed a wider vision and a broader range of activities. This is true in two senses. First, the contraction of advisory services in line with prescriptions set out in the 1997 White Paper is beginning to be worrying. It has reached the point where curriculum specialisms, especially in the arts, have virtually disappeared from the advisory services of many LEAs (Hendy 1998). It must be a question as to where, in the future, specialist support to schools will be nurtured and sustained. Moreover the statutory 'Code of Practice on LEA–School Relations' (DfEE 1999a) further specifies and delimits the activities of advisory services – even to the point of defining how many visits to schools in the course of a year should be the norm (three, apparently). This is said to flow from a concept of school improvement based on challenge and support – with advisory service monitoring visits providing the former, and purchased services the latter. In reality it stemmed from the need to reassure the former grant-maintained sector. The then Minister for Standards (Stephen Byers) remarked to the committee scrutinising the relevant section of the Bill, 'there were concerns that [an LEA] might intervene and meddle in the day-to-day running and operation of individual schools. . . . Perhaps there will be an over-zealous LEA that wants to flex its muscles . . .' (Hansard, 3 March 1998, col. 795).

The controls are financial as well as procedural. The 'Fair Funding' arrangements (DfEE 1999b) ensure ever increasing devolution of funds to schools. The combined effect is to squeeze out the scope for nurturing, identifying, validating and disseminating good practice and innovation. These will not flourish without the appropriate support. Is the establishment of a website a good enough alternative?

Second, the narrow definition of activity deemed to contribute to school improvement focused on advisory service work, at the expense of other (primarily structural) activities. How can you ensure that all schools are good schools if some are structurally disadvantaged by unfair competition in a rigged market? Perhaps 'joined-up' thinking and planning was necessary. In due course the new government did acknowledge the need for infrastructural planning, and the fact that the LEAs were best placed to manage it. Incrementally, a series of other plans were required of LEAs, most of them statutory and subject to ministerial or DfEE approval. At the time of writing, these can be illustrated graphically as in Figure 14.1.

The plans shown are only those newly required by the government. The arrangement of these plans on the figure is mine, intended to demonstrate areas of overlap. This has been an *ex post facto* task, however, since LEAs have had to respond to an accumulating set of directives and requirements from various divisions within the DfEE pursuing Ministers' wishes to see

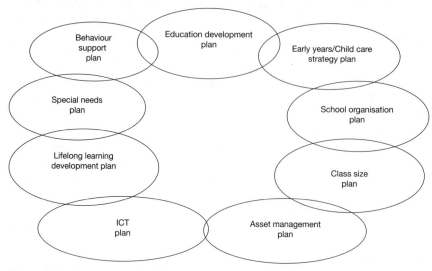

Figure 14.1 Plans required of local education authorities

action by LEAs on a number of fronts – but under licence. What is striking is the hole in the middle. It is arguable that the space is there for LEAs to pull together the growing number of disparate plans into a coherent shape through an overarching strategic vision (cf. Audit Commission 1998). In addition, the planning framework described above needs somehow to be located within the broader system of local 'performance plans' demanded of local government in the quest for a more corporate approach. In a sequence of six Green Papers and the White Paper *Modern Local Government: In Touch with the People* (DETR 1998), enacted in the Local government Act 1999, the Government required local authorities to consult and respond to local communities and develop coherent approaches to problems. The developing tension with the top-down approach in education went unremarked.

Scrutiny

Finally, the degree of control of LEAs is completed by the establishment of a scrutiny system *pour encourager les autres*. The system of LEA inspection (and potential intervention) became perhaps the defining characteristic of the relationship between central and local government. LEA inspection, invented by the Tories, was enthusiastically embraced by New Labour, primarily as its principal means of dealing with 'under-performing' LEAs. The School Standards and Framework Act gave the Secretary of State unprecedented new powers to intervene in cases where an LEA 'fails adequately to carry out its duties in relation to school education'. The joint OfStEd/Audit Commission system of LEA inspection, begun on a statutory basis in 1998, was accelerated by the government in 1999 such that by September 2001 all 150 LEAs will have been inspected. By spring 2000 two substantial contracts for the outsourcing of LEA services had been let to the private sector (in Hackney and Islington) as a result of government intervention, and more were plainly set to follow. The School Standards Minister announced in November 1999 that she anticipated (it was unclear on what basis) fifteen 'major interventions' in failing LEAs.

So a major casualty of the 'drive' of New Labour has been the pluralism which characterised much educational advance in our history (Tomlinson 1993). it included a profoundly important contribution from the teaching profession itself. That too has been reduced. So far as local democracy in education is concerned, the scope for local discretion and choice has been reduced almost to the point of disappearance. The major choice which once confronted councillors (how much to spend on what) has also virtually evaporated. First, the government announced that it expected local authorities to 'passport' funding improvements through to schools, irrespective of other pressures – or risk criticism. Second, the Secretary of State adopted the power to limit, through capping, the amount councils plan to spend on central services such as special educational needs and access – formerly a matter for their discretion.

The New Labour project of 'modernising' local government has been described as a 'Jekyll and Hyde' approach (Reed 1998). Whilst conferring new duties and possibilities on local authorities, a battery of reserve powers has been assembled which, in the event of inadequate compliance with the prescribed agenda, could have a terminal effect on local democracy more generally.

Alongside this muting of the elected local voice in education there are new exhortations, or requirements, to construct local 'partnerships' where the LEA is one actor among a number. Among the many examples of these are: School Organisation Committees (to consider School Organisation Plans); Admissions Forums (to debate the admission arrangements of the plethora of school admissions authorities); Early Years and Child-care Partnerships (to co-ordinate multi-provider coverage and expansion); Strategic Lifelong Learning Partnerships (to seek some coherence in the chaotic post-16 sector) and (most high-profile) Education Action Zones. The stated intention is to involve all 'stakeholders' in devising local solutions (within set parameters) and resolving local conflicts. The private and voluntary sectors have an established place. Whether these new social forms of governance and decision making will be effective is unpredictable. Certainly they will be bureaucratic. But perhaps some experimentation was overdue.

Investing in equal opportunities

No assessment of New Labour in government should ignore the issue of how far its education policies redirected resources and attention towards the disadvantaged. Whilst fundamental redistribution was never on the agenda, the *public* system of education was deteriorating to the point where it was ceasing to be the choice of many of the middle classes. New Labour recognised the need to reinvest in the infrastructure of the public service. Acknowledging this, and beginning to address the scale of the deficit, has been immensely important to those who work in the service and those who use it. It is very difficult at this point, however, to assess how far action has matched the need. Thus far, financial settlements for local government have delivered very little real-terms improvement in the actual spending position of schools and other LEA services (particularly Adult and Youth). In any case, revenue funding levels for the school system had sunk so low that in the last year of their administration even the Tories began a modest improvement. The Comprehensive Spending Review of 1998, however, promised an average 5.1 per cent (5.7 per cent in SSA) real (cash) terms increase over the years 1999–2002. What will this mean?

The proportion of gross domestic product (GDP) allocated to education will increase from 4.8 per cent in 1996–7 to 5 per cent in 2001–2. However, all developed countries are increasing their investment in education. Analysis of government's published spending plans (Hale 1998) shows that:

- Inflation, increased pupil numbers and higher pay settlements will consume large proportions of the new resources.
- Significant sums of the 'new money' will be spent on central government projects (though a number of these do focus on equal opportunities, e.g. Sure Start, Excellence in Cities and the Ethnic Minorities Achievement Grant).
- The opportunity has not been seized to define a basic per-pupil spending entitlement across all LEAs to even out the inequities of the flawed Standard Spending Assessment (SSA) system.

Against this are some important achievements and signals. The government has:

- eliminated outside toilets from all schools;
- established 'New Deal' capital spending on schools to address the worst of the decrepit building stock;
- diverted money (from the assisted places scheme and elsewhere) to create smaller classes in the early years (notwithstanding the caveats set out above);
- expanded early years provision, with increased funding for 3 and 4 year olds.

In one sense, New Labour would argue, a central thrust of its education project is directed at equal opportunities, since its 'standards agenda' is an attack on underachievement. The focus of action has been on 'underperformance' (of teachers, of schools, of LEAs): linkages with poverty have not been closely examined. No serious efforts at redistribution of resources have occurred. The flagship policy which the government has adopted to address the issue of educational disadvantage is that of Education Action Zones. The study of the evolution of this idea is fascinating. From a concept which focused on schools in 'challenging circumstances', it became one which sought to create testbeds for new ideas (in pedagogy, governance and management). The initiative was driven through at great speed. Learning from previous research (for example, on the Education Priority Areas of the 1970s) was not apparent. Partnerships bidding to run zones were expected to tackle deep-seated and intractable problems, and they were given some confusing messages. They were expected to be, at one and the same time, 'creative, flexible, innovative and safe' (Riley *et al.* 1998).

The most notable of all New Labour's initiatives in relation to equal opportunities addresses 'social exclusion'. Here the government deserves immense credit in bringing to the fore the problems of those whom the education service (along with many others) fails, and whose problems have been unnamed and unprioritised for too long. The effort to address them is authentic and serious. New Labour's policies are requiring those at local level to work together more effectively and give thought to new approaches. It is a disgrace that too many local authorities held little information and had poor coordination of services to groups such as Children Looked After and the permanently excluded.

Widening the vision

Since the initial focus on schools at its election to government New Labour has begun to widen the span of its thinking. Three years is but a short time in government, and it hardly seems reasonable to criticise: yet, from the LEA perspective, the determined focus on school improvement and somewhat narrow definitions of 'achievement' had initially led to some tunnel vision. Now there appears to be some recognition that creating a learning society (if that is to be a meaningful aspiration) entails not just considering the learning which goes on outside school, in families and throughout life. It also points to the need to have inclusive conceptions of 'achievement'. The work of many LEAs was once informed by that vision.

New Labour, in its second year of office, turned its attention to these connections. Major new advisory groups were convened to consider broader concepts of achievement than had been the focus of the powerful Standards Task Force (the first group external to the DfEE assembled to advise the Secretary of State). Advisory groups on Citizenship and on Creative and Cultural Education were asked to report on aspects of learning not usually associated with the 'standards' agenda. Other committees and groups followed on the themes of Sustainability and on Personal, Social and Health education. The lifelong learning White Paper (DfEE 1999c), built on the work of the National Advisory Group for Continuing Education and Lifelong Learning, looked beyond schools (and indeed institutions) to consider what needed to be done to widen participation and extend achievement. The first audit of the Youth Service (1998) signalled a significant revival of interest in the purposes and possibilities of that undervalued service. And the coffers of the Lottery were raided to establish funding for significant developments in out-of-school learning and child care, 'summer universities', study support and residential opportunities.

Conclusion

There is no question but that the first years in office of the New Labour administration marked a further fundamental shift in recasting the roles of central and local government in education, and that a new constitutional settlement of the remaining anomalies and tensions would probably now be helpful. The changes may be spun as 'modernising' or criticised as centralising/controlling. To return to the values identified at the beginning of this chapter, an appraisal of New Labour after its full term – or possibly two terms – in office will be the time to judge whether gains in achievement and equality of opportunity outweigh the loss of pluralism.

References

Audit Commission (1998) *Changing Partners*, London: Audit Commission.

Blair, T. (1998) *Leading the Way: A new Vision for Local Government*, London: IPPR.

Byers, S. (1998) *School Standards and Framework Bill: Code of Practice on LEA–School Relations*, remarks made by the Minister of State for School Standards to the Commons Standing Committee examining the Bill (Hansard, 3 March 1998, col. 795).

Department for Education and Employment (1997a) *Diversity and Excellence*, London: HMSO.

Department for Education and Employment (1997b) *Excellence in Schools*, London: HMSO.

Department for Education and Employment (1998) *The Learning Age: A Renaissance for Britain*, London: HMSO.

Department for Education and Employment (1999a) *Code of Practice on LEA–School Relations*, London: HMSO.

Department for Education and Employment (1999b) *'Fair Funding': The Financing of Maintained Schools Regulations 1999*, London: HMSO.

Department for Education and Employment (1999c) *'Learning to Succeed': A New Framework for post-16 Learning*, London: HMSO.

Department of the Environment, Transport and the Regions (1998) *Modern Local Government: In Touch with the People*, London: HMSO.

Hale, R. (1998) 'Education: The Financial Framework', unpublished presentation to Joint Society of Education Officers/PricewaterhouseCoopers seminar, London.

Hendy, J. (1998) *Fourth Survey of LEA Advisory and Inspection Services*, Reading: EMIE/NFER.

Kogan, M. (1999) 'Myth: good education requires strong central direction', in B. O'Hagan (ed.) *Modern Educational Myths*, London: Kogan Page.

Labour Party (1994) *Opening Doors to a Learning Society*, London: Labour Party.

Lane, G. (1998) 'The new and exciting role of LEAs', *Education Review* 12 (1), 10–12.

National Youth Agency/Department for Education and Employment (1998) *England's Youth Service: The 1998 Audit*, London: HMSO.

Reed, D. (1998) *The Local Government White Papers: An Analysis*, London: Local Government Information Unit.

Riley, K. and Skelcher, C. (1998) *Local Education Authorities: A School's Service or a Local Authority Service?* London: Local Government Management Board.

Riley, K., Watling, R., Rowles, D. and Hopkins, D. (1998) *Some Lessons learned from the first Wave of Education Action Zones*, London: Education Network.

Tomlinson, J. (1993) *The Control of Education*, London: Cassell.

Widdicombe report (1986) *The Conduct of Local Authority Business*, Cmnd 9797, London: HMSO.

Acknowledgements

I should like to thank Margaret Maden, Peter Mortimore and Peter Housden for their comments on a draft of this chapter.

Part V

Rethinking the roles and realities of educational research

15 Revitalising educational research

Past lessons and future prospects

David H. Hargreaves

> In public policy making, many suppliers and users of social research are dissatisfied, the former because they are not listened to, the latter because they do not hear much they want to hear.
>
> Lindblom and Cohen (1979: 1)

> Time and again we come across reports of social scientists complaining about not being listened to and policy makers complaining about being provided with too little worth listening to . . . Why is it that this supposed 'dialogue between producers and users of social research' so often degenerates into a series of loosely coupled monologues?
>
> Wittrock (1991: 335)

> If the purpose of educational research is . . . to inform educational decisions and educational actions, then our overall conclusion is that the actions and decisions of policy-makers and practitioners are insufficiently informed by research . . . The lack of an effective dialogue and understanding between researchers, policy-makers and practitioners is illustrated by the fact that while most of the researchers felt that the balance of the research agenda was too skewed towards policy and practice, the practitioners and policy-makers thought the opposite.
>
> Hillage *et al.* (1998: 46–8)

Doubtless the same is being said in some quarters to this day. Now, when educational research, both in the United Kingdom and internationally, has been under close scrutiny and vigorous debate, is there any hope of ending this disheartening and debilitating lack of dialogue through new relationships, cultures and structures out of which better research and better policy making might arise? It is too early to say: the New Labour government's policy on educational research emerges slowly but steadily. To appreciate the possibilities for, and constraints on, the future of UK educational research and its relation to policy and practice, we might usefully go back some fifty years to examine the views of some leading social scientists.

Tensions within the social sciences and their relation to policy and practice were neatly captured in Robert Lynd's influential *Knowledge for what?* (1939), published on the eve of the great advance in applied social science which occurred during the Second World War and after. Lynd distinguished between the *scholar*, who is at risk of becoming remote from life and disengaged from social problems, and the *technician*, who is in danger of accepting policy makers' definitions of social problems and their short-term solution. He himself was committed to policy application: he saw the purpose of social science as helping human beings continually to understand and rebuild their culture, and in this regard he identified himself with the founding fathers of social science. As Alvin Gouldner has insisted (1957: 94): 'Whatever their many differences, Marx, Durkheim and Freud share the applied social scientist's concern with bringing social science to bear on the problems and values of laymen with a view to remedying their disturbances.'

In the post-war period the tensions between 'pure' and 'applied' became more acutely felt. Edward Shils (1949) noted that it was now easier to chart the complex history of how university-based social science progressively distanced itself from the concern with application in favour of the academic preference to develop a coherent, autonomous corpus of knowledge. This estrangement from policy application was, moreover, compounded by a widespread commitment to model this corpus on the natural sciences and by the consequent need to engage in basic research which would yield the theories and generalisations out of which applications might be made. Whilst in this period some leading figures, notably Kurt Lewin, believed it possible to develop both good social scientific theory and powerful applications for social amelioration, his distinguished disciples conceded the intellectual difficulties of achieving both concurrently (e.g. Likert and Lippitt 1954).

By the 1970s, a generation later, and to the consternation of most, it was becoming apparent that the optimistic hopes of successful application of research to public policy were being dashed in most fields (Myrdal 1968; Orlans 1971, 1976; Fay 1975; Russell and Shore 1976; Rein 1976; Weiss 1977, and later, in education, Cohen and Garet 1975; Nisbet and Broadfoot 1980; Kallen *et al.* 1982; Husén and Kogan 1984; Finch 1984). The evidence was that the influence of research on policy was rare, partial and often indirect, a case of academics casting their research bread upon policy waters. The applied social scientist's conventional model of the relation between research and policy was evidently simplistic. First, it misrepresented the complexity of the relationship between policy maker and researcher in assuming that:

> policy makers who were crafting new policies would occasionally stumble across areas of ignorance. To remedy the ignorance, they would call upon the policy sciences, which would come up with the knowledge that enabled them to design wiser policy. It was assumed that policy actors would automatically use the new knowledge, that ensuring use

was simply a matter of communicating relevant information to the appropriate people. Needless to say, common experience was very different.

(Wagner *et al.* 1991: 18)

Second, the approach was often founded on a naive positivism:

Social science, the most recent of all the sciences, which deals with phenomena of the greatest complexity, tries to model itself on the oldest of the natural sciences, physics, which deals with phenomena of the least complexity . . . There is an assumption that social scientific theory has to have a high degree of generality, like, presumably, physics theory . . . The results are usually trivial from the point of view of theory, and much too abstract to be useful in practice . . . The proper model for this kind of work is clinical medicine or engineering . . . because in practice social science research is often pursuing action-oriented goals similar to those in clinical medicine or engineering . . . The question is not whether the clinical–engineering model should be adopted or not, but how it can be adopted most effectively.

(Ben-David 1973: 39–44)

Gouldner (1965: 19) noted an important difference between the *engineer* and the *clinician* as models for applied social scientists:

From an engineering standpoint the problems as formulated by the client are usually taken at face value; the engineer tends to assume that his client is willing to reveal the problems which actually beset him. The clinical sociologist, however, makes his own independent diagnosis of the client's problems. He assumes that the problems as formulated by the client may often have a defensive significance and may obscure, rather than reveal, the client's tensions. Not only does the clinician assume that the client may have some difficulty in formulating his own problems but he assumes, further, that such an inability may in some sense be motivated and that the client is not entirely willing to have these problems explored and remedied. The clinician, therefore, does not take his client's formulations at their face value, any more than he does comments made by an ordinary interviewee; but he does use them as points of departure in locating the client's latent problems.

Gouldner clearly favoured the clinician model, but in two penetrating essays (1962, 1965) on the issues of whether social science could be value-free and of the extent to which a social scientist is inevitably partisan, he brilliantly explored the subtlety of the choices and challenges facing researchers and their relation to policy. Whilst the pretension that it is not the business of social scientists to make value judgements could be used to justify acceptance of research contracts from clients with dubious ethical motives, it could also be used to defend themselves against engagement with the real world and research relevant to current human problems. Such researchers:

> feel impotent to contribute usefully to the solution of [society's] deepening problems, and even when they can, they fear that the terms of such an involvement require them to submit to a commercial debasement or narrow partisanship, rather than contributing to a truly public interest . . . Estranged from the larger world, they cannot escape except in fantasies of posthumous medals and by living huddled behind self-barricaded intellectual ghettoes . . . [under] the soothing illusion . . . that their exclusion from the larger society is a self-imposed duty . . .
>
> (1962: 208)

This approach appealed to many left-wing educationists who felt alienated and neglected during the Thatcher years; under New Labour the postmodern hermits defend themselves on the grounds that the policy environment remains unchanged. Before the last general election the whole question of bias in educational research was a claim made or assumed by politicians of the right against researchers of the left. When claims of left-wing partisanship came from a (right-wing) 'insider', Tooley (1998), commissioned by Chief Inspector Chris Woodhead, the charges could not be swept lightly aside. However, both Tooley's own approach and defensive responses by those whom he attacks as partisan (e.g. Hodkinson 1998; Atkinson 1998) display apparent ignorance of Gouldner's powerful and enduring insights. Elsewhere (Hargreaves 1996) I bewail the failure of educational research to be cumulative, a problem commonly acknowledged in other areas of social science (e.g. Shils 1949: 228; DiMaggio 1997: 192); equally worrying is the failure of educational researchers to acquire cumulative wisdom about our craft from our illustrious forebears.

Morris Janowitz (1970), following Zetterberg (1962), took a rather different line in distinguishing between the engineering and enlightenment models. The engineering model was, in this version, essentially positivistic: to develop and test a logico-deductive system of hypotheses, to identify specific cause-and-effect relations, and to collect empirical data on request to solve specific problems. The enlightenment model, by contrast, focuses on generating different kinds of knowledge and creating the intellectual conditions for problem solving, rather than the actual solving of problems, shaping the way people think in relation to policy rather than policy itself. Janowitz detected both models in operation among his contemporaries. Psychologists incline to the engineering model, but 'sociology is basically a teaching profession with implicit commitment to the enlightenment model . . . the requirements and pressures of the teacher move the sociologist in the direction of the enlightenment model' (p. 255).

Today the crude linear and positivistic model once assumed by many applied social scientists is patently naive. Janowitz himself inclined to the enlightenment model, for he could not envisage how an engineering model could be modified to take account of emerging complexities. The motives of policy makers have many sources and their decision making is based on a wider range of influences and interests than just relevant research. Policy makers usually have a great deal of knowledge about an issue or area in which policy is to be made and need to take account of a wide range of possible consequences, including political ones, of adopting a particular policy. In this sense social scientific knowledge deriving from research should never be seen as more than additional knowledge that serves as a supplement to, not a substitute for, the policy maker's existing knowledge (Lindblom and Cohen 1979).

The continuing failure of research to exert direct influence on policy led some social scientists, including educational researchers, to see indirect impact or 'enlightenment' as the *usual* relation between research and policy making. In Weiss's (1986: 37) words:

> it is not the findings of a single study nor even of a body of related studies that directly affect policy. Rather it is the concepts and their perspectives that social science research has engendered that permeate the policy-making process.

It is then but a short step to regarding enlightenment as a necessary or even desirable aim of research. Brown (1997: 84) has argued that:

> if the aim is for educational research to have some impact on practice, its ideas and findings have to change educators' *understandings*, and that will not be achieved overnight. It is only when the ideas enter into the common-sense discourse of communities' policy makers and practitioners that impact is achieved . . . In general, it will take five to ten years for such ideas to take hold and no one will remember, recognize or celebrate their research origins. Researchers have to be patient and accept that their rewards will come from intrinsic satisfaction that eventually their ideas have been taken up rather than from any public acclaim.

Research does indeed exert part of its influence through permeation of the wider climate of opinion. But this uncontentious fact can easily be taken as encouragement and consolation for the hermit stance in which the researcher shuns the messy world of short-term, practical problems in favour of penning intellectual obscurities masquerading as profundities whilst dreaming of academic recognition. Moreover, it cannot be assumed that when ideas percolate through to common sense the effect will be beneficent. Most social scientists in the field of education are paid primarily as teachers, not researchers. Until recently they exercised a monopoly over the intellectual basis of initial teacher training, and it is arguable that their attempts to 'enlighten' novice teachers with the ideas of, say, Piaget, Bernstein or Skinner, have led to distortions and illegitimate applications of these ideas and thus to untold damage on teachers' professional practices. Teaching theory to teachers is dangerous unless a sound body of empirical evidence to inform their routine practices accompanies it.

The extensive literature on the relation between social science research and social policy and practice often deals in too monolithic a conception both of research and of policy/practice. There are many different kinds of research directed at answering different kinds of questions; there are many different kinds of policy and ways of forming or implementing policy; and there are significant differences between policy and practice. In consequence, there is no single model that applies to all cases in every circumstance and for all time, nor could there ever be one. The implications of this lesson have yet to be adequately addressed in educational research and policy making.

If a fraction of the time and energy that the British Educational Research Association spent on defending educational research from criticism by Hargreaves (1996), Tooley (1998) and Hillage *et al.* (1998) had instead been devoted to working out how Bulmer's (1982) *six* kinds of applied social research or Wittrock's (1991) *eight* models could illuminate the very different ways that research relates to educational policy, depending on the nature of the problem, the circumstances of its being commissioned, and its eventual impact on the policy-making process, then relations between policy makers and researchers would be healthier and more productive. Problems which have hitherto been badly neglected by both sides, such as the tension between 'blue skies' and applied research, need to be openly debated. Researchers too often react to demands for better applied research by defending the importance of basic research and researchers' professional autonomy, but without tackling problems such as the appropriate balance between basic and applied research, the criteria by which basic research should be funded – and the simple fact that much educational research is neither genuinely basic nor usefully applied.

In this sense, the creation of a National Educational Research Forum, charged with developing a strategy for educational research, to help to shape its direction and coordinate programmes of work, is essential to revitalising educational research. Whilst such a forum has not been welcomed by all researchers – it was attacked by one as 'Stalinist centralisation' – its establishment, with a mixed membership of researchers and users, will stimulate the dialogue between researchers, policy makers and practitioners on which greater mutual understanding and cooperation depend. The complaints noted in the epigraphs at the opening of this chapter need to be brought to a rapid end, for only in a very different climate can the limitations of research be better understood, the factors that shape policy and practice be taken into account, and the potential social and professional value of educational research be most fully realised. It is a sad fact that disillusionment in the 1970s about the relations between research and policy never led to profitable discussion among the parties: mutual suspicion, defensiveness and even hostility and recrimination persist to this day. The Forum creates the conditions for orderly and regular multilateral debate and negotiation, helped by exchange among the parties of information, interests and intentions. The Forum is in my view a precondition of progress, and commitment and patience on all sides will be needed to make it a success.

But there is another element in the new government's approach which gives rise to optimism, namely its pragmatic approach to 'what works' and to the rapid dissemination of 'good practice' throughout the education service. This is highly compatible with an evidence-based approach to professional practice in education, to parallel what is happening in medicine (Hargreaves 1997). 'The time has come,' said the Minister with responsibility for educational research, 'to look forward and demonstrate a commitment to developing evidence-based policy and practice' (Clarke 1998). This orientation is guiding the most exciting opportunity for British educational research, the £12 million fund for research on teaching and learning, managed by the Economic and Social Research Council, according to whose chief executive, Professor Amann (1998), 'This new programme will be seeking to develop evidence-based teaching showing what works best and why it does so.'

These developments are controversial precisely because the concept of evidence-based teaching is controversial among educational researchers. But the new ministerial policy towards research flows naturally from an important shift. Hitherto, discussions about the relationship between research and its application typically refer rather loosely to *policy* and *practice* as if the two were much the same. In one sense they are similar, for in both cases there is an attempt to give research a role in solving practical problems, which have three essential elements (Merton and Devereux 1971):

- a perceived discrepancy between an existing state of affairs and the goal of the individual or organisation;
- an expressed or felt need for adjustive activity or corrective action;
- a puzzle element or an awareness of ignorance or doubt about what to do.

In other ways the practical problems of policy and the practical problems of practice are very different. *Policy* problems usually mean major policy decisions by central government on large issues concerned with levels and types of resource allocation – decisions that, once taken, are difficult to undo. Problems of *practice* mostly refer to the relatively small-scale professional practices of teachers in schools and classrooms, which can usually be easily revised. More has been written about the difficulties of relating research to policy, but problems and limitations in this sphere do not necessarily pertain when research is applied to professional practice (or vice versa).

What is new under David Blunkett, as Secretary of State for Education and Employment, is that these two worlds are now conjoined, because government action, as in the Literacy and Numeracy Strategies, *is making professional practice the direct target of policy making.* In England and Wales policy makers were formerly limited, or limited themselves, mainly to decisions about the structure of the education service; the internal activities of what teachers did in classrooms, even the curriculum itself, were largely left to the discretion of teachers enjoying a high level of professional autonomy. Today a new link is being forged between what hitherto have been mainly distinct areas, and it marks an end to the convention by which politicians remain distant from classroom practice.

Policy makers' intervention in classroom activities will, I suspect, increase, especially if the national literacy and numeracy strategies are succeeding in raising the levels of students' measured achievement. Ministers now recognise that standards of teaching and learning are unlikely to be raised by policy action that never penetrates classrooms. This is less dangerous than it initially appears, as long as Ministers retain some distance by a pragmatic attention to 'what works' and by an acknowledgement that the discovery of 'what works' is more a matter of evidence, not just ideology or political preference. In both education and health the raising of professional standards is seen to entail political intervention in professional practice, and at such a time a sound evidence base for professional practice is a vital protection.

We should not, perhaps, use the term 'evidence-based', for it is something of a misnomer even in medicine. Decisions are not based on research evidence alone; the evidence is but one (albeit important) element in decision making, which also has to take into account a range of unique contextual factors (Sackett *et al.* 1996). To avoid any implication that teachers or educational policy makers should not, in making decisions, take account of (1) the quality and strength of the research evidence and (2) the contextual factors relating to that decision, we should, I suggest, speak of evidence-*informed*, not evidence-based, policy or practice (cf. Brown *et al.* 1998). Policy makers cannot always postpone their decision making until the evidence is in; and even when it is, they are constrained in their decisions by much other knowledge in their possession and by many factors concerned with public perceptions and political consequences. Although teachers are also constrained by other knowledge, particularly their existing craft knowledge, they enjoy far greater autonomy in making their decisions and are more free to experiment with and modify new ideas suggested by research: the error element of their professional trial-and-error learning is rarely consequential. We need to turn teachers' habitual classroom tinkerings into a much more trustworthy form of research evidence (Hargreaves 1998).

The implications of both the government's current orientation to educational research and my estimation of it may now be illustrated. This government, like its predecessors, takes the relations between home and school as an important arena for raising standards. Since Douglas's (1964) study it has been known that parental support of children's learning has beneficial effects on their achievements in school. Since then, literally hundreds of ideas and so-called 'good practices' have been urged on teachers.

When teachers are overstretched, both policy makers and practitioners would benefit from answers to the following questions:

- What is the effect size of home–school partnerships on children's achievement?
- Which of the many ways in which partnerships could be created have the greatest effect size?
- Which combination of two or three ways of building such partnerships are most likely to be effective and in what circumstances?
- Which combinations have the highest leverage (that is, have greatest effect for the least input level from teachers)?

These are demanding questions, but if we had evidence, even in a provisional form, on some of them, government policy, thus evidence-informed, would be far more supportive of, and acceptable to, the teachers who implement the policies. In fact the guidelines on homework, issued in November 1998, are evidence-informed, and contain an appendix summarising relevant research evidence. The guidance on home–school agreements, issued at the same time, contains no such appendix, because relevant evidence is lacking.

Providing better evidence for policy issues is not easy. Even with a significant change of emphasis and direction from researchers, no simple recipes for policy would emerge. But none is needed, since the object is to inform, not determine, policy and practice. Meeting the demands will entail more experimental studies, and for some problems a series of randomised controlled trials on which a meta-analysis could be based (Glass *et al.* 1981; Kulik and Kulik 1989; Maynard and Chalmers 1997). This does not mean a return to the abandoned, simplistic notions of science or a tidy, linear relationship between research and policy, but rather:

- Readiness to investigate some 'reasonably stable relationships' without the deductive logic of classical positivism (Miles and Huberman 1994: 4), combined with:
- Recognition that scientific conclusiveness is a matter of degree (Lindblom and Cohen 1979: 42), and so:
- Understanding that discovering 'what works' is not a search for universal laws but an uncovering of ever changing practices through a research process that is itself endless, since the inevitable exceptions to 'what works' become the basis of further research, and
- Commitment to making research evidence about 'what works' both cumulative and readily available in accessible forms to those who can benefit from it, through an educational equivalent to the Cochrane collaboration in medicine.

The government has started to implement the recommendations of the Hillage report, has established a National Educational Research Forum and several specialist research centres, is increasing the budget devoted to educational research, and, following the pioneering work of the Teacher Training Agency, is directly funding more schools and practising teachers to engage in educational R&D, leading to new forms of partnership between schools and researchers in universities (Hargreaves 1998). It is an act of faith that, following the critical reviews, the quality and relevance of educational research will be improved; it is thus a total rejection of Chief Inspector Chris Woodhead's contention that all educational research is a waste of money. The change of direction in government policy does, however, leave researchers with some issues to resolve. An outstanding example is the place of 'blue skies' or basic research. Researchers often appeal to this as a defence against pressure for more applied research. The terms 'blue skies' and 'basic' cover a range of possibilities, including:

- research that is in some sense fundamental and which cannot be expected to lead to applications in the near future, but perhaps eventually;
- research that will never itself lead to application, but nevertheless may move the research field forward, e.g. the development of theory;
- research that will not lead to applications but will influence the field of policy and practice by changing the agenda or the concepts in which an issue is understood, e.g. critiques of policy and practice;
- research that is of clear value in its own right but by definition is unlikely to have much direct bearing on policy or practice, e.g. research in the history of education.

Educational researchers should spend more time debating how much of the total research effort and budget should be devoted to basic and applied research – my own view is that most of the basic research will be done in mainstream social science departments rather than Schools of Education – to achieve a balance which can justify the £60 million to £70 million currently spent on educational research. What is surely unacceptable is the use of the terms 'basic' and 'blue skies' by academics to defend their right to choose topics that interest them, entirely unfettered by legitimate demands for wider accountability for their use of public money. A healthy research community continually debates the criteria of 'good' research – and involves their funding bodies and 'user' communities in those deliberations.

Educational researchers begin the new century with a level of government support, both moral and financial, far beyond their expectations. If the research community contributes positively to the emergent policy on educational research, then in a decade's time it may be possible to report that the epigraphs at the head of this chapter have been consigned to history. Educational research, educational policy making and the professional practice of teachers will all be the better for it.

References

Amann, R. (1998) reported in *Social Sciences*, 39, 1.

Atkinson, E. (1998) 'Partisan research and the pursuit of truth', *Research Intelligence*, 66, 18–19.

Ben-David, J. (1973) 'How to organize research in the social sciences', *Daedalus* 102 (2), 39–51.

Brown, M., Askew, M., Baker, D., Denvir, H., and Millett, A. (1998) 'Is the National Numeracy Strategy research-based?' *British Journal of Educational Studies* 46, 362–85.

Brown, S. (1997) respondent comment, in: S. Hegarty (ed.) *The Role of Research in Mature Education Systems*, Slough: National Foundation for Educational Research.

Bulmer, M. (1982) *The Uses of Social Research*, London: Allen & Unwin.

Clarke, C. (1998) 'Resurrecting research to raise standards', *Social Sciences* 40, 2.

Cohen, D. K. and Garet, M. S. (1975) 'Reforming educational policy with applied social research', *Harvard Educational Review* 45 (1), 17–42.

DiMaggio, P. (1997) 'Epilogue: sociology as a discipline', in K. Erikson (ed.) *Sociological Visions*, Lanham MD: Rowman & Littlefield.

Douglas, J. W. B. (1964) *The Home and the School*, London: MacGibbon & Kee.

Fay, B. (1975) *Social Theory and Political Practice*, London: Allen & Unwin.

Finch, J. (1984) *Education as Social Policy*, London: Longman.

Glass, D. V., McGaw, B. and Smith, M. L. (1981) *Meta-analysis in Social Research*, London: Sage.

Gouldner, A. W. (1957) 'Theoretical requirement of the applied social science', *American Sociological Review* 22 (10), 92–102.

Gouldner, A. W. (1962) 'Anti-Minotaur: the myth of a value-free sociology', *Social Problems* 9, 199–213.

Gouldner, A. W. (1965) 'Explorations in applied social science', in A. W. Gouldner and S. M. Miller (eds) *Applied Sociology*, New York: Free Press.

Hargreaves, D. H. (1996) *Teaching as a Research-based Profession: Possibilities and Prospects*, London: Teacher Training Agency.

Hargreaves, D. H. (1997) 'In defence of evidence-based teaching', *British Educational Research Journal* 23, 405–19.

Hargreaves, D. H. (1998) *Creative Professionalism: the Role of Teachers in the Knowledge Society*, London: Demos.

Hillage, J., Pearson, R., Anderson, A. and Tamkin, P. (1998) *Excellence in Research in Schools*, London: Department for Education and Employment.

Hodkinson, P. (1998) 'Naiveté and bias in educational research', *Research Intelligence* 65, 16–17.

Husén, T. and Kogan, M. (1984) *Educational Research and Policy*, Oxford: Pergamon.

Janowitz, M. (1970) *Political Conflict*, Chicago IL: Quadrangle Books.

Kallen, D. B. P., Kosse, G. B., Wagenaar, H. C., Kloprogge, J. J. J. and Vorbeck, M. (eds) (1982) *Social Science Research and Public Policy Making*, London: NFER–Nelson.

Kulik, J. A. and Kulik, C. C. (1989) 'Meta-analysis in education', *International Journal of Educational Research* 13, 221–340.

Likert, R. and Lippitt, R. (1954) 'The utilization of social science', in L. Festinger and

D. Katz (eds) *Research Methods in the Behavioural Sciences*, London: Staples Press.

Lindblom, C. E. and Cohen, D. K. (1979) *Usable Knowledge*, New Haven CT: Yale University Press.

Lynd, R. S. (1939) *Knowledge for What?* Princeton NJ: Princeton University Press.

Maynard, A. and Chalmers, I. (1997) *Non-random Reflections on Health Services Research*, London: BMJ Publishing.

Merton, R. K. and Devereux, E. L. (1971) 'Practical problems and the use of social science', in I. L. Horowitz and C. Nanry (eds) *Sociological Realities*, New York: Harper & Row.

Miles, M. B. and Huberman, M. (1994) *Qualitative Data Analysis*, London: Sage.

Myrdal, G. (1968) 'The social sciences and their impact on society', in H. D. Stein (ed.) *Social Theory and Social Invention*, Cleveland OH: Case Western Reserve University Press.

Nisbet, J. and Broadfoot, P. (1980) *The Impact of Research on Policy and Practice in Education*, Aberdeen: Aberdeen University Press.

Orlands, H. (1971) 'Social science research policies in the United States', *Minerva* 9 (1), 7–31.

Orlans, H. (1976) 'The advocacy of social science in Europe and America', *Minerva* 14 (1), 6–32.

Rein, M. (1976) *Social Science and Public Policy*, Harmondsworth:, Penguin Books.

Russell, B. and Shore, A. (1976) 'Limitations on the governmental use of social science in the United States', *Minerva* 14 (4), 475–95.

Sackett, D. L., Rosenberg, W. M., Gray, J. A. M., Haynes, R. B. and Richardson, W. S. (1996) 'Evidence based medicine: what it is and what it isn't', *British Medical Journal* 312, 71–2.

Shils, E. (1949) 'Social science and social policy', *Philosophy of Science*, 16, 219–42.

Tooley, J. (1998) *Educational Research: a critique*, London: Office for Standards in Education.

Wagner, P., Weiss, C. H., Wittrock, B. and Wollman, H. (eds) (1991) *Social Sciences and Modern States*, Cambridge: Cambridge University Press.

Weiss, C. (1977) *Using Social Research in Public Policy Making*, Lexington MA: Lexington Books.

Weiss, C. (1986) 'The many meanings of research utilization', in M. Blumer (ed.) *Social Science and Social Policy*, London, Allen & Unwin.

Wittrock, B. (1991) 'Social knowledge and public policy: eight models of interaction', in P. Wagner, C. H. Weiss, B. Wittrock and H. Wollman (eds) *Social Sciences and Modern States*, Cambridge: Cambridge University Press.

Zetterberg, H. L. (1962) *Social Theory and Social Practice*, New York: Bedminster Press.

16 Restructuring educational research for the 'Third Way'?

John Elliott and Paul Doherty

Under the successive Conservative administrations of the 1980s and 1990s a somewhat piecemeal, but nonetheless neo-liberal, radical restructuring of educational provision took place. The educational 'reformers' adopted similar strategies: deficiencies were identified; blame was allocated; a 'cure' was prescribed. Ball (1997) has depicted the language which accompanied these reforms as the 'discourse of derision'. Stronach and MacLure (1997) point out that with each cycle of 'blame and cure' different professional groups were thrust under the spotlight. First it was teachers, then local education authorities, then teacher educators and now it is the turn of educational researchers. Could it be that New Labour is simply completing the unfinished business of the previous administration? What indications are there that their policy-making agenda represents a break with a neo-liberal agenda and is forging an authentic third way?

The neo-liberal agenda for educational reform

The neo-liberal reform agenda may be characterised quite simply as the subordination of educational policy to economic imperatives. Within the neo-liberal state the educational system merely functions as part of the economy to produce learning outcomes that have commodity value for the labour market. The role of the state is to guarantee these learning outcomes and the role of the school is to produce them.

The neo-liberal mechanisms for improving the commodity value of educational outcomes are associated with the market, namely competition (parental choice), transparency (performance indicators) and comparison (league tables). However, the educational policies of the Conservative government constructed a quasi-market rather than a free market. The latter would have implied a radical programme of privatisation and a degree of curriculum diversity between schools. Instead there was growing standardisation and centralisation – evidenced both in a national curriculum and in its assessment arrangements. New Labour therefore inherited a somewhat contested, ambiguous and incomplete neo-liberal project.

One could read the Prime Minister's post-election promise that he would place 'Education, education, education' at the centre of his government's agenda as indicative of his intention to continue the neo-liberal policies of the previous administration, albeit with greater ferocity. Education, it could be said, is one of the few levers left to the nation state as it struggles to exercise some control over the 'relentless' expansion of global capital. Indeed, the idea of a Third Way may simply be a case of government 'spin', permitting New Labour to appear committed to its traditional values while masking its impotence in the face of global capital.

School improvement and the restructuring of educational research under New Labour

New Labour appears to share at least two of the concerns of the neo-liberal right: the first is the improvement of standards in schools; the second is the discrediting of professional identities that stand in the way of that process. At the time of writing we are witnessing the continued discrediting of educational research and of sections of the research community (see Hillier *et al.* 1998; Tooley and Darby 1998). Researchers are accused of researching topics that are 'irrelevant', of communicating their findings in impenetrable 'theory-laden' jargon, and of being 'politically motivated'. The Secretary of State for Education feels free to pour scorn on research simply because he disagrees with its findings (Reeves 1999). These attacks would be tedious were they expressions of personal prejudice, but is not a much more insidious process taking place, one that seeks to redefine what education research can and cannot be, what educational researchers can and cannot do? Government policy appears to be based on the assumption that improving the commodity value of learning is the *sole* task of the research community. Hence the mechanisms of the educational market are left intact.

However, there is a subtle and significant departure in New Labour's approach: its insistence that any improvements in standards (in the commodity value of learning) should not be achieved at the expense of increased inequality; school improvement should be a socially inclusive process. Schools are therefore responsible for enhancing the nation's economic performance *and* for overcoming any negative effects of social exclusion (when high levels of social exclusion appear to correlate with unfettered capitalist economies). In relation to both responsibilities New Labour has cast educational researchers in the role of midwife. It is the task of educational research to produce evidence about how schools and teachers can improve the commodity value of learning for *all* students.

From a policy-making perspective the 'problem' with some research is that it points to the influence of factors outside the school on actions within it: school improvement is given a social dimension. Research may suggest the need for strong affirmative action in order to reduce social or educational exclusion by redistributing scarce resources to the point of need. To act on such research may require increased taxation, and that would limit the accumulation of capital, so affecting economic 'growth'. To act on such evidence may be to privilege egalitarian values over economic values, and this may explain the recent attacks on sociologically oriented educational research. The process of evidence production therefore falls under the spotlight and the desire to restructure research may indicate a desire to promote a single discourse of school improvement.

Restructuring educational research, in a form which will provide evidence of how schools and teachers can improve the commodity value of learning outcomes for all their students, adds a new and interesting component to the 'quality assurance' system in education. It enables the government to hold schools and teachers to account, whilst the government (which continues to profess social democratic values while embracing the logic of economic performativity) is 'let off the hook'. With the assistance of restructured educational research New Labour is able to rationalise a reduced commitment of resources to the just distribution of education as a social good. In exercising control over what counts as research and what counts as actionable research evidence it can have its cake and eat it.

A number of measures for restructuring educational research have already been put in place or are being entertained. The Teacher Training Agency (TTA) has been promoting the idea of teaching as an 'evidence-based profession' following Hargreaves's (1996) influential lecture. A national 'Teaching and Learning Research Initiative' has been launched by the Economic and Social Research Council (ESRC), with £15 million set aside from higher education funding for educational research. The Department for Education and Employment's (DfEE) Standards and Effectiveness Unit is undertaking the groundwork for establishing a national database for educational research that can be accessed by schools and teachers (along the lines of the Cochrane collaboration in the Medical Research field). The DfEE has also established a National Educational Research Forum to forge policies regarding the future direction of Educational Research. Finally, the Education panel of the 2001 Research Assessment Exercise (RAE) has been restructured to include 'user group' representation. A consistent thread running through these policy interventions is the emphasis on the practical utilisation of research findings. However, who gets to decide what is to count as useful evidence? Is it teachers or is it government?

Can we argue, then, that this latest cycle of 'blame and cure' is not simply business as usual but the realignment of research to a Third Way, one that seeks to improve the commodity value of learning *and* redress social disadvantage? However, it may be that the Third Way simply prevents the neo-liberal economic agenda from being disrupted or undermined by addressing social exclusion. The Third Way could be a neo-liberal educational agenda after all, containing an 'inclusive' dimension within its boundaries.

Education for social inclusion: Rawls, Stenhouse and 'New Labour'

The philosophical groundwork of New Labour's Third Way policy option was developed by John Rawls (1971: 62). In his liberal egalitarian *Theory of Justice* Rawls states that: 'All primary social goods – liberty and opportunity, income and wealth, and the basis of self-respect – should be distributed equally unless an unequal distribution of any or all of these goods is to the advantage of the least favoured.' His theory of justice balances the twin principles of *equality* and *difference*. Just as inequalities in social circumstances are a morally arbitrary basis for distributing social goods, so are inequalities in natural talents and endowments. Hence, all other things being equal, goods like education should be equally distributed. No one deserves a better education than others by virtue of their natural endowments (as a libertarian might argue). For Rawls the *only* basis for distributing social goods unequally is to benefit the least favoured. However, his principle of difference is not exactly the same as the egalitarian principle of redress. The latter implies a levelling out of opportunities, whereas the principle of difference may justify allocating educational resources in favour of the *better* endowed in order to improve the long-term expectation of the least favoured.

Rawls argues that 'the value of education should not only be assessed in terms of economic efficiency and social welfare' (p. 101). With respect to the distribution of education as a social good, it should not be defined entirely in terms of its commodity value. Equally, if not more, important is the role education plays in enabling people to enjoy the culture of their society and to take part in it as active citizens, providing them with a secure sense of self-worth. 'Enhanced self-esteem' and 'respect' are values that are central to Rawls's idea of benefit for the least favoured. In relation to education they lead him to conclude that educational resources should 'not be allotted mainly according to their return as estimated in productive trained abilities, but also according to their worth in enriching the personal and social life of citizens, including here the less favoured' (p. 107).

Rawls's principle of difference resonates with Stenhouse's (1967) emphasis on providing all students with equality of access to culture regardless of their natural abilities and aptitudes in a form that enhances their 'individuality' and 'autonomy'. Stenhouse, like Rawls, is opposed to an education organised solely for the purposes of productive enterprise. Such an education implies an outcomes-based model of curriculum planning which distorts culture by rendering it an instrument for the production of commodity value, rather than valuing culture as a resource for students to use in constructing their personal and social identities in a democratic society. For Stenhouse, achieving equality of access to the culture in a form that enhances students' 'autonomy' and 'individuality' (values closely allied to those of 'self-esteem' and 'respect') was a matter of attending to the quality of teaching and learning processes. Here 'quality' is judged in terms of the consistency of the processes with such values, rather than in terms of their instrumental effectiveness in producing predetermined outcomes. Such judgements are best left in the final analysis to 'insiders', given the complex configurations of factors that shape teaching and learning processes in particular contexts of action. Like Rawls, Stenhouse did not disregard the importance of training for the purposes of productive enterprise in schools. Nor did he dispute the appropriateness of the 'objectives model' for curriculum planning in this respect. What he objected to was the subordination of the school curriculum as a whole to these purposes.

Rawls's liberal egalitarian theory of justice provides us with a framework for evaluating the authenticity of New Labour's education policies as expressions of a Third Way. It accommodates the egalitarian principle of redress without treating it as absolute. It also accommodates the libertarian view that tends to underpin the neo-liberal agenda while rejecting the grounds on which it is justified. Unequal distributions of education in favour of the well endowed can be just, but not on the grounds of desert. From what may be called a Third Way liberal egalitarian perspective, New Labour's criterion for a just distribution of educational resources, that the arrangements should improve the commodity value of education for all, implies a very narrow interpretation of the liberal egalitarian principles of distributive justice. Indeed they *hardly differ* from the libertarian principle of just deserts, inasmuch as it implies that inequalities in social circumstances alone are no basis for distributing educational resources. Improving the commodity value of learning for all students in schools, up to the limits of their natural ability, is an aim many libertarians would endorse.

A genuine Third Way would have to accommodate a conception of the value of education which goes beyond that of producing commodity value for the labour market. The latter forms no basis for an education that gives the individual a secure sense of his or her own worth. Genuine Third Way policies would pay more than lip service to the value of enhancing the lives of students, in relation both to their culture, and to preparing them for active participation in a democratic form of social life.

New Labour, school effectiveness research and Rawls's principles of justice

The form of research that is providing New Labour with a benchmark for restructuring educational research is school effectiveness research (SER). The growth of SER over the past twenty-five years was motivated by an interest in discovering the 'mechanism' that would enable schools to control and shape students' educational attainments (see Hamilton 1994). Early grounds for optimism were provided by the studies of Edmonds (1979) in the United States and of Rutter *et al.* (1979) in the United Kingdom. These studies were influential in challenging the findings of Colman *et al.* (1966), Jenks *et al.* (1971) and Willis (1977) that schooling made little difference to educational attainments and that the variance in levels of attainment is largely due to the influence of socio-economic background factors. One of the preoccupations of SER has been to discover those 'in school' factors which enable schools to 'add value' to children's attainment level. Therefore SER took on board one of the major mechanisms employed by the education market in its analysis of schooling. It used 'performance indicators' in the form of outcome measures to assess the value of the education provided by the school. SER 'back-mapped' from outcomes to see whether it could identify those factors operating in the school environment that it could correlate with differences or changes in these outcome measures. In doing its research from the 'back end' it avoided 'front-end' considerations of the goals of education and the values embedded in it.

If we look at SER in the light of Rawls's principles we can discern a difference between the early studies carried out in the United States and the later studies in the United Kingdom (see Elliott 1998). The US research focused on how schools might equalise the achievements of children in areas such as literacy and numeracy. The aim was to discover ways of redressing inequalities of life opportunities by the levelling of learning outcomes. As critics have pointed out, the outcome measures used by the researchers to assess the effectiveness of teaching and learning had the perverse effect of 'dumbing down' the quality of the teaching and learning (see Perrone 1989: 44). Teachers discovered that they could become 'effective' teachers if they asked more low-level questions, did not pick up on or amplify students' responses, did not encourage self-initiated questions and comments, and spent most of their time whole-class teaching. Therefore, although it was egalitarian in intent, the early SER in the United States was clearly inconsistent with the expression of democratic values at the pedagogical level (see Howe and Howe 1995). Indeed, from a Rawlsian perspective these early school improvement interventions constituted a procedurally *unjust* way of distributing education as a social good.

School effectiveness research in the United Kingdom implied no such equalising intention. It is a sufficient condition that schools can be shown to be adding commodity value to the learning of all children across a range of outcomes, however unequal the final level of attainment. If evidence of progress in learning can be demonstrated for all children, the influence of social background factors is being reduced for those most disadvantaged. Such an intention appears to reflect Rawls's principle of difference, inasmuch as the effective school is one which research shows to have benefited *all* its children, irrespective of their level of attainment. However, SER in the United Kingdom does not go beyond the very narrow interpretation of the principle of difference, one that the libertarian may find acceptable. It is this inter-pretation which underpins much of New Labour's current vision of school improvement. Although SER claims to embrace a wide range of learning outcomes, including social as well as academic outcomes, it fails to grasp the value of education in terms of its contribution to the personal and social development of students, and that attention needs to be paid to the quality of teaching and learning processes. This kind of attention is not shaped by outcome specifications but informed by values that are constitutive of a democratic form of social life. Thereby SER, like New Labour's education policies, distorts liberal egalitarian principles by confusing the personal and social ends of education with outcome specifications. In doing so they reduce *all* educational values to commodity value. Ironically, a recent example of this reductionism in policy making is the outcomes-based framework proposed for a new curriculum in citizenship education (see Elliott 1999). Such a framework, if taken seriously, requires teachers to teach democracy undemocratically.

In the late 1990s SER in the United Kingdom tended to shift its focus from schools to classroom teaching. This reflected the findings of related research that used multi-level modelling to suggest that the size of school effects is much smaller than originally reported and that it is difficult to differentiate school effects from classroom effects. Much of the variation between schools appeared to be due to classroom variation, and the influence of factors in the school environment beyond the classroom appeared to be very small (see Reynolds 1994: 23–4). The impact of such findings has been to reinforce a focus on classroom practice and to restructure educational research through the discourse of evidence-based teaching.

The idea of evidence-based teaching: trajectories of meaning

The shift of interest among school effectiveness researchers towards the classroom as a site of school improvement broadly coincided with an impending change of government. It provided them with a new horizon of opportunity. The idea of evidence-based teaching was attractive to a new government and promised to provide school effectiveness researchers with a solution to a long-standing problem: that of getting teachers to apply the findings of SER in classrooms. However, such attractiveness at the level of both research and policy has a price: 'evidence-based teaching' has become something of a contested concept. Hargreaves (1997) has fielded much of the debate, for it was he who floated the idea in the first place.

When we examine his writings we can see that a consistent thread has been the assertion that the role of educational research is to provide 'decisive' and 'conclusive' evidence 'that if teachers do X rather than Y in their professional practice there will be significant and enduring improvement in outcome' (1997: 412). Such evidence, he argues, yields actionable knowledge of 'what works' and it will be couched in terms of statistical probability. His preference is therefore for more experimental studies and random controlled trials in educational research (in parallel to clinical trials in medicine). From this point of view the future of educational research lies in more quantitative, outcomes-based research.

Hargreaves favourably compares this 'engineering' model of educational research with a more theoretically oriented 'enlightenment model' that aims to change the way people understand the processes of schooling. The latter, Hargreaves (1999) argues, with sociologists of education particularly in mind, has at best only an indirect influence on people's actions and decisions. It does not count as actionable knowledge.

The 'engineering' model of educational research fits a neo-liberal educational agenda very well, inasmuch as it legitimates policy intervention to directly shape, or 'reform', what teachers do in their classrooms to improve the commodity value of students' learning. It is a picture that Reynolds endorsed in a subsequent TTA lecture (1998). Hargreaves (1999: 107) writes:

> Ministers now recognise that standards of teaching and learning are unlikely to be raised by policy action that never penetrates classrooms. This is less dangerous than it initially appears, as long as Ministers retain some distance by a pragmatic attention to 'what works' and by an acknowledgement that the discovery of 'what works' is more a matter of evidence, not just ideology or of political preference.

It is interesting that Hargreaves sees the question of what works as free of ideology or of political preference. However, in contrast to Reynolds, his account of 'evidence-based practice' becomes very much more complex when he examines the relationship between research evidence and its use by teachers and policy makers. In spite of the claim that it is the task of research to generate 'decisive' and 'conclusive' evidence for practice Hargreaves paradoxically insists that research evidence informs rather than displaces professional judgement. Research evidence enhances judgement but cannot displace professional and personal knowledge of *what works* with whom in which situations. He recognises that this kind of situational understanding of cases is central to professional judgement and that at best the kind of evidence he depicts as useful is only an additional component of judgement. In discussing the relationship between research and policy decisions he argues that the latter are context-bound and that research knowledge, of the kind he considers relevant, 'serves as a supplement to, not a substitute for, the policy maker's existing knowledge'.

There appear to be two 'trajectories of meaning' in Hargreaves's writings. On the one hand 'actionable knowledge' provides 'conclusive' and 'decisive' evidence of what works. On the other hand it is knowledge that informs the teacher's judgement of what works. Here it is the teacher who decides whether the evidence 'constitutes actionable knowledge'. The two trajectories collide on the question of research methodology.

In spite of his preference for quantitative research, Hargreaves argues (1997: 412) that he is open in principle to a diversity of research methods. What matters is not the specific methodology but the *purpose* of the research. He acknowledges the benefits to practice of Stenhouse (1975) and his associates' attempts to link a particular form of interactionist studies with the development of teaching through the development of the idea of the 'teachers as researchers'(see Rudduck and Hopkins 1985). Such studies have engaged teachers in research and not simply with research, but according to Hargreaves the problem is that they yield only 'private' and 'personal' knowledge that is not 'actionable' generally because it is not generalisable and cumulative. Teachers benefit only as individual 'reflective practitioners' rather than as a professional body.

It is here that, despite the concern with the purpose of research (with 'what works' across contexts), we find Hargreaves building in specific methodological presuppositions as to what constitutes actionable knowledge. It must be couched in terms of generalisations that are open to revision in the light of exceptions and changing circumstances. He assumes that only statistically based probabilistic studies produce knowledge of this kind.

It may be the case that generalisations from clinical trials in the field of medicine are cumulative, but in the field of education we are dealing with relationships between human actions and their social consequences. MacIntyre (1981) points to an important difference between statistically based social science generalisations and those which obtain in the physical sciences (see Elliott 2000). Exceptions need not expose deficiencies in the original generalisation and do not therefore constitute counterfactual evidence. Nevertheless, MacIntyre argues, probabilistic generalisations in the social sciences can inform human action, and by implication constitute 'actionable knowledge', without the people who make use of them feeling that exceptions provide a reason for abandoning or improving upon them. They simply acknowledge that there are limits on the extent to which human affairs can be rendered predictable.

Hargreaves's assumption that probabilistic generalisations about what works in classrooms are cumulative well matches the neo-liberal policy maker's interest. It recognises or acknowledges no empirical or moral limits on the extent to which the outcomes of teaching can be made more predictable. It is an assumption that explains why he has little problem with policy interventions to shape teachers' classroom practices. The more evidence can be accumulated about 'what works' in most cases the more one can justify strong policy interventions. Hargreaves's assumption that there are no limits (in principle) on the extent to which educational research can render learning outcomes predictable appears to be in tension with his view that research evidence can only inform and not displace teachers' judgements. This latter point of view would suggest that there are, and always will be, limits on the extent to which learning can be made predictable by teachers. Even if there were no empirical limits, one could always argue, in the light of Rawls, that there are moral limits. Indeed, in the context of meaningful social interaction it is difficult to distinguish empirical from moral limits, since values are embedded in action.

This overriding concern with rendering the outcomes of teaching predictable leads Hargreaves to neglect the role of non-probabilistic generalisations in educational research. Teachers have used case studies to inform their own judgements and decisions – a process known as 'naturalistic generalisation' (see Stake 1996). Teachers have also examined their practices in the light of formal generalisations about the conditions of teaching and learning across a range and variety of contexts. Generalisations of this kind are developed by the application of methods of comparative analysis to case study evidence. Such methods are quite different from those of statistical aggregation. They attend to relationships between factors evidenced within a range of contexts, as opposed to establishing a general relationship by isolating factors from their contexts.

Teachers' action research studies have been used as a basis for generalisation in both the above senses, and have demonstrated that they can support the development of a professional, as opposed to a personal and private, knowledge base (see Elliott and Adelman 1974; Elliott and MacDonald 1975; Ebbutt and Elliott 1985; Elliott 1977). Much of the case for claiming that the evidence from experimental studies is more actionable than evidence from teachers' action research is simply evidence of bias towards the neo-liberal outcomes-based education agenda, a bias that remains hidden by refusal to address 'front-end' issues of the values in and purpose of education. The paradoxes of the link between research and teaching get 'resolved' through the operation of this bias. What is really at stake is the very thing that Hargreaves denies, namely that what counts as evidence about 'what works' is ideologically and politically constructed. In this respect Hargreaves conforms to the tendency of most school effectiveness researchers: he avoids those values and interests that underpin *all* research procedures. In portraying education as an apolitical and uncontested arena the meaning context of action is neglected. The researcher focuses on outcomes of actions, rather than the complexities and ambiguities participants experience in making sense of their situation. This deliberate retreat from ambiguity and complexity masks the moral dimension of teaching, and in doing so enables the control values embedded in the research procedures to appear as a pragmatic concern to discover 'what works'.

The focus on outcome dovetails with a neo-liberal agenda, but it cannot avoid the need to rejoin with context. It is in the calls to action made on the basis of research that those values avoided at the 'front end' have to be confronted. The technique serves to mask the values of the researcher until others are asked to act on the basis of their findings, when the values embedded in those findings are exposed. The move toward evidence-based practice may therefore be resisted by teachers because the values embedded in the concept of evidence may stand in opposition to the philosophical basis of their own practice.

Educational action research, of the kind associated with Stenhouse, also rests on a bias that is broadly liberal-egalitarian, namely that there are empirical and moral limits on the extent to which teachers can and should make the learning outcomes of their students predictable. Hence the quality of teaching and learning should not and cannot be judged solely in these terms.

Concluding comment

Teacher effectiveness research, like SER, in its efforts to improve the predictability of learning outcomes, will tend to either ignore or distort the personal and social ends of education. These 'ends' refer to those values governing the processes of teaching and learning; to the manner in which teachers represent knowledge and ideas to their students and the ways in which students engage with it as learners. When teachers asks, 'What works in *my* classroom?' they do not divorce the empirical from the ethical. Teachers experience classrooms as empirically complex and morally ambiguous arenas (see Doherty and Elliott 1999) in which they have to balance the requirement to produce 'commodity value' against the requirement to engage students in processes that respect their personal autonomy and individuality. There *are* questions to be asked about the quality of these interactions with students as future citizens of a democratic social order, in addition to questions about the instrumental effectiveness of teaching interventions. They are inseparable from a consideration of 'what works'. Evidence about the consistency of classroom interactions and the values that define an educationally worthwhile process needs to be weighed against any evidence of their effectiveness. At the micro-level of the classroom this kind of enquiry is an expression of a genuine commitment to a liberal egalitarian view of justice in education.

From a liberal egalitarian point of view, then, it is difficult to understand how educational research into what works in classrooms could be carried out with teachers simply being cast in the role of a 'user group'. It requires active collaboration in determining what counts as useful evidence, in the collection of that evidence, and in interpreting its significance for classroom practice (Doherty and Elliott 2000). Evidence-based teaching involves not only engaging teachers with research, but also engaging them *in* research. We can see that Hargreaves's notion of 'evidence-informed teaching' reflects a position articulated by Stenhouse (1979) over twenty years ago. It is that a condition of teachers using research evidence is that they do research into what works in their *own situation*. Indeed, we would argue that evidence of statistical probabilities is no more 'actionable' than the kind of interactionist 'enlightenment' research that Hargreaves criticised. By the engagement of teachers *in* and *with* research, within their own classrooms and within a reflective and self-critical community, educational research may produce knowledge that is both actionable and meaningful.

Collaborative research, with teachers, is central to the development of a genuine Third Way to ensure the just distribution of education as a social good, accessible to all. New Labour's attempts to develop a Third Way in educational policy exhibit a number of internal contradictions and must surmount a number of external obstacles. Government must trust the quality of teachers' judgements; it must avoid interventions that may undermine, override or displace their professional judgements. The active engagement of practitioners is a necessary condition of establishing a high-trust system of quality assurance. Were such research relationships supported and developed, we suggest, the quality of educational experiences could be defined within the profession – by those committed to it. The assurance of quality would be through the engagement of teachers *in* and *with* research: as members of a professional community and as active participants in the production of knowledge.

References

Ball, S. (1997) 'Policy sociology and critical social research: a personal review of recent policy and policy research', *British Educational Research Journal* 23 (3), 257–84.

Coleman, J. S., Hobson, C. J., McPartland, J., Mood, A. M., Weinfeld, F. D. and York, R. L. (1966) *Equality of Educational Opportunity*, Washington DC: US Government Printing Office.

Doherty, P. W. and Elliott, J. (1999) 'Engaging Teachers in and with Research: the relationship between context, evidence and use', British Educational Research Association, Annual Conference, Brighton: University of Sussex, 2–5 September.

Doherty, P. W. and Elliott, J. (2000) 'What Counts as "Applied Research" in Education? Linking evidence to context for use', Current Issues in Qualitative Research Conference, Norwich: University of East Anglia, 24–5 July.

Ebbutt, D. and Elliott, J. (eds) (1985) *Issues in Teaching for Understanding*, London: Longmans/Schools Curriculum Development Committee.

Edmonds, R. (1979). 'Effective schools for the urban poor', *Educational Leadership* 37 (1), 15–24.

Elliott, J. (1996) 'School effectiveness research and its critics: alternative visions of schooling', *Cambridge Journal of Education* 26 (2), 199–224.

Elliott, J. (1977) 'Developing hypotheses about classrooms from teachers' practical constructs: an account of the work of the Ford Teaching Project', *Interchange* 7 (2), 2–22.

Elliott, J. (1998) *The Curriculum Experiment: Meeting the Challenge of Social Change*, Buckingham and Philadelphia: Open University Press.

Elliott, J. (2000) 'How do teachers define what counts as "credible evidence"? Some reflections based on interviews with teachers involved in the Norwich Area Research Consortium'. Paper presented at the annual conference of the British Educational Research Association, University of Cardiff, September.

Elliott, J. (in press) 'Revising the National Curriculum: a comment on the Secretary of State's proposals', *Journal of Education Policy*.

Elliott, J. and Adelman, C. (eds) (1974) Ford Teaching Project Publications, Norwich: CARE, University of East Anglia.

Elliott, J. and MacDonald, B. (eds) (1975) *People in Classrooms*, CARE Occasional Publications 2, Norwich: University of East Anglia.

Hamilton, D. (1994) 'Clockwork Universes and Oranges', Annual Conference of the British Educational Research Association, Oxford: University of Oxford.

Hammersley, M. (1997) 'Educational research and teaching: a response to David Hargreaves' TTA lecture', *British Educational Research Journal* 23 (2), 141–61.

Hargreaves, D. H. (1996) *Teaching as a Research-based Profession: Possibilities and Prospects*, London: Teacher Training Agency annual lecture.

Hargreaves, D. H. (1997) 'In defence of research for evidence-based teaching: a rejoinder to Martyn Hammersley', *British Educational Research Journal* 23 (4), 405–19.

Hargreaves, D. H. (1999) 'Revitalising educational research: lessons from the past and proposals for the future', *Cambridge Journal of Education* 29 (2): 239–49.

Hillier, J., Pearson, R., Anderson, A. and Tamkin, P. (1998) *Excellence in Research on Schools*, Research Report 74, London: Department for Education and Employment.

Howe, K. and R. (1995) 'Democracy, justice and action research: some theoretical developments', *Educational Action Research Journal* 3 (3): 347–49.

Jenks, C., Smith, M., Acland, H., Bane, M. J., Cohen, D., Gintis, H., Heyns, B. and Michelson, S. (1971) *Inequality: A Reassessment of the Effect of Family and Schooling in America*, New York: Basic Books.

MacIntyre, A. (1981) *After Virtue: A Study in Moral Theory*, London: Duckworth.

Perrone, V. (1989) *Effective Schools and Learning: Reflections on Teachers, Schools and Communities*, New York: Teachers' College Press.

Rawls, J. (1971) *A Theory of Justice*, London: Oxford University Press.

Reeves, A. (1999). 'Academics dub Blunkett a tyrant in row over research', *Observer*, 21 November, p. 9.

Reynolds, D. (1994) 'School effectiveness and quality in education', in P. Ribbens and E. Burridge (eds) *Improving Education: Promoting Quality in Schools*, London: Cassell.

Reynolds, D. (1998) *'Teacher Effectiveness': Corporate Plan Launch, 1998–2001*, London: Teacher Training Agency.

Rudduck, J. and Hopkins, D. (1985) *Research as a Basis for Teaching: Readings from the Work of Lawrence Stenhouse*, London: Heinemann.

Rutter, M., Maughan, B., Mortimore, P. and Ouston, J. (1979) *Fifteen Thousand Hours: Secondary Schools and their Effects on Children*, London: Open Books.

Stake, R. E. (1996) *The Art of Case Study Research*, London and New Delhi: Sage.

Stenhouse, L. (1967) *Culture and Education*, London: Nelson.

Stenhouse, L. (1975) *An Introduction to Curriculum Research and Development*, London: Heinemann.

Stenhouse, L. (1979) 'Using research means doing research', in L. Dahl, A. Lysne and P. Rand (eds) *Spotlight on Educational Problems*, Oslo: University of Oslo Press.

Stronach, I. and MacLure, M. (1997) *Educational Research Undone: The Postmodern Embrace*, Buckingham: Open University Press.

Tooley, J. and Darby, D. (1998) *Educational Research: A Critique*, London: Office for Standards in Education.

Willis, P. (1977) *Learning to Labour*, Farnborough: Saxon House.

Part VI
International perspectives

17 The two solitudes

Policy makers and policy implementers

Dean Fink

I often ask the groups of educators I work with around the world to identify paradoxes, ironies, or oxymorons in their educational contexts. They have few problems developing long lists. In Britain, educators particularly enjoy oxymorons like 'fair funding', 'head teacher' and 'local authority'. In virtually every country I've visited, these paradoxes, ironies and oxymorons reflect a deep disconnect between policy makers and the people who have to implement their policies, teachers and school heads – there exists in many countries 'a dialogue of the deaf' between these two groups. In Canada, some years ago, a book was written which described the relationship between French and English-speaking Canadians as *Two Solitudes*. I would submit that in most Western countries there are two solitudes in education that endanger the longevity of important changes and threaten to undermine state-supported education. In virtually all cases, well intentioned, highly motivated people, both policy makers and policy implementers, seek in their own ways to create the very best educational experiences for young people. Unfortunately, they have become so caught up in their own 'solitude', 'paradigm' or 'mind set' that they are unable or unwilling to see the perspective of others, or to acknowledge that their way may not support pupils' learning. As one who frequently and regularly interacts with British educators, it is my observation that the 'two solitudes' exist in the British context and undermine many of the Labour government's commendable educational goals and policies. At the same time, I do not pretend to be an expert on British educational policies and practices. I therefore offer the following observations of the 'two solitudes' from an international perspective as a modest contribution to building bridges to the productive changes necessary for pupils to function in a world that is dramatically different from the one in which most of us grew to maturity.

Sources of change

When 'the wall' came down in 1989 the international order of things changed profoundly. Before the fall of the Berlin Wall and the end of the Cold War, virtually all international and national policies pertained in some way to the confrontation between the 'West' and the 'East'. As Friedman (2000) points out, the power blocs were like two sumo wrestlers – pushing each other around amid much grunting, groaning, and ritualistic posturing. Now, as the result of information technology and the disappearance of the 'old rules' of international engagement following the fall of the 'wall', nations and states, to continue Friedman's sporting metaphor, are in 100 metre races against each other, but no sooner is one race completed than another begins. The 'race' is not for advantage in a Cold War, but rather to achieve economic benefit in a globalised world (Rifkind 2000). Not only are national economies, cultures, and politics, for better or for worse, becoming increasingly globalised, so is education. Policy makers, aware of this shifting international terrain, must focus on policies they believe will help their nation, province or state to participate and survive in a strange and somewhat chaotic game in which the rules keep changing. Much of the rhetoric I hear about education as I travel is that 'we' (and you can fill in the 'we') must improve our educational system so that 'our' nation, province, state or district (and you can fill in the 'our') can compete in this changing economic world. The language of 'world class' education, whatever that means, is part of the international discourse. The connection between education and economic success is tenuous at best and unproven. Certainly the success of the US economy and that nation's dismal showing on international comparisons of achievement challenge this 'conventional' wisdom for massive educational changes. This economic argument has led policy makers internationally to speak in the language of failure – that is, our educational system has failed our young people, our economy, and us. It certainly is an easier argument to make than pointing fingers at corporate elites or government economic policies. I think a better argument and a more honest argument for educational change is that educational systems in most Western countries have delivered what society has historically wanted them to deliver, but now these educational systems are obsolete and must change. Not only is this a more accurate reflection of the global situation, it also would encourage a more enthusiastic and supportive response from the people who have to implement change – teachers and Heads.

Unlike policy initiators, who often see children as mere statistics, policy implementers face the reality of promoting the learning of a specific group of children, with all their diversity and complexity. Moreover, each context creates a set of variables with which policy implementers must contend, and about which some policy initiators seem unaware, unimpressed, or uncaring. Poverty, for example, does affect children's learning in spite of political protestations to the contrary – the evidence is overwhelming. Efforts by some policy makers to obfuscate this reality are unhelpful at best and downright dishonest at worst. One need only read Nick Davis's (1999) description of Sheffield in the *Guardian* to understand the significance of context to pupils' learning. Pupils do not come in the neat little categories that policy makers and academics like to create. Teachers face not only issues of social class, but also issues of race, ethnicity, gender, and sexuality. Moreover, each child comes equipped with his or her own set of needs, interests, and abilities. While policy makers ask, 'How are we going to improve our system to compete in the emerging economy?' teachers ask, 'How am I going to get this particular reluctant child to read and write?' The goals may be similar but understanding of each other's reality appears to be lacking.

To policy makers and many academics, teachers are usually viewed as technicians.

> Central to this notion of teaching is the belief that if procedures are correctly defined, clearly detailed and correctly monitored, most major teaching decisions can and should be prescribed through policy mandates that alter school schedules, programs, assessment, and teaching responsibilities. . . . When a technical view of teaching is influential, reformers assume that educators have the capacity and ability to teach in different and more effective ways but are either lazy, unknowledgeable, unfocused or resistant to change.
>
> (Bascia and Hargreaves 2000: 5)

Technical approaches to teaching may work when the purpose is to teach a narrow band of low-level skills, but to teach each child a rich, intellectually challenging curriculum, however, requires teachers who are able to:

- deal with the complexity of continually updating their knowledge of subject matter, child development, and assessment strategies;
- work collaboratively with colleagues, and engage in positive ways with the social-emotional lives of each child in their care (Hargreaves and Fink 2000);
- create meaning for themselves and their pupils in the learning process.

In comparison with other professions, there is clear evidence that teaching ranks high in task complexity (Rowan 1994).

Orientation to change

Policy makers removed from this day-to-day reality tend to espouse broad philosophies based on their own experience, ideological inclination, or educational background. I was forcefully struck by Kenneth Baker's admission that major policy initiatives in England that have influenced countless pupils and teachers were based on personal whim and prejudice (Davis 1999). Whether it is blind adherence to the wisdom of the market as the solution to all problems, or unwavering adherence to progressive approaches to curriculum and teaching, clearly 'one size does not fit all'.

Nonetheless, policies that are often based on political theories are pursued with zealous certitude, with little real thought as to the consequences for 'real' pupils in 'real' schools with 'real' teachers. The law of unintended consequences can be cruel. I'm sure, for example, that when it initiated its reform agenda by blaming its teachers for most of the educational ills of society the government of Ontario in Canada did not intend to unify its teachers into a broad coalition which staged a two-week strike. I'm sure successive British governments did not want to create teacher and leadership shortages or to precipitate a serious morale issue among teachers. I'm also sure that the government of Texas did not intend to further exacerbate the gap between 'have' and 'have not' children when it introduced its standards-based curriculum (McNeil 2000).

Policy implementers have a different orientation to the change process from policy initiators. Teachers, in particular, and Heads tend to operate based on the 'practicality ethic' – does it work for my pupils in my classroom, or for my pupils in my school (Doyle and Ponder 1977)? In my work with colleagues at the International Centre for Educational Change at OISE/University of Toronto we have succeeded in our change efforts where teachers have considered the approaches to educational change that we have introduced made a difference to them and their pupils in their classrooms. Our experience in working through recent dramatic changes to Ontario secondary schools, however, indicates that teachers tend to retreat to their departments and classrooms in the face of multiple changes and have difficulty looking at change on a school-wide basis, let alone more widespread systemic change. Indeed, we are seeing teachers withdraw from school-wide committees, extra-curricular activities and adopting a siege mentality as they experience one change after another. This pattern is not unique to Ontario (Riley 2000). Similarly, many of our very best leaders are retiring early because of their profound disenchantment with the directions of the Ontario government's so-called 'common sense' revolution. The loss of experience and wisdom is showing up daily as inexperienced and unprepared leaders learn by trial and error. There is a growing leadership crisis in Ontario and many US states because good people are either leaving the profession or choosing alternative career paths. This is, I am told, an issue in the United Kingdom. In addition, Ontario schools have jettisoned school development plans and other school improvement strategies to manage the onslaught of often ill conceived government changes. Interestingly, outside mandates do appear to energise those few schools that have had a very limited history of school improvement (Hargreaves *et al.* 2000). It would seem that mandated 'top-down' reform is inversely related to a school's prior record of improvement (Hargreaves *et al.* 2000). Mandates, therefore, may help less successful schools but tend to inhibit more successful schools. The long-term result of top-down change efforts appears to be a merging of schools in the mediocre middle.

Intellectual paradigm

As suggested, policy makers tend to look on education as a technical exercise that can be improved by a mandate here, a new policy there, and lots of accountability procedures to coerce the unwilling or the incapable. In this paradigm, educational change is quite straightforward – define 'what' the pupils must learn, divide the learning into convenient chunks, establish time frames, develop a testing regimen, organise suitable materials, then tell teachers how to achieve predetermined targets. When governments add the requirement that teachers and Heads learn the correct way to do what is mandated by enrolling on in-service sessions, euphemistically called 'professional development', and then impose plenty of measures to check that they faithfully carry out the policy makers' designs, we have the major ingredients of educational change in most Western jurisdictions. This conventional wisdom is logical, linear and quite consistent with Western intellectual thought for the past 400 years. René Descartes said, 'I think, therefore I exist,' and set in motion an intellectual revolution that underpins all of our major institutions, especially schools. Reason and rationality have become the only acceptable ways of knowing. Since he didn't say, I feel, I sense, I intuit, I believe, feelings, intuition, memory, ethics, and common sense have been largely cast out of intellectual discourse (Saul 1993). When Cartesian rationalism is combined with the Newtonian mechanical school of physics that suggested that we live in an orderly universe that was knowable through rational scientific methods, we have the basis for much of Western thought. Within this intellectual paradigm the world is knowable through logical, linear, cause–effect techniques. If we can just take things apart and then put them together again the object of study, be it the universe, the human body, or a child's learning needs, is knowable. Faith in science, progress and technology underpins this way of thinking. This kind of reductionism has brought us untold scientific and technological triumphs, from the splitting of the atom to the unlocking of the genetic code. It has also brought us the arms race, environmental devastation, and grinding poverty for most of the world's population (Capra 1983; Saul 1993).

Our businesses, schools, and other social organisations reflect this way of thinking. For example, a pupil who attends virtually any secondary school is looked upon not as a whole living, breathing, feeling person, but in terms of his or her parts – the history part, the science part, the maths part, and so on. The pupil proceeds in a perfectly linear, logical way from class to class, each of which is organised into a period of equal length regardless of the learning programme. The pupil then progresses in assembly-line fashion from year to year until he or she leaves school. This has proved to be a very efficient way to educate large numbers of pupils. Its effectiveness, however, is another matter. Similarly, 'Fordist' approaches to manufacturing have provided efficient if not effective ways to mass-produce consumer goods. In both examples, however, reductionism has focused attention on the parts of the process and not on the entire process. Departments and ministries of education as well as schools of education are departmentalised, compartmentalised, and fragmented. Organised bureaucratically, they tend to see the world in terms of rules, roles, and responsibilities. Individuals and groups within these organisations often work in isolation from one another and at cross-purposes, and frequently send out conflicting and confusing messages to policy implementers. As a foreigner, I find the negativity of the inspectoral system and particularly the former Chief Inspector, for example, strangely at odds with the more positive, progressive rhetoric of other policy officials.

Since the early 1970s the newer sciences such as quantum physics, molecular biology, *Gestalt* psychology, and ecology have challenged the conventional rational–linear paradigm (Capra 1983). Their proponents have argued that rationality must be balanced by an ecological approach that looks at human and natural systems holistically, and rather than just knowing them through their parts attempting to understand their interrelationship and connections within larger systems. For example, the universe is now recognised as chaotic and knowable only through the patterns of relationships and connections among its components (Wheatley 1994; Stacey 1995). Unlike the mechanical, watch-like universe of Newton, the universe of the systems thinker is like a 'bubbling bowl of porridge' that is chaotic but produces patterns of activity that are knowable. Within this paradigm, pupils are seen as whole persons who operate in particular contexts and are knowable and therefore teachable only if one is conversant with the patterns which affect the individual's life. While the implications of this view from a contemporary perspective are truly revolutionary, we must in the words of Michael Fullan (1991) 'start small' but begin to 'think big' (p. 167). This requires an educational vision that anticipates changing social forces (Stoll *et al.* forthcoming) and not merely 'polishing yesterday's paradigm' (Peters 1999: 25).

Implementers face a non-rational, non-linear, complex and, some would even suggest, chaotic reality (Stacey 1995). Teachers deal with whole classes of diverse and complex human beings. It is one thing to criticise middle years teachers in the abstract (Barber 2000); it is quite another to recognise that teaching young adolescents (Hargreaves *et al.* 1996) is a challenging, unpredictable, and often frustrating job. Similarly, school Heads don't deal just with curriculum departments, or special education departments, or professional development; they must attend to the complex interconnections and interrelationships in an entire organisation. Effective Heads see whole schools, not just their parts (Fink 2000).

Policy makers, because they are politically more powerful, can insist that implementers conform to their reality. Unless the policy makers are prepared to understand the influence of context, micro-politics, school culture, the emotions of teaching and learning and leadership styles on educational change in schools, they are 'doomed to tinkering' (Fullan 1991). Policy makers need to understand more than just the content of the changes they mandate, they must grasp the complexities and subtleties of the change process (Tyack and

Tobin 1994; Tyack and Cuban 1995; Stoll and Fink 1996). To bridge the 'two solitudes', policy makers need to address both the content and the processes of change simultaneously (Sergiovanni 2000). They must 'shift their efforts from designing controls intended to direct the system to developing capacity that enables schools and teachers to be responsible for student learning and responsive to diverse and changing student and community needs, interests and concerns' (Darling-Hammond 1998: 643). Policy implementers and particularly teachers' unions, for their part, must come to grips with the shifting international and national contexts that affect schools and grasp the opportunity, when it offers, to reinvent schools and schooling.

Change strategy

The prevailing change strategy, as mentioned, emanating from many government offices has been a top-down compliance model. An international pattern has emerged – first manufacture an educational crisis by naming, blaming and shaming educators for real and alleged failures of the system; design a curriculum with more content and 'higher' standards; change structures of governance to reduce local political control, and reduce funding in the name of efficiency. The 'conventional wisdom', propagated by the popular press, corporate leaders, and ambitious politicians, is that teachers and other educators are the source of most problems. They must, therefore, be obliged to comply with mandates through elaborate and usually expensive accountability measures.

More recently, in some jurisdictions, the failure of such policies has gradually led to policies that are no less controlling, but at least make some effort to recognise the complexity of the change process and the need for more collaborative approaches between policy makers and policy implementers. I applaud, for example, the British government's intent, if not its methods, to improve programmes for inner cities and to reduce social exclusion by improving access to good education for all. The literacy and numeracy initiatives do appear to be genuine attempts to provide teachers with good materials and appropriate assistance as they adjust to new ways of doing things. My interactions with many school Heads and academic colleagues in both of our countries suggest that these efforts tend to be more of a doing 'with' approach than similar change projects in the past or in other juris-dictions internationally. Many questions remain, however. One that interests me is how testing and other accountability measures will affect the intent of the strategy. When senior British policy officials use North Carolina and particularly Texas as exemplary change models there should be reason for profound concern. The evidence in some of the US states that appear to have influenced British policy suggests that the 'testing tail will wag the teaching and learning dog' (Jones *et al.* 1999; McNeil 2000), and further discriminate against minorities and the less advantaged. The ultimate test for the literacy and numeracy strategies in Britain, of course, will come when the accountability pressure is reduced and the funds begin to dwindle, as they inevitably will. Will the strategies become institutionalised as 'part of the way we do things around here', or will they disappear as so many large-scale change efforts have over time? Will the traditional 'grammar of schooling' (Tyack and Tobin 1994) reassert itself? How adaptable is the strategy to changing national and international contexts? It will be interesting to see whether this change initiative is able to balance pressure and support. More significantly, will the initiative promote 'deep' learning and under-standing or merely low-level test taking skills? There is evidence that technicist approaches based on a behaviouristic view of learning promote some basic skills and raise test scores (Reynolds 2000). This narrow and shallow perspective on teaching and learning, however, contributes little to pupils' desire to imagine, create, appreciate, and think critically (Orfield and Kurlaender forthcoming; Earl and LeMahieu 1997; Galton 2000).

We know from a vast body of international research that pupils construct their learning (Perkins 1999). There is, unfortunately, not a great deal of room in most of the test-driven reform agendas internationally for pupils to construct knowledge, and to demonstrate their creativity, imagination, and innovativeness. Clearly, knowledge workers must possess these qualities to function effectively in a changing economic climate. This raises an interesting paradox. On one hand schools must prepare their charges for a world of complexity and indeterminacy. In a knowledge society pupils will have to be more creative, imaginative, resilient, and persistent. Paradoxically the people who must prepare them in this way are treated like skilled tradespeople: they are told what to teach, when to teach it, how to assess the results, and more recently how to teach. I saw a recent report which stated that GCSEs were in large measure a test of memory. If the report is indeed true, this finding would be consistent with testing internationally. A major challenge for policy makers, then, is to develop accountability procedures that assure the public of the value of its investment in education, without turning teachers and Heads into rather dull-witted robots and our pupils into shallow memorisers.

Purposes of change

At the root of the 'two solitudes' between policy makers and policy implementers is that they focus on different and in some cases conflicting purposes for education and educational change. Brouilette (1996) has summarised the four most common ways of viewing the purposes of education as humanist, social efficiency, developmentalist, and social meliorist. To the *humanist* the purpose of education is to prepare pupils for citizenship so that they understand the values and traditions embodied in their societies' institutions. To that end, pupils must be sufficiently literate to communicate with their fellow citizens and have the knowledge necessary to comprehend current issues and cast their vote appropriately. In practice this has tended to be interpreted as an emphasis on the teaching of the liberal arts with a focus on the 'basics' – grammar, spelling, and an understanding of Western, eurocentric values and traditions.

To those who advocate *social efficiency*, the purpose of schools is to prepare students for jobs, and to contribute to the economic well-being of society as a whole. The concept of students as 'human capital' evolves from this point of view. Business-oriented politicians tend to focus on the non-college-bound students and enquire into their employability. While this view places an emphasis on the basics and sees education as a very linear 'input–output' process, it does stress the need for vocational education and education to prepare pupils to make a living.

The *developmentalist* position holds that education should help individual students to develop their personal potential, 'so that they are prepared to be creative, self-motivated lifelong learners who are effective problem-solvers, able to communicate and collaborate with others, and to meet the varied challenges they will encounter in their adult lives' (p. 224). While humanists and developmentalists have similar aspirations for students, they diverge on where to put the emphasis in curricula. The humanist is much more concerned with forms and precision than the developmentalist. The developmentalist would entertain invented writing and focus more on the content and ideas of a student's work than on the syntax and spelling. To focus too early on what they might see as cosmetics, they would argue, inhibits a student's creativity and imagination.

The purpose of education to the *social meliorist* is to bring about a more just society, 'through using the schools to help those children whose background puts them at risk, to get the resources they need to succeed, and through teaching all students about diverse cultures and ethnic heritages, thus helping them to grow into open-minded, tolerant adults' (p. 224). Those who advocate this view would see the humanist approach to be narrow, traditional, elitist, overly eurocentric, and perpetuating the tyranny of the majority. In a similar vein they would view the social efficiency perspective as exploitive and 'unthinking replication of social injustice'. The developmentalist view with its focus on individual growth and development, from a social meliorist point of view, tends to ignore the social context and social ills that prevent students from taking advantage of opportunities. The developmentalist emphasis on cooperation can easily mean cooptation with forces that should be confronted. These positions help to explain the challenge of developing shared meaning in a community, a school, or among governors where all four purpose positions often coexist somewhat uneasily. In general, people in schools who must implement policies tend to emphasise developmentalist and social meliorist goals, whereas policy makers, who are more in tune with international and national trends and less directly involved with schools and pupils, tend to emphasise humanist and particularly social efficiency goals. Certainly the rhetoric of your Chief Inspector reflects his belief in traditional approaches to teaching and learning. It is also no coincidence that the division of government charged with responsibility for education in the United

Kingdom is called the 'Department for Education and Employment' and the same department in Ontario is the 'Ministry of Education and Training'.

Success criteria and change

The 'two solitudes' are also inclined to assess the results of reform in quite different ways. The policy maker will want clear, measurable evidence that change has occurred. Standardised testing and/or inspections provide evidence of change. Interestingly, scores on standardised tests almost invariably go up on the second administration of a test. Policy makers will often use this as evidence of the correctness of their policies. Similarly, the results of inspections the second and third time around usually show improvement. This pattern suggest the question – are these gains the result of the policy initiatives or of the fact that teachers and pupils have become better at handling the accountability procedures? A second criterion for success from a policy maker's perspective is the fidelity with which the reforms are carried through in the classroom. Are the implementers implementing in the ways in which the change was intended? Surely this is what OfStEd is all about. The third criterion for policy makers is popularity (Cuban 1998). Are the changes politically popular? Often the pressured climate created by policy makers is intended to produce tangible results before another election. They will speak in the language of crisis and urgency. In Ontario the government has done such an effective job of demeaning the teaching profession that its solution of teacher testing proved politically very popular in the last election. The fact that there are few if any examples of teacher tests that contribute to quality makes little difference when political advantage is to be gained. Similarly, the mania for standardised pupil testing has swept the world because it is efficient, popular, inexpensive, supported by powerful vested interests, and can be carried out with fidelity. To teachers in the classroom, success is not an array of disembodied statistics on tests of questionable utility; they judge the efficacy of a change initiative on whether it can be adapted to their individual context and works with their pupils in their classroom. Similarly, Heads find change that they can adapt to their unique communities more useful. Kindergarten as a concept has spread throughout the world because it could be adapted to many different contexts (Tyack and Cuban 1995). Many teachers use a version of cooperative group learning, but its use differs widely from the original literature on the topic. Implementers also like changes with some staying power. In Ontario, where one change has followed another in rapid succession, policy implementers have become very cynical and are just hoping that – like a kidney stone – changes they find painful will pass. They do what they have to do and little more. As for most secondary teachers in Ontario, they find little meaning in the changes. This is once again not a unique phenomenon in Ontario.

Conceptions of change

Another source of the 'two solitudes' is based on differing concepts of time. Policy makers tend to operate within a monochronic time frame. Monochronic time is concerned with doing one thing at a time in discrete segments, in an organised and scheduled manner. Most policy makers operate on monochronic time. Their focus is on the completion of schedules, perhaps to the exclusion of context, and the building of relationships with people. Most Western organisations operate on monchronic time because that is the traditional way to get business done, and achieve results (Hargreaves 1994).

Teachers, particularly primary teachers, operate on polychronic time. As anyone who has spent time in a primary classroom will know, there are many things going on at once to which the teacher must attend within the immediate context. According to Andy Hargreaves (1994) 'it is a world deeply grounded in intense, sustained, and subtly shifting interpersonal relationships among large groups of children and between these children and their teacher' (p. 104). Heads also tend to operate on polychronic time. Days are often a series of unrelated events, crises, and occasionally planned activity. Misunderstanding and poor policy implementation can occur when policy makers who tend to operate on monochronic time fail to consider the polychronic concepts of time of the people who have to implement changes. Certainly, my observation based on many interactions with British teachers and Heads is that they feel overwhelmed by the sheer number of change initiatives, and swamped by demands on their time. This appears to be an international condition for teachers and Heads.

Building bridges

While the preceding discussion has tended to dichotomise the world of the 'policy maker' and the world of the 'policy implementer', the challenge for the future is to create and maintain bridges of understanding between these two realities as the way to build a 'state of the art' educational system. There is an old Indian proverb 'You think because you understand one you must understand two, because one *and* one makes two. But you must also understand *and*' (Wheatley 1994: 9). What then does *and* consist of?

Policy makers attend to what Sergiovanni (2000) calls the 'systemsworld'. This is the world of structures, accountability, policies, and protocols. These provide the order and direction for complex organisations. 'In schools leaders and their purposes, followers and their needs, and the unique traditions, rituals, and norms that define a school's culture comprise the lifeworld' (Sergiovanni 2000: 61). Change efforts that focus only on the 'systemsworld' or the content of change, and ignore the 'lifeworld' or processes of change, will shine brightly as long as the pressure to change is maintained, but over time will fade away as so many change efforts have in the past. Andy

Hargreaves and I have argued (2000) that joining the content *and* processes of educational change requires change agents to look at change from three interrelated and often conflicting dimensions:

- Does the change have depth? Does it improve important rather than superficial aspects of pupil learning? Does it address 'powerful, high performance for understanding that prepares young people to participate in today's society' (p. 30)?
- Does it have length? Is it sustainable over long periods of time?
- Does it have breadth? Can it be extended beyond a few schools, networks or showcase initiatives? (p. 30).

Only policy makers and policy implementers who understand each other's world, and work together to enhance the educational experiences of all pupils in their care, can address such complex questions productively.

References

Barber, M. (2000) 'High expectations and standards for all no matter what', *Times Educational Supplement*, 7 July, 22–4.

Bascia, N. and Hargreaves, A. (2000) *The Sharp Edge of Educational Reform*, Dordrecht: Kluwer.

Brouilette, L. (1996) *A Geology of Reform: The Successive Restructuring of a School District*, Albany NY: State University of New York Press.

Capra, F. (1983) *The Turning Point: Science, Society, and the Rising Culture*, New York: Bantam Books.

Cuban, L. (1998) 'How schools change reforms: redefining reform success and failure', *Teachers' College Record* 99 (3), 453–77.

Darling-Hammond, L. (1998) 'Policy and change: getting beyond bureaucracy', in A. Hargreaves, A. Lieberman, M. Fullan and D. Hopkins (1998) *International Handbook of Educational Change*, Dordrecht: Kluwer, pp. 642–67.

Davis, N. (1999) 'Schools in crisis', *Guardian*, 14, 15, 16 September.

Doyle, W. and Ponder, G. A. (1977) 'The practicality ethic in teacher decision-making', *Interchange* 8 (3), 1–12.

Earl, L. and LeMahieu, P. (1997) 'Rethinking assessment and accountability', in A. Hargreaves (ed.), *Rethinking Educational Change with Heart and Mind*, Arlington VA: Association for Supervision and Curriculum Development, pp. 149–68.

Fink, D. (2000) *Good Schools/Real Schools: Why School Reform doesn't Last*, New York: Teachers' College Press.

Friedman, T. (2000) *The Lexus and the Olive Tree*, New York: Anchor Books.

Fullan, M. G. (1991) *The New Meaning of Educational Change*, New York: Teachers' College Press.

Galton, M. (2000) 'Big change questions: should pedagogical change be mandated? Dumbing down on classroom standards: the perils of a technician's approach to pedagogy', *Journal of Educational Change* 1 (2), 193–8.

Hargreaves, A. (1994) *Changing Teachers, Changing Times*, London: Cassell.

Hargreaves, A. and Fink, D. (2000) 'The three dimensions of education reform', *Educational Leadership* 57 (7), 30–4.

Hargreaves, A., Earl, L. and Ryan, J. (1996) *Schooling for Change*, London: Falmer Press.

Hargreaves, A., Shaw, P., Fink, D., Retallick, J., Giles, C., Moore, S., Schmidt, M. and James-Wilson, S. (2000) *Change Frames: Supporting Secondary Teachers in Interpreting and Integrating Secondary School Reform*, Toronto: Ontario Institute for Studies in Education/University of Toronto.

Jones, M. G., Jones, B., Hardin, B., Chapman, L., Yarborough, T. and Davis, M. (1999) 'The impact of high stakes testing on teachers and students in North Carolina', *Phi Delta Kappan* 81 (3), 199–203.

McNeil, L. (2000) 'Creating new inequalities', *Phi Delta Kappan* 81 (10), 729–34.

Orfield, G. and Kurlaender, M. (eds) (forthcoming) *Raising Standards or Raising Barriers: Inequality and High Stakes Testing in Public Education*, New York: Century Foundation.

Perkins, D. (1999) 'The many faces of constructivism', *Educational Leadership* 57 (3), 6–11.

Peters, T. (1999) *The Circle of Innovation: You can't Shrink your Way to Greatness*, New York: Vintage.

Reynolds, D. (2000) 'Big change questions: should pedagogical change be mandated? Can and should pedagogical change be mandated at times?', *Journal of Educational Change* 1 (2), 193–8.

Rifkind, J. (2000) *The Age of Access: The new culture of hypercapitalism where all of life is a paid-for experience*, New York: Putnam.

Riley, K. (2000) 'Leadership, learning and systemic change', *Journal of Educational Change* 1 (1), 57–75.

Rowan, B. (1994) 'Comparing teachers' work with work in other occupations: notes on the professional status of teaching', *Educational Researcher* 23 (60), 4–17.

Saul, J. R. (1993). *Voltaire's Bastards: The Dictatorship of Reason in the West*, Harmondsworth: Penguin.

Sergiovanni, T. (2000) 'Changing change: toward a design and art', *Journal of Educational Change* 1 (1), 57–75.

Stacey, R. (1995) *Managing Chaos*, London: Kogan Page.

Stoll, L. and Fink, D. (1996) *Changing our Schools: Linking School Effectiveness and School Improvement*, Buckingham: Open University Press.

Stoll, L., Fink, D. and Earl, L. (forthcoming) *It's about Learning and it's about Time*, London: Routledge/Falmer.

Tyack, D. and Cuban, L. (1995) *Tinkering toward Utopia: A Century of Public School Reform*, Cambridge MA: Harvard University Press.

Tyack, D. and Tobin, W. (1994) 'The grammar of schooling: why has it been so hard to change?' *American Educational Research Journal* 31 (3), 453–79.

Wheatley, M. (1994) *Leadership and the New Science*, San Francisco CA: Berrett-Koehler.

18 Managing the myth of the self-managing school as an international educational reform

John Smyth

Recent media reports set my mind racing that Australians appear to have a fascination with myth – perhaps because of yearning for a greater sense of history than has been possible in 200 years of European settlement. It seemed to me that this absence can sometimes erupt in odd ways. For example, the Tasmanian Tiger (or Thylacine) was hunted to extinction in the 1920s in my country and its demise well documented scientifically. But lately there have been some quite bizarre attempts (literally and metaphysically) to engineer its return. From museum remains, some scientists have seriously suggested that it would be relatively easy to reconstruct it from DNA. Others claim frequent but unsubstantiated sightings of the animal in various parts of the country.

The reason I invoke this seemingly irrelevant example is that the self-managing school as an international phenomenon is a centrepiece of the design and reality of contemporary Western education policy. In the context of such confusion even intelligent people sometimes suspend rational thinking. Australians are not alone in their preparedness to suspend rational judgement in dismantling established and proud comprehensive public education systems in favour of untried ideologically driven market alternatives. To understand this we have to turn to the literature explaining why sensible people are prepared to engage in leaps of faith and place unwarranted trust in the paranormal (see Humphrey 1996, a devastating critique). Humphrey (1996) attributes this to 'paranormal fundamentalism' – the unshakable belief that, whether there is evidence or not, there is still a deep-seated mind–body dualism around some issues that says 'There must be something out there': 'in the developed world, between a third and two-thirds of the population still attest to the reality of such phenomena as telepathy, precognition, interaction with spirits of the dead, reincarnation and the paranormal effects of prayer' (p. 3).

The fallacy I am seeking to expose here is the international retreat from equitably provided public schooling to individually managed, competitive, hermetically sealed, consumerist and choice-oriented stand-alone schools. O'Hagan (1999: 8) puts the proposition compellingly:

How is it that giving power (through local management of schools), responsibility (through attention to outcomes rather than processes) and accountability (through annual reports, inspections and league tables) to institutions has occasioned fragmentation and disintegration within these institutions?

In trying to find a way out of the miasma created by ill conceived reforms, it is clear that the educational carpetbaggers[1] who have conceived and introduced school reform of a particular persuasion with such zealotry have taken us down educational policy pathways making it impossible to put the genie back in the bottle. For a host of good reasons we would not want to do that, largely because we need to avoid a 'sentimental attachment to an imagined "golden age" of comprehensive education [that never really existed]' (O'Hagan 1999: 3). We cannot 'return to past structures and methods . . . [O]nly the future, not the past, can replace the present' (p. 3). If 'there can be no going back', then the challenge confronting us is the question: 'Where are the signs of fresh growth' (p. 8) in controversial areas like the self-managing school? How can this concept be refashioned so as to reclaim and reaffirm a more comprehensive ideal (see Pring and Walford 1997)?

But first, to address my concern of how the self-managing school came to be. The self-managing school is a notion that has bedazzled the elite of the global educational policy community for the past decade or more with such consistency and ferocity that it would not be unreasonable to label it the Viagra of school reform (to borrow a colourful analogy from Fielding 1999a). In country after country, public education has been assailed with claims that not to become self-managing is tantamount to an act of educational dereliction. But, in all of this, there is an absence of evidence showing that dismantling public schools (Blackmore 1999a) in the manner that is occurring actually produces any better learning for students (Angus 1994). Angus and Brown (1997) note that in the case of Victoria, Australia, where the self-managing school has been pushed to greater extremes than anywhere else through schools taking on responsibility for setting priorities around resourcing, 'there is little if any reference to educational processes, pedagogy, teaching or learning styles, or relations among students and teachers' (p. 6). Something is going on here, but it is certainly not going on with an educator's intent or for pedagogical reasons.

I want to move now to unravel something of the complexity of this phenomenon, why it is occurring now, what it is up to, and why it has not attracted the attention it deserves. What needs to be done about it will be sketched only briefly – the detail will have to await another paper.

The starting point has to be a preparedness to think radically outside the frame in the sense of seeing the self-managing school as a complex creation of the inability of the state to handle the continuing decision overload brought about by the post-World War II international restructuring of capitalism we call globalisation. But before I come to this I have first to deal with the issue of disbelief, because it is central to what has happened around this reform.

Writing about how the category of 'youth' 'gets articulated as an absent presence', Roman (1996: 1) argued that the discursive category of 'youth' is constructed as an object of disparagement and a kind of convenient 'landscape for journalists, social workers, media, social scientists, and educators', while the 'inaudible voice in public debates over concerns that crucially affect its conditions of existence' (p. 1) go unheard. Roman's argument is that, because of unequal power relations, those who have a particular agenda are able to go about contributing to a 'burgeoning discourse of "monological deficit" assumptions' (p. 3) largely immune from any ideological or semiotic unpicking of the 'moral panics' they are perpetrating. This idea of 'moral panics' first appeared in the work of Cohen (1972) to describe campaigns designed to try and police supposedly unruly youth by portraying them as 'folk devils' of society and therefore in need of social control.

Another way of referring to moral panic in the context of school reform is what Berliner and Biddle (1995) call a 'manufactured crisis'. The argument, at least in part, is that Western economies are experiencing economic restructuring difficulties because of the past inadequacies of their education systems, and that schools are part of the 'cause' as well as the 'solution' – what is needed to make schools do their economic work (after they have been appropriately demonised) is a healthy blast of competition and free enterprise in the form of self-managing schools.

What are the claims?

It is worth while briefly summarising some of the claims and what research has had to say about them. In those countries where it has been most warmly embraced the self-managing school is promoted as a way of:

- allegedly making public schools more immediately accountable and responsive to parents and students;
- removing supposed inefficiencies that exist in the form of bureaucratic red tape;
- enabling schools and their local communities to make decisions in their own best interests because such decisions are taken closer to the point of learning;
- giving parents greater curriculum choices for their children by construing them as 'customers';
- bringing schools much more into the orbit of the competitive practices of the business sector.

What we are not being told, and what is being kept from us, as the research is beginning to demonstrate, is that:

- There is as yet no demonstrated or substantiated improvement of learning attributable to shifts to the self-managing school, even after a decade of such policies.
- Where it has been introduced, the self-managing school has generally been accompanied by financial enticements to schools to induce them to 'take up' the initiative, but thereafter such funding quickly disappears as schools have to find more of their resources from other sources.
- Schools tend to respond to the ideology of competition and market forces that accompany the self-managing school by resorting to conservative pedagogies, through pursuing image and impression management strategies (for example, through advertising, school uniforms and discipline policy).
- Schools that have access to the necessary cultural and financial capital to stand alone benefit, but the least advantaged schools are considerably worse off.
- In order to maintain standards, there is a recentralisation of control through curriculum and policy frameworks, and through the use of performance indicators such as testing, league tables, performance pay, and the like.
- There is an increasing hierarchy and distancing of principals and other senior managers in schools from classroom teachers as the former exert more control over what happens.
- There is a very marked intensification in the work load of principals and a qualitative shift in the nature of the work as they become more like 'chief executives' than educational leaders.
- Classroom teachers experience increasing managerialisation of their work, with the accompanying emphasis on paperwork that comes with accountability.

A complication here is that policy processes like that of the self-managing school have appeal precisely because they constitute somewhat flexible and diffuse categories capable of multiple interpretations. Lingard (1999), utilising Rizvi (1994), has argued that 'school-based management has no stipulative meaning but rather . . . is a concept that is rearticulated over time in changing political contexts, while also being contested at any time' (p. 1). As Lingard (1999) put it, 'As with most policies . . . school-based management statements involve a suturing together of multiple and competing discourses' (p. 1). Lingard notes that three of the competing discourses alluded to by Rizvi are the 'social democratic', the 'corporate managerialist' and the 'market', and the latter two are frequently accompanied by claims that school-based management 'will lead to improved student outcomes' (p. 1), a position that still remains unsubstantiated.

In part we can understand what is occurring with the self-managing school if we focus on the nature of the 'game' being played here. The adult game in reform, Wirt (1991) notes, is a political game concerned with 'a struggle for power to decide dominant symbols, to secure resources, to employ facilitative structures and to express historical influences' (pp. 39–40). In contrast, the children's game is about children's learning and focuses on curriculum and pedagogy. 'The cold truth is that there is no convincing evidence that these US and UK reforms have played the children game successfully' (p. 40). Some of the frustration in schools about school-based management is probably about the disjuncture between these two circuits of reform and the need to link them in some way (p. 6).

How did we get into this situation?

The path by which we arrived at the self-managing school as an international educational policy option is rather a complex one (see Smyth 1992). Even though it may look as though several countries simply copied one another, in point of fact there is a good deal more to it than that.

In this part of the chapter I want to pursue the explanation from the vantage point of the crisis of the state in which Habermas (1976) argues, and as Codd *et al.* (1997) note, 'political problems are converted into technical ones, with technical solutions' (p. 266). The consequence is 'depoliticisation' as 'decisions are taken over by "experts"', with choices at the local level being circumscribed to the implementation of means about educational ends formulated elsewhere – a process that Giroux and McLaren (1992) aptly term 'the politics of erasure'.

One way of explaining the apparently consistent breakout of the self-managing school around the world lies in the wider political/economic conditions that have gripped the (mostly Western) world over the 1980s and 1990s in what O'Connor (1984) labels 'the crisis of the state'. Such an explanation needs to focus on the role of the state in supporting and fostering 'capital accumulation' and 'legitimation' (Habermas 1976, 1979). Offe (1984) summed this up in terms of two simultaneous and contradictory activities: on the one hand, the role of the state in supporting and fostering capital accumulation (through, for example, the provision of infrastructure) while, at the same time, operating in ways that sustain, maintain and legitimate its own position through popular support, particularly electoral support. What is occurring here is a process of wider structural adjustment as the state tries to ameliorate the worst effects of the pendulum-like actions of the business cycle.

Held (1982) says that in this inherent contradiction 'the capitalist state must act to support the accumulation process and at the same time act, if it is to protect its image as fair and just, to conceal what it is doing' (p. 184). But, as Habermas (1976, 1979) notes, the irony is that the more the state intervenes in seeking to provide rational, technical and scientific administrative solutions (in the process generating a *rationality* crisis) the more it is required to listen to and acknowledge the cultural norms and interests of widely disparate groups, and concomitantly, the greater the risk it runs of losing credibility because of its ultimate inability to deliver promised solutions in a situation of complex decision overload (which is to say, a *legitimation* crisis). According to Habermas, it is these two interlocking crises (the growing inability of the state to bring about widespread and equitable social change because of insufficiency of resources, coupled with the incapacity of large bureaucracies to make increasingly complex decisions) that in turn give rise to a crisis of *motivation* characterised by individuals' growing sense of powerlessness, alienation, loss of meaning and general feelings of exclusion from discourse about the resolution of these issues.

Devolution in the form of the self-managing school becomes an attractive option in these circumstances, because as Codd *et al.* (1997: 265) note:

> As the state's institutions extend their sphere of activity in order to sustain capitalist expansion, there is a parallel expansion of state budgets with increasing problems of fiscal management . . . This crisis can be resolved only by savage reductions in state expenditure, but the policies required to bring this about tend to undermine mass loyalty . . .

In the case being spoken about of New Zealand by Codd *et al.* (1997) the rationale is that devolution 'produces greater flexibility and responsiveness, but it also produces a structure in which decisions can be more effectively controlled' (p. 268). The way this occurs is by 'shifting responsibility for the way funds are spent to the institutional level', with any dissatisfaction being 'vented at the local level and thus diverted from central government' (p. 269). In other words, 'the legitimation crisis is transported downwards' in circumstances where any pressure for increased spending on education 'can no longer be readily applied through established channels at the national level' (p. 269) but has to be worn at the level of each individual school.

This is an interesting explanation, made even more so because of its obvious disparity with official accounts of why we have to have self-managing schools. There are more than a few elements of slippage here that deserve serious discussion, the foremost of which is why the deception – but this is an issue I will not go into here (see Smyth 2000 for a discussion).

If we are to take up Fielding's challenge in the title of this volume of 'taking education really seriously', what would we need to do in order to refashion the notion of the self-managing school so as to embrace a set of more educative, socially just, democratic and inclusive ideals than have been incorporated into versions experienced hitherto?

I want to begin the process of very tentatively mapping the territory upon which it may be possible for some modest reclamation to occur. As George Marcus said in *Ethnography through Thick and Thin* (1998), what I have here is not a well crafted, finely honed argument so much as a set of ideas in need of elaboration. Like Marcus, I hope these ideas have the 'order of progression and coherence that I intend' (p. 35). My focus is what a democratic self-managing school might look like (and I use the terms 'socially critical' and 'socially just' interchangeably with 'democratic').

The forces operating on teachers' work

As already indicated, the terrain upon which this chapter is constructed is one on which the forces of globalisation are operating ideologically and practically in shaping the self-managing school (see Smyth and Shacklock 1998; Helsby 1999; Menter *et al.* 1997; Blackmore 1999b; Woods *et al.* 1997). There is little to be gained as Henry *et al.* (1999) argue, in continuing to feed the pessimistic view of 'globalization as an uncontrollable juggernaut' (Holton 1997: 86). I want to argue the need to search for a space of 'engagement with globalization . . . [within which it is possible to pursue] a renewed emphasis on democratic politics at the level of communities . . .' (p. 86) – which, in my instance, is schools and the work of teachers, broadly defined.

My starting point is that the economic version of the self-managing school – with its centrepiece of markets, choice, competition, surveillance, performance indicators and accountability – is intellectually vacuous, educationally bereft, deeply polluted and quite likely the instrument for the ultimate destruction of public (i.e. state-provided) schools as we know them.

The idea that schools should be given a measure of meaningful control over how they live their educational lives is a good one, but it is not occurring in the current context where schools are:

- stripped of resources and made to compete against one another for students and funding;
- forced to follow a narrowly conceived National Curriculum and be ranked against one another on the basis of league tables of test results;
- cut loose from central support of the work of teachers that has historically been aimed at redressing social and economic inequities.

What is required instead, and it seems almost trite to mention it, are schools where teachers feel valued, their views are listened to, and where human relations are central to everything that occurs. In the end, good schooling occurs only where teachers are respected, and respect for teachers is at a historic low at the moment, in circumstances where they are treated by policy makers with extreme distrust. As Bastian *et al.* (1985: 47) put it:

> Almost every in-depth study of school practice concludes that a central determinant of good schooling is good teachers. Yet we must be clear that what makes most teachers good is not a mystical talent to rise above adversity, but the ability to shape the conditions and consequences of their work.

The idea I have in mind is disarmingly simple: a restoration of the notion of the teacher-as-teacher ! – rather than as some adjunct of industry. In the socially just version of the self-managing school we need to claw back the pedagogical essence of what schools are fundamentally about. Current policy agenda have all but expunged teachers' views of the primacy of teaching and learning from the agenda of schooling, leaving in their place the toxic waste of managerialism, outcomes and accountability measures.

Why the reclamation of the self-managing school has to be pedagogical

With the mounting evidence worldwide that the prevailing economic version of the self-managing school is having devastating effects on teachers, students and equity/social justice agenda, I want to pursue the argument as to why the reclamation has to be pedagogical. Given that the ground to date has been totally captured by an impoverished and fiscally anorexic version of the self-managing school, we need a sustained process of 'daring to imagine' what other more robust and equitable alternatives might look like through 'unlock[ing] the voices of dissent and possibility' (O'Loughlin 1995).

Reforming schools is always a process of 'changing hearts and minds', and particular managerialist versions can hold sway only for a limited period – we need to make the current version transparent. The territory on which this needs to be fought are ones that are already familiar to teachers, like:

- *teaching*, which is coming to mean the technical application of procedures, strategies and curriculum developed outside (and at some distance from) classrooms;
- *collegiality*, which is being hollowed out and used as an instrument of 'management by stress' in the post-Fordist restructured work organisation of the school;
- *community*, which is coming to refer to 'the guys from the big end of town';
- *evaluation*, which is being conducted by people who hold a diminished or non-existent background in pedagogy;
- *school effectiveness*, which amounts to a boiled-down version of 'what works', to the exclusion of socio-political context;
- *professionalism*, which is being corrupted and equated with notions of managerialism;
- *assessment*, which has come to mean narrow measurement against predetermined targets, omitting much of the richness and diversity of what occurs in classrooms;
- *leadership*, which is coming to mean entrepreneurialism that is amputated from the educative agenda of the school;
- *school development planning*, which is increasingly being used as a means of imprinting, transmitting and implementing 'core values' (Ball 1997) decided externally.

None of this is to suggest that teachers are hapless victims of some grand scam. In many instances they *do* have considerable agency, and there is some compelling evidence of it. With questions being asked at the moment as to whether practitioner research (Cochran-Smith and Lytle 1998) constitutes the 'new paradigm war' (Anderson and Herr 1999), it is important to acknowledge the nature and status of this work in moves to reclaim the self-managing school. Some of the codes being used as signifiers of the 'socially critical version of the self-managing school' (Smyth 1993, 1996) are terms like 'democratic schools' (Apple and Beane 1995; Wood 1992; Bastian, *et al.* 1986), 'multicultural education' (May 1994; McLaren 1997), although 'grass-roots school reform' (Goodman 1994) conveys the sentiment just as well.

The 'enunciative spaces' for a critical theory of teachers' work

The kind of revitalised and reinvigorated teacher professionalism I have in mind as an antidote to the hegemonic view of the self-managing school is one that embraces five elements (Figure 18.1).

Working the global/local dialectic

The notion here is that thought and action in schools are not only related to but embedded in wider social issues and occurrences, and events in the world

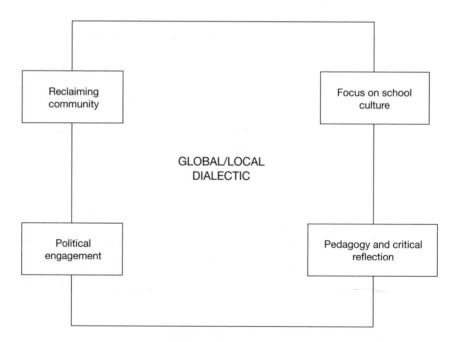

Figure 18.1 Elements of a critical theory of teachers' work

are also deeply implicated in shaping what happens locally in schools. As Bottery (1996: 191) puts it, this involves schools working in ways in which teachers place 'themselves within a wider picture'. Put most directly, 'teachers . . . to be able to defend themselves better, have to understand themselves better . . . But part of this also comes from an understanding of themselves *vis-à-vis* the society in which they live' (p. 190).

In the broad, this would encompass:

- exposing the fallacy that teaching is not simply about following individual preferences and styles in teaching and learning, but is profoundly shaped by wider dominant discourses;
- creating democratic processes inside the school that pursue wider structural issues of racism, poverty, central power and other social inequities emanating from outside schools;
- acting according to the view that, while agendas for action need to be set within the school, they cannot be pursued without acting in the global context.

Reclaiming community

This is not another plea, as Abowitz (1999: 143) put it, for a 'smoothing over of difference', uniting divisions, healing broken relationships or restoring moral responsibility. The aim is not to produce some largely unattainable state of harmony in schools, but rather to promote instead the 'public' dimension of teaching in such a way that teachers are seen as having 'duties and concerns . . . [that focus on the] collective life as opposed to individual interests' (Bottery and Wright 1996: 82).

Some of what is involved here would entail:

- moving beyond 'feel good' notions of community to ones that focus on power and how it works (May 1994);
- exposing the superficiality of the imposition of targets that come with the self-managing school, and positing instead a broad range of agendas that deal with access, opportunity and outcomes based on social justice (Beane and Apple 1995);
- integrating worthwhile community projects into the curriculum, not only for reasons of relevance but as a way of working back to redress structural inequality (Beane and Apple 1995).

Focusing on school culture

Schools have quite complex and intriguing cultural geographies and ecologies that need to be excavated in order to understand how they work. Having the occupants analyse the culture of the school is an indispensable first step in unravelling what kind of place a school is, how it came to be that way, and what forces are operating to keep it that way or change it.

Here teachers would need to:

- take on the 'black box' (Ball 1999: 201) view of what goes on inside school, by insisting on processes based on a visible rendering of complexity;
- create structures that work for the least advantaged, in a context of shared governance and a wider sense of common purpose;
- endorse forms of leadership that are not only 'provisional' (in the sense of being based on who holds knowledge) but also profoundly educative and sceptical of superficiality (May 1994).

Pedagogy/reflection

Naming and reframing issues of teaching, learning and school organisation in moral, ethical and political terms are crucial to moving schools beyond hollowed-out notions of collegiality, consumption and marketisation. The more important question, as Fielding (1999a: 281) put it in response to cries for schools to be responsive, is 'Whose relevance? Whose meaning?'

Put succinctly, pursuing this involves:

- exploiting the dislocation between 'the culture of pedagogic discourse and the management culture' (Bernstein 1996: 75);
- making an ethical commitment to theorise about teaching and to share that with others who are also 'meaning makers';
- a pedagogy that starts from the presumption that the 'other' may have something of value and worth knowing.

Political engagement

Confronting, adapting, rejecting and responding to the 'policy hysteria' (Stronach and Morris 1994), the 'policy pathology' (Fielding 1999a) and the 'policy epidemic' (Levin 1998) reining in on teachers requires courageous action on their part. We need more and better 'counter-narratives of teachers' work' (Neilsen 1999) as they exploit the disjuncture between official policy and their own spaces and influences over policy production (Ball 1990).

This would amount, among other things, to:

- publicly and pointedly highlighting instances of 'overinterpretation' (Radnor 1998) of impositional versions of the self-managing school;
- through counter-narratives of teachers' work (Neilsen 1999) dispelling the widely held myth that teaching is a commonsense activity that can be rendered down to the measurement of performance;
- asking how and in what ways policy will benefit children.

Conclusion

The argument I have advanced in this chapter is that the way to start strategically extricating ourselves from the quagmire of the accountants' anorexic view of the self-managing school is to focus on a reconstrual of the nature of teachers' work through the notion of teacher professionalism or teachers' work. I don't underestimate the difficulty of doing this, but it is the only option open to us, because the policy option has largely been hi-jacked. Teachers around the world have been systematically excluded for the past couple of decades from having a say in educational reform. We need 'a new professionalism for "new times"', one in which there is a reinvigorated 'collaborative culture among learning professionals' (Quicke 1998: 323). If we take professionalism to mean 'work which is not just done for a living but [which] gives meaning to life itself, and is carried out with standards set by the community of autonomous workers for the benefit of society as a whole' (ibid.) – then what is happening to the work of teaching through processes like the self-managing school needs to be examined and reconstructed by teachers themselves in the light of new times, characterised by 'inequality', 'erosion of community', 'fragmentation of culture', 'social breakdown' and a general absence of 'reflection on the relation to a wider society of solidarity based on an awareness of common values expressed in similar life histories' (Quicke 1998: 326).

But, if we are to be truly serious about taking up my opening claim about 'a preparedness to think radically outside the frame', not only will we have to bring teachers into the frame, as I have suggested here, but, as Fielding (1999b) notes, such a democratic aspiration must also involve parents and students as well in a 'redefined professionalism responsive to democratic society' (p. 28). As I have been at pains to argue here, any self-managing school worth its salt must be attentive to the three touchstones of the dialogic school referred to by Fielding (1999b): first, that as teachers we ought to learn 'not only from our peers but also from our students, parents and members of the community'; second, that these occasions 'ought to transcend the coincidental . . . [and] be intended and nurtured'; third, that the kind of reciprocal learning implied here should be 'a central part of a radical collegial ideal . . . supportive of an increasingly authentic democracy' (p. 28). Only when we begin to construct a more 'inclusive collegiality' (Fielding 1999b) along these lines will it be possible to confront the most corrosive and inauthentic aspects of the self-managing school through 'taking education really seriously'.

Note

1 The carpetbagger is a peculiarly American political term coined in the post-Civil War era to describe unscrupulous politicians who came from the North seeking lucrative office in the ravaged South, bringing their belongings in carpetbags. It is a term loaded with scorn and mistrust of metropolitan fakery, and is generally

used to describe interlopers. In that sense it is a most apt description for those of an economic and accountancy persuasion who peddle their wares under the banner of school reform that does not have an educator's sensibility.

References

Abowitz, K. (1999) 'Reclaiming community', *Educational Theory* 49 (2), 143–59.

Anderson, C. and Herr, K. (1999) 'The new paradigm wars: is there room for rigorous practitioner knowledge in schools and universities?' *Educational Researcher* 28 (5), 12–21, 40.

Angus, L. (1994) 'Sociological analysis and educational management: the social context of the self-managing school', *British Journal of Sociology of Education* 15 (1), 79–91.

Angus, L. and Brown, L. (1997) *Becoming a School of the Future: the Micro-politics of Policy Implementation*, Melbourne: Monash University.

Apple, M. and Beane, J. (1995) *Democratic Schools*, Alexandria VA: Association for Supervision and Curriculum Development.

Ball, S. (1990) *Politics and Policy Making in Education: Explorations in Policy Sociology*, London and New York: Routledge.

Ball, S. (1997) 'Good school/bad school: paradox and fabrication', *British Journal of Sociology of Education* 18 (3), 317–36.

Ball, S. (1999) 'Labour, learning and the economy: a "policy sociology" perspective', *Cambridge Journal of Education* 29 (1), 195–206.

Bastian, A., Fruchter, N., Gittell, M., Greer, C. and Haskins, K. (1985) Choosing Equality: the case for democratic schooling, *Social Policy*, spring, 34–51.

Bastian, A., Fruchter, N., Gittell, M., Greer, C. and Haskins, K. (1986) *Choosing Equality: The Case for Democratic Schooling*, Philadelphia: Temple University Press.

Beane, J. and Apple, M. (1995) 'The case for the democratic school', in M. Apple and J. Beane (eds) *Democratic Schools*, Alexandria VA: Association for Supervision and Curriculum Development, pp. 1–25.

Berliner, D. and Biddle, B. (1995) *The Manufactured Crisis: Myths, Fraud and the Attack on America's Public Schools*, Reading MA: Addison-Wesley.

Bernstein, B. (1995) *Pedagogy, Symbolic Control and Identity: Theory, Research, Critique*, Bristol PA: Taylor & Francis.

Blackmore, J. (1999a) '"Privatising the public": the shifts in priorities in self-managing schools away from public education and social justice', *Curriculum Perspectives* 19 (1), 68–75.

Blackmore, J. (1999b) *Troubling Women: Feminism, Leadership and Educational Change*, Buckingham: Open University Press.

Bottery, M. (1996) 'The challenge to professionals from the new public management: implications for the teaching profession', *Oxford Review of Education* 22 (2), 179–97.

Bottery, M. and Wright, N. (1996) 'Cooperating in their own deprofessionalisation? On the need to recognise the "public" and "ecological" roles of the teaching profession', *British Journal of Educational Studies* 44 (1), 82–98.

Cochran-Smith, M. and Lytle, S. (1998) 'Teacher research: the question that persists', *International Journal of Leadership in Education* 1 (1), 19–36.

Codd, J., Gordon, L. and Harker, R. (1997) 'Education and the role of the state:

devolution and control post-Picot', in A. Halsey, H. Lauder, P. Brown and A. Wells (eds) *Education: Culture, Economy, Society*, Oxford: Oxford University Press, pp. 263–72.

Cohen, S. (1972) *Folk Devils and Moral Panics: the Creation of the Mods and Rockers*, London: MacGibbon & Kee.

Fielding, M. (1999a) 'Target setting, policy pathology and student perspectives: learning to labour in new times', *Cambridge Journal of Education* 29 (2), 277–87.

Fielding, M. (1999b) 'Radical collegiality: affirming teaching as an inclusive professional practice', *The Australian Educational Researcher* 26 (2), 1–34.

Giroux, H. and McLaren, P. (1992) 'America 2000 and the politics of erasure: democracy and cultural difference under siege', *International Journal of Educational Reform* 1 (2), 99–109.

Goodman, J. (1994) 'External change agents and grassroots school reform: reflections from the field', *Journal of Curriculum and Supervision* 9 (2), 113–35.

Habermas, J. (1976) *Legitimation Crisis*, London: Heinemann.

Habermas, J. (1979) *Communication and the Evolution of Society*, Boston MA: Beacon Press.

Held, D. (1982) 'Crisis tendencies, legitimation and the state', in J. Thompson and D. Held (eds) *Habermas: Critical Debates*, London: Macmillan, pp. 181–95.

Helsby, G. (1999) *Changing Teachers' Work: The 'Reform' of Secondary Schooling*, Buckingham: Open University Press.

Henry, M., Lingard, B., Rizvi, F. and Taylor, S. (1999) 'Working with/against globalization in education', *Journal of Education Policy* 14 (1), 85–97.

Holton, R. (1997) 'Some myths about globalization', in the *Proceedings* of papers presented at the Higher Education Research and Development Society of Australia, Adelaide, July, pp. 141–59.

Humphrey, N. (1996) *Leaps of Faith: Science, Miracles and the Search for Supernatural Consolation*, New York: Springer.

Levin, B. (1998) 'An epidemic of educational policy: (what) can we learn from each other?' *Comparative Education* 34 (2), 131–42.

Lingard, B. (1999) 'Developments in School-based Management: The Specific Case of Queensland, Australia', paper presented at the Australian Association for Research in Education, Melbourne.

Marcus, G. (1998) *Ethnography through Thick and Thin*, Princeton NJ: Princeton University Press.

May, S. (1994) *Making Multicultural Education Work*, Clevedon: Multilingual Matters.

McLaren, P. (1997) *Revolutionary Multiculturalism: Pedagogies of Dissent for the New Millennium*, Boulder CO: Westview Press.

Menter, I., Muschamp, Y., Nicholls, P., Ozga, J. and Pollard, A. (1997) *Work and Identity in the Primary School: A post-Fordist Analysis*, Buckingham: Open University Press.

Neilsen, A. (ed.) (1999) *Daily Meaning: Counternarratives of Teachers' Work*, Mill Bay BC: Bendall.

O'Connor, J. (1984) *Accumulation Crisis*, London: Blackwell.

O'Hagan, B. (1999) *Modern Educational Myths: The Future of Democratic Comprehensive Education*, London: Kogan Page.

O'Loughlin, M. (1995) 'Daring the imagination: unlocking voices of dissent and possibility in teaching', *Theory into Practice* 34 (2), 107–16.

Offe, C. (1984) 'Social policy and the theory of the state', in J. Kane (ed.) *Contradictions of the Welfare State*, London: Hutchinson.

Pring, R. and Walford, G. (eds) (1987) *Affirming the Comprehensive Ideal*, London: Falmer Press.

Quicke, J. (1998)'Towards a new professionalism for "new times": some problems and possibilities', *Teacher Development* 2 (3), 323–38.

Radnor, H., Ball, S. and Vincent, C. (1997) 'Whither democratic accountability in education? An investigation into headteachers' perspectives on accountability in the 1990s with reference to their relationships with their LEAs and governors', *Research Papers in Education* 12 (2), 205–22.

Rizvi, F. (1994) 'Devolution in education: three contrasting perspectives', in R. Martin, J. McCollow, L. McFarlane, G. McMurdo, J. Graham and R. Hull (eds) *Devolution, Decentralisation and Recentralisation: The Structure of Australian Schooling*, South Melbourne: Australian Education Union, pp. 1–5.

Roman, L. (1996) 'Spectacle in the dark: youth as transgression, display, and repression', *Educational Theory* 46 (1), 1–22.

Smyth, J. (1992) 'Teachers' work and the politics of reflection', *American Educational Research Journal* 29 (2), 267–300.

Smyth, J. (ed.) (1993) *A Socially Critical View of the Self-managing School*, London: Falmer Press.

Smyth, J. (1996) 'The socially just alternative to the "self-managing school"', in K. Leithwood, J. Chapman, D. Corson, P. Hallinger and A. Hart (eds) *International Handbook of Educational Leadership and Administration* II, Dordrecht, Boston MA and London: Kluwer, pp. 1097–31.

Smyth, J. (2000) 'The self-managing school: the reform we had to have?' submitted to *Educational Researcher*, April.

Smyth, J. and Shacklock, G. (1998) *Remaking Teaching: Ideology, Policy and Practice*, New York & London: Routledge.

Stronach, I. and Morris, B. (1994) 'Polemical notes on educational evaluation in the age of "policy hysteria"', *Evaluation and Research in Education* 8 (1–2), 5–19.

Whitty, G., Power, S. and Halpin, D. (1997) *Devolution and Choice in Education: The State School and the Market*, Buckingham: Open University Press.

Wirt, F. (1991) 'Policy origins and policy games: site-based management in the United States and the United Kingdom', in G. Harman, H. Beare and G. Berkley (eds) *Restructuring School Management: Administrative Reorganisation of Public School Governance in Australia*, Curtin ACT: Australian College of Education.

Wood, G. (1992) *Schools that Work: America's Most Innovative Public Education Programs*, New York: Dutton.

Woods, P., Jeffrey, B., Troman, G. and Boyle, M. (1997) *Restructuring Schools, Reconstructing Teachers: Responding to Change in the Primary School*, Buckingham: Open University Press.

Acknowledgement

Some of the ideas contained in this chapter come from a considerable reworking, expansion and condensation of ideas in: J. Smyth, 'Towards a Critical Theory of Teachers' Work in the Context of Devolving School Management', presented to the annual meeting of the British Educational research Association, University of Sussex, 1999, and J. Smyth, 'The self-managing school: the reform we had to have', submitted to the *Educational Researcher*, 2000. Research in this chapter was supported by funding from the Australian Research Council.

Index